THE MONK

PAUL
WILLIAMS

ALSO BY PAUL WILLIAMS

Almost the Perfect Murder
Murder Inc.
Badfellas
Crime Wars
The Untouchables
Crimelords
Evil Empire
Gangland
Secret Love (ghostwriter)
The General

THE MONK

THE LIFE AND CRIMES OF IRELAND'S MOST ENIGMATIC GANG BOSS

PAUL WILLIAMS

ALLEN&UNWIN

In memory of Lawrence 'Larry' Williams
10 August 1937–8 June 2019

First published in Great Britain and Ireland in 2020 by Allen & Unwin

Picture credits: images 1, 2, 10 and 15 © Derek Speirs; 6, 17 and 36
© Charlie Collins/Collins Photographic Agency; 8, 11 and 39 © *Irish
Independent*. The remaining photographs have been sourced by the author.

Every effort has been made to trace or contact all copyright holders. The
publishers will be pleased to make good any omissions or rectify any
mistakes brought to their attention at the earliest opportunity.

A CIP catalogue record for this book is available from the British Library.

Trade paperback ISBN 978 1 91163 079 1
E-Book ISBN 978 1 76087 425 4

Printed and bound in Great Britain by Clays Ltd, Elcograf S.p.A.

10 9 8 7 6 5 4 3 2 1

CONTENTS

Prologue

The couple and their two children blended seamlessly in the throng of high-spirited passengers disembarking the packed flight from Dublin in César Manrique Airport, Lanzarote on 28 December 2015. They were there as part of the seasonal invasion of Irish folk seeking a sunny post-Christmas respite from the cold and the darkness back home.

The family teamed up with a friend who had arrived on the island the previous day with his girlfriend. Just before Christmas the two men had presented their respective partners with an unexpected gift of an all-expenses paid holiday to ring in the New Year on the Spanish island. As the women looked forward to a week's fun in the sun, their dangerous partners had a more pressing objective – and it didn't involve lying by the pool sipping sangria.

The women were blissfully unaware that their seasonal escape had been paid for by the men's boss, Daniel Kinahan, the leader of one of Europe's biggest crime cartels, and that this was to be a busman's holiday.

Kinahan had dispatched the experienced hit men – what Colombians call *sicarios* – on a high-risk, top-secret mission. The enormity of this decision would be remembered as a seminal event in the history of organized crime back home in Ireland.

The two killers from the north side of Dublin had already proved their ability as cold-blooded, fearless professionals who were prepared to kill anyone just as long as the price was right. And this particular hit held out the promise of a very substantial bounty because it was to be, in gangland terms, a premier league job.

Their target was Gerard 'Gerry' Hutch, aka the Monk, one of the most infamous and powerful godfathers in Irish organized crime: in Mafioso parlance, a man of 'respect' who no one dared to cross. The relatively few who had foolishly stepped over the line in the past had ended up on mortuary slabs.

Hutch was one of the country's best-known criminals who had earned celebrity gangster status after masterminding some of the biggest cash heists in Irish history – and getting away scot-free with millions in used, untraceable bank notes.

In the eyes of the law the clever crime boss was not so much untouchable as uncatchable. The people in his old inner-city neighbourhood saw him as a Robin Hood figure while to the wider public, who watched his portrayal in a Hollywood blockbuster and read about his exploits in the media, he was the object of morbid curiosity and fascination.

To Daniel Kinahan, however, Hutch was nothing more than a pre-cancerous spot that required excision before it developed into a terminal tumour. Hutch was a threat to his continued survival and the cartel boss had decided that the Monk was a dead man walking.

By 2015 Ireland's most successful armed robber had retired from his extensive criminal activities, spending most of the year in Lanzarote where he owned a villa in Puerto del Carmen in the south of the island. After a festive visit back to Dublin Hutch had returned to Lanzarote on 28 December with his wife. The gang boss had a lot on his mind. Dramatic unforeseen events during the year had pulled Hutch reluctantly into the midst of a simmering feud that was not of his making and beyond his ability to control. Unwavering loyalty to family and the transgressions of the younger hot-headed generation had propelled the head of the crime family into the firing line of an increasingly inevitable confrontation with one of Europe's most powerful gangs.

The seeds of conflict took root over a year earlier when the Monk's volatile nephew, Gary Hutch, had organized a hit on his one-time close pal and boss Daniel Kinahan in Marbella in August 2014.

The attempt was an unmitigated disaster with the would-be assassin shooting an innocent man by mistake. The finger of suspicion quickly landed on Gary Hutch and he was held prisoner while the crime boss investigated his near miss.

At the insistence of Daniel Kinahan and his father, Christy Senior, the Dapper Don, Gerry Hutch was dragged into the negotiations to save his nephew's life. A peace deal was hammered out which, in return for Gary's life, included a payment of compensation and the punishment shooting of the suspected gunman. Pragmatism and reason seemed to have prevailed as both sides withdrew from the brink – or so thought the Monk.

In the end the agreement was nothing more than a ruse to buy time as far as Daniel Kinahan was concerned. He was just waiting for the best moment to take his revenge and it came in September 2015 when Gary Hutch was executed at his apartment complex in Estepona, Spain.

In the months since the murder Kinahan had made a number of approaches to Hutch requesting a parley and further sit downs but the Monk had ignored them. Hutch's silence had rattled Daniel

Kinahan who knew he had awakened a very deadly foe and there was only one way to neutralize the threat – a hit man's bullet. And that was what brought two of the most effective contract killers in Dublin to Lanzarote on what was supposedly a festive break.

Darkness had fallen on New Year's Eve when Hutch and his wife arrived in the bar in Puerto del Carmen where he had celebrated his fiftieth birthday two years earlier. The bar was full of revellers partying through the last remaining hours of what had been the Monk's *annus horribilis*.

The hit men had already reconnoitred the popular Irish pub, situated just off the main strip on the seafront, where they had the best chance of cornering their wily target when he least expected it. By nature Gerry Hutch was cautious and alert even when at his most relaxed, and the gradual escalation of hostilities between the two sides since the murder had him on his guard. Although he felt relatively safe on the island he knew his enemies had contacts everywhere.

As the Monk scanned the crowd, his eyes locked onto two guys who had just walked in and were ordering a drink at the bar. His body tensed when he recognized the pair. The Monk knew one of them to be a former friend of his nephews and a member of the republican crime gang, the INLA. He had a reputation as a contract killer and a Kinahan loyalist. The pair at the bar pretended not to see their target but a momentary glance in his direction confirmed Hutch's suspicions – they had come to kill him.

Satisfied that they had their target housed, the hit men promptly left the pub to pick up the murder weapons. They would have plenty to celebrate by the time the clock struck midnight and 2016 arrived.

A few minutes later the killers returned wearing balaclavas and, clutching the automatic weapons under their jackets, made for the spot where Hutch had just been sitting. But the seats were empty and there was no sign of the Monk or his wife. For a moment the killers seemed confused and looked around distractedly, before they fled to the street and vanished.

As the killers left the pub Hutch was already being informed about the drama he had narrowly avoided. His legendary feral street instinct had paid off.

The following day Hutch returned to view the pub's CCTV footage to get a look at his would-be assassins. It wasn't difficult to work out who they were – the two men in balaclavas were wearing the same clothing as when they entered the pub looking for their target.

Looking at the CCTV images Hutch realized that a line had been crossed that changed everything and proved beyond all doubt just how perfidious and treacherous the Kinahans were. He knew they would not stop until they had killed him. To get his revenge there was only one law for Gerry Hutch to follow – the gangland law of meeting fire with fire.

The Monk phoned a close confidante to tell him of the events of the previous night and of his next move: 'Fuck them … if that's what they want, then that's what they're going to get.'

CHAPTER ONE

CLASH OF THE CLANS

On New Year's Day 2016 veteran criminal Gerry Hutch was facing the biggest single crisis of his fifty-two years. The two most powerful family-based gangs in Ireland – led by Irish godfathers Christopher Kinahan Senior and Gerard Hutch – were on a one-way collision course with disaster. The murder of the Monk's nephew Gary Hutch in September 2015 and the New Year's Eve attempt against Gerry Hutch himself had ruled out any prospect of reasoning with his one-time close allies. A line had been crossed and they were now deadly enemies.

Hutch, however, had no intention of breaking with his code of omerta to seek help from his old foes, the gardaí, or of instructing his lawyers to threaten legal action. He had no interest in the way disputes are settled in the civilized world beyond gangland's cultural boundaries. The only law he would invoke was the primal law of vengeance: an eye for an eye. In the immediate aftermath of the failed execution attempt, he disappeared into the shadows to plot the manner and timing of his revenge, beyond the reach of the assassins the Kinahan cartel would surely keep sending until they finally succeeded in closing his eyes – permanently. He knew that when it came to the strike back it would have to be executed with the same meticulous planning and ruthless efficiency of his celebrated heists.

The sensational story of the Monk's close call in Lanzarote was widely reported in the media back in Ireland. The news was greeted with genuine astonishment by experienced cops, criminals and reporters alike. As crime stories go it could not get any more sensational than that – or so we thought. If someone twelve months earlier had predicted such a confrontation they would, to paraphrase the comedian Billy Connolly, have been sent to the funny farm without getting home for their pyjamas.

Hutch and Kinahan Senior were two of the most devious and intelligent godfathers in Irish organized crime; traits which had helped them to prosper and survive. They had known each other since the early 1980s when they embarked on their respective career paths: Hutch as a street thief turned professional armed robber; Kinahan as a suave petty fraudster turned drug trafficker. Both criminals had been clever enough to learn from the mistakes of their contemporaries who had ended up dead or in prison.

One of the secrets to the Monk's successful criminal career lay in his talent for self-preservation which involved strategically manipulating circumstances to ensure that he always maintained total control over events. These skills had been the hallmark of his multiple robberies. Losing control inevitably meant failure and the prospect of a long stint behind bars or worse – losing control was not an option. Another secret to his success was that Hutch adopted a pragmatic, methodical approach to solving problems, commenting: 'When you are in trouble your first priority is to get out of it. Once you have done that you can worry about other things.' On 1 January 2016 his priority was to regain control of the febrile situation before it was too late.

The master thief's adherence to a reasoned, non-confrontational approach in business had successfully shielded him from the endemic volatility and treachery that characterized the psyche of the new breed of criminal on Dublin's streets. It was a tragic irony that it was these same capricious traits in his hot-headed nephew which had ultimately engulfed the Monk's peaceful world in flames.

It may seem counter-intuitive in the eyes of law-abiding civilians, but Gerry Hutch was an ethical villain who observed a certain code of honour. He exemplified the qualities of a so-called Ordinary Decent Criminal (ODC) – an all but extinct criminal type these days – who played a straight game and kept his word. The ruthless capacity that lurked behind the benign, conciliatory image burnished his reputation as an ODC and a man of 'respect'. But it was well-known this brutal reaction was only ever deployed when all other avenues of common sense and reason had failed. As a result, the elusive Monk straddled the razor wire fence between gangland and civilized society; he could walk freely on either side and never have to look over his shoulder.

Gardaí who have been trying to catch Gerard Hutch for decades share that view of his character. One veteran cop remarked: 'He is undoubtedly a villain and one who is capable of vicious violence. But he is also honest, and I think that he was wise enough never to make the mistake of considering himself as being invincible. He is also very focused. He has always been able to compartmentalize problems, dealing with them separately, one at a time.'

In Hutch's bible treachery was an unforgivable, mortal sin. It breached his strongly-held moral code, an approach he once explained in an interview with crime journalist Veronica Guerin: 'My philosophy in life is simple enough. No betrayal. That means you don't talk about others, you don't grass and you never let people down.'

As far as the Monk was concerned the Kinahan gang had broken this code. Five months earlier, Christy Senior, the Dapper Don, and his son, Daniel, had made a solemn, inviolate pact with Gerry Hutch that in return for financial compensation and a promise of no further retaliation, his nephew Gary's safety was guaranteed and there would be peace between the two families. The two godfathers had reportedly agreed that they would each keep control on the younger generation to avoid unnecessary bloodshed. It was easy to see why Gerry Hutch was confident that he had a deal and afterwards, according to a friend, warned Gary to stay out of trouble before his impetuous nephew returned to the Kinahan's stronghold in Puerto Banus in Spain's Costa del Sol.

And so, when the Kinahans broke the accord by executing Gary and then turning their hit men on the Monk, it was an unconscionable, devastating act of betrayal from which there was no going back. From Gerry Hutch's point of view, extreme violence was the only option left open to him, with all the unavoidable bloody consequences that would surely follow.

A close friend of the Monk who spoke to him after the failed execution commented:

> Gerard was not a guy to come out all guns blazing like the other hotheads because his instinct was to sort out potentially dangerous situations peacefully, talking the problem through with both sides in a calm collective way, a bit like a real-life Don Corleone. He didn't want people blowing one another up because he was wise enough to know that one killing just leads to another and then another. That's why he has only ever been connected

to a few killings in his time and they were ones that couldn't be avoided. Gerard always believed that there's a way of solving problems other than ending up in a casket. But this situation changed everything.

After that [assassination bid] and Gary's murder he knew he couldn't trust the Kinahans and everyone around him all agreed with that. The Kinahans are treacherous vipers, especially Daniel, and he got that from his father Christy. Gary had told Gerard of all the people who had been double-crossed by Daniel and his father. Gerard said Christy was 'a cheap, fuckin' fraud man who'd do his own mother… you can't trust him or any of his clan'. In the weeks after the thing in Spain Daniel and Christy denied that they had anything to do with the attempt on his life and they kept trying to arrange meetings with him to talk peace but he knew they only wanted to set him up. He was the one man they feared most because they knew what he was capable of. For Gerard there was no going back. He was in a corner and to protect himself and his family it was a case of kill or be killed. His old way of doing things wouldn't help him this time. He had a big crew of very able lads around who were more than willing to back him up.

In the first weeks of the New Year, in the midst of much media speculation about the escalating tensions between the two tribes, an eerie calm descended. The Monk had ordered his gang to maintain a low profile while he plotted the next move. This total silence made Daniel Kinahan and his father nervous. Hutch escaping a bullet in Lanzarote was a disaster. They were well aware that he made for a lethal enemy. The wily gangster would never allow them to come so close to killing him again. The Kinahans continued to make overtures to Hutch but they had more immediate concerns.

In a joint venture with UK boxing promoter Frank Warren, Daniel was involved in organizing the WBO European Lightweight title fight which was scheduled to take place in Dublin in early February. Over the years Daniel had been using his dirty money to pursue an ambition of becoming a legitimate international boxing promoter. He had entered a partnership with British-Irish champion boxer Matthew Macklin and set up the MGM gym – Macklin Gym Marbella – from his base in Puerto Banus. Kinahan also managed a stable of boxers. The last thing Daniel wanted was for the highly lucrative venture to be marred by a member of the Hutch gang taking a pot shot at him. There had been much coverage and speculation in the media that the expected escalation in the feud might coincide with the timing of the big fight when the cartel leadership would be together in one place.

In the weeks before the event Kinahan sent two of his closest associates, who had once been close friends of Gary Hutch, to talk with Eddie, the Monk's elder brother. Eddie 'Neddie' Hutch was six years older than the Monk and had been one of his criminal mentors growing up. He brought his younger brother on his first armed robberies when he was still a teenager. Although long since retired, and no longer involved in organized crime, Neddie was still his infamous brother's eyes and ears. He was the only line of communication the Kinahans had to Gerry who had gone to ground. The young boxing promoter wanted to convince Gerry Hutch that the cartel had nothing to do with the attempt on his life and that they were seeking a truce. Christy and Daniel Kinahan also spoke to Eddie on the phone in an effort to de-escalate the situation and seek assurances that there would be no trouble at the forthcoming boxing title fight. Eddie Hutch agreed to pass the message on to his younger brother who rebuffed the offer because he said the Kinahans could not be trusted. At the same time, the Monk was secretly preparing for vengeance.

When Gerry Hutch made his move a few weeks later, it was unprecedented and ferocious. Just before 2.30 p.m. on a storm-lashed, gloomy Friday afternoon on 5 February 2016 – thirty-six days after the botched hit in Lanzarote – a five-man assassination squad stormed the Regency Hotel in Dublin's northside. In the ballroom about 200 spectators had gathered to attend the much publicized weigh-in for the big fight, billed as the 'Clash of the Clans', which was due to take place the following night in the National Stadium, in Dublin's south inner city. Kinahan and his top lieutenants, including Liam Byrne who ran the cartel's Irish operation, were there for the big event. The Monk, however, had orchestrated an alternative clash of the clans which wouldn't conform to boxing's Queensberry rules.

Three of the killers were kitted out as members of the Garda Emergency Response Unit (ERU), complete with paramilitary-style fatigues, balaclavas, Kevlar helmets and bullet-proof vests emblazoned with the word 'Garda'. The only difference was that these guys were brandishing AK-47 military assault rifles, the weapon of choice of the IRA. The other two hit men were armed with handguns and posed as a couple, with one of them dressed as a woman.

The 'Garda' squad burst into the front lobby of the busy hotel while the 'couple' came through a back door into the ballroom. The plan was to trap Daniel Kinahan and his sidekicks by forcing them to flee from the ballroom straight into the path of the waiting 'ERU' team who would riddle them with high velocity bullets. Gerry Hutch intended it to be the Irish equivalent of Al Capone's infamous St Valentine's Day massacre. Like the fictional Don

Corleone in *The Godfather*, a movie Daniel Kinahan was obsessed with, Gerry Hutch was determined to sort 'all family business' in a single devastating blow.

The attack was designed to cause maximum shock and use brutal, overwhelming force to wipe out the cartel's top management tier in Ireland. With them out of the way the organization would be left powerless and in complete disarray. The Kinahan cartel would be no more. Equilibrium could be restored and peace would prevail.

The 'couple' fired a series of shots in the air, creating pandemonium in the ballroom as panicked men, women and children scrambled for the exit doors. On the other side of them, the sight of the fake 'ERU' team added to the confusion, giving the spectators the impression that the gardaí had arrived to restore order. But even the best laid plans by successful criminal brains are susceptible to going awry. Daniel Kinahan and his associates fled through an emergency door and got away as the gunman in drag could be heard shouting: 'He's not fuckin' here...I can't fuckin' find him.'

The hit team did find David Byrne, the younger brother of Liam Byrne, who was a major player in the cartel. One of the 'Garda' team shot David Byrne as he ran with the panicked crowd through the reception area in the lobby. He fell to the ground and tried to crawl for cover. Two of Byrne's associates were also shot and injured. A second fake 'Garda' fired more rounds into Byrne as the other gunmen could be seen on CCTV searching the bar, adjoining rooms and the rear exits for their targets amongst the chaos of the terrified crowd. Reviewing the footage afterwards the shooters seemed calm and completely focused on their task – it was clear they knew who they were looking for.

One of the garda imposters was shown jumping onto the reception desk and pointing his rifle at a journalist who had sought refuge behind it. Satisfied that the terrified man wasn't a member of the cartel, the gunman casually turned and fired again into David Byrne's prone body. The thirty-three-year-old criminal was shot a total of six times in the face, stomach, hand and legs. He was so badly disfigured that his family were unable to have an open casket at his funeral.

Realizing that the main targets had escaped, and time had run out, the killing squad retreated to a waiting van outside the front entrance and sped away. The blitz attack was over in six minutes.

Gerry Hutch had established a new inauspicious record for the most audacious attack ever seen in Irish gangland history. His terrorist-style offensive elevated him to a higher level of notoriety. The killers had avoided shooting or injuring any innocent people which illustrated their level of focus and discipline. When examined from the cold-blooded perspective of a terrorist or hired assassin, the attack had been a top-notch professional job.

But after the chaos had subsided and the cordite fumes had dissipated from the lobby of the Regency Hotel, the Monk had to face the realization that it had been a spectacular failure. The senior members of the Kinahan cartel had been left untouched and were already gearing up for a merciless backlash. And Gerry Hutch knew that they had the money, weaponry and soldiers to wage war. He had lost the biggest gamble of his life and the world as he knew it was about to implode.

The attack seemed a reckless escapade given the fact that the links between the pre-fight weigh-in and the Kinahan organization had been so widely publicized. The Monk and his crew would have had to factor in the distinct possibility that armed gardaí would be monitoring the patrons at the Regency Hotel, heightening the risk of a shoot-out. Strangely, however, despite being an obvious public security risk, no gardaí were assigned to monitor the event. It was later deemed an embarrassing and inexplicable oversight. Garda chiefs had planned a major security operation around the National Stadium for the big fight but had not considered the weigh-in a likely flashpoint. It was the only bit of luck the Hutch gang had that day.

While garda management had not considered it necessary to keep an eye on the country's biggest drug trafficking gang at a major public spectacle in the midst of a simmering feud, photographers and reporters from the *Irish Independent* and the *Sunday World* certainly did. They had intended snapping pictures of Daniel Kinahan and his henchmen but what they got instead was a sensational – and terrifying – scoop. As they left, the killers pointed their weapons at the journalists but did not open fire.

The shocking and dramatic images captured by the courageous photographers of the 'Garda' team storming the entrance with AK-47s at the ready and the 'couple' running from the building with automatic pistols clearly in sight flashed around the world. Such pictures were normally associated with narco-terrorism in Mexico or Colombia but not on the streets of a civilized EU democracy.

The publication of the stark iconic images caused a major public outcry. The uproar could not have come at a more inconvenient time for government politicians who were in the middle of a keenly-contested general election campaign. As questions were asked, it became clear that in the eight years since the economic collapse An Garda Síochána had been starved of resources and one of the consequences was that criminal intelligence gathering had fallen between the cracks. The outgoing government got the blame for plunging Ireland into a policing crisis as outrage grew that criminals were prepared to carry out such brazen, violent acts on the streets of Dublin in full public view.

The government's immediate response was to open the purse strings and give gardaí whatever resources they required to launch a counter-offensive and bring the offenders to justice. The embarrassment over events at the Regency Hotel also stiffened the resolve of the gardaí to regain public confidence by launching a large-scale assault on the feuding mobs. The Kinahan/Hutch feud, as it became known, would be a three-sided conflagration involving the two gangs and the State. Having enjoyed a long absence, Gerry Hutch was now back at the top of Ireland's 'Most Wanted' list.

But the reaction from the State was the least of his worries. The Monk had factored in an inevitable visit from the gardaí after the shooting. That didn't bother him; he was adept at picking out a spot on the wall and saying nothing for days on end while in custody. It was the expected backlash from the Kinahans and Byrnes that most concerned him and his associates.

The ferocity of the Regency attack had shocked the Kinahans and their associates. They knew Hutch was dangerous but had never dreamt that he would launch such an audacious paramilitary-style strike. It took them 24 hours to regroup and assess their next move. The Byrne gang, made up of close family relations, was traumatized by the murder of David and was baying for blood. The night after the murder a female relative of the dead man, in her quest for someone to blame, settled on the media and demanded that two journalists be shot. But cool heads prevailed after the threat leaked back to gardaí and they reminded the Byrnes of what had happened to the Gilligan gang after they murdered journalist Veronica Guerin twenty years earlier. In any event there were plenty of others to hold accountable.

Apart from his own anger and upset at the murder of his friend, not to mention the attempt to kill him, Daniel Kinahan was also counting the financial cost of the attack. Within hours of the incident senior gardaí ordered the cancellation of the big fight. The young mob boss had lost out on an event which would have given him a big pay day and a lot of prestige in the boxing game. The presence of the hated media had also led to another negative repercussion. The dramatic images of the attack at the pre-fight weigh-in made headlines around the world focusing an uncomfortable spotlight on the contamination of the sport by an organized crime boss.

Daniel Kinahan and Liam Byrne wanted immediate and implacable vengeance. They issued orders to wipe out Gerry Hutch and everyone belonging to him. The cartel was about to unleash a small army of contract killers in an unprecedented cycle of bloodletting and violence that would turn Hutch's north inner-city home turf into a war zone. Anyone bearing the name Hutch, or those aligned to them, was fair game in the hostilities that were about to erupt – and they wasted no time getting started.

Just three days after the attack, Gerry's brother Eddie was gunned down at his apartment at Poplar Row in the heart of the Hutch stronghold in Dublin's north inner city. The killer showed no mercy as the fifty-eight-year-old taxi driver was shot several times in the head. His murder was greeted with shock and revulsion by local people and gardaí. Eddie Hutch was described by those who knew him as a friendly, harmless individual; he was a soft target who bore the Hutch name. It would later transpire that Eddie was not quite as uninvolved as everybody thought.

It wasn't that surprising the cartel went after Eddie as he had been acting as an intermediary between his younger brother and the Kinahans. Detectives described the killing as 'very personal', highlighting the fact that the assassin deliberately tried to inflict similar horrific facial injuries to those suffered by David Byrne. It was intended as a grotesque reciprocal gesture so that the Hutches, like the Byrnes, could not have an open casket at Eddie's funeral.

The murder was a shattering blow for Gerry Hutch who had been very close to his brother. Eddie and another older brother, Patsy, Gary Hutch's father, had been role models for the Monk when they were kids. They were well established as local thieves when eight-year-old Gerry came of age and got caught for the first time by the police.

The night after Eddie's shooting the Monk sat alone in total darkness in the front room of his home in the seaside suburb of Clontarf, in north-east Dublin. He was watching for his enemies as he tried to work out his next move. Although he did not show any emotion, he was in turmoil. A friend who spoke to him that evening said: 'Gerard didn't show emotion because he was programmed that way, but you knew he was on fire inside. It was probably the only time in his life that he seemed to be losing control of things.'

The murders of his nephew and brother had swept away the old assumptions – Gerry Hutch was no longer untouchable. He was still a man to be feared and respected but the protective screen that his standing in the criminal hierarchy had provided to his family and friends lay shattered in smithereens. Now every wannabe gangster who could handle a gun would be lining up to have a pop at the gangland legend. To borrow from the observations of W. B. Yeats on the fallout of a more honourable conflict, all had 'changed, changed utterly'.

CHAPTER TWO

——

CARNIVAL OF CRIME

The streets where Gerry Hutch grew up in north inner-city Dublin were swarming with police as hundreds turned out for the funeral of his brother Eddie on 19 February 2016. It was probably the first time in the Monk's criminal career that he was glad to see the gardaí.

Before the funeral, garda sniffer dogs had swept Our Lady of Lourdes Church on Seán McDermott Street for explosives. A similar search had been carried out in Glasnevin cemetery. Officers from the real Emergency Response Unit, whom Hutch's gang had dramatically imitated exactly two weeks earlier, toted machine guns and automatic pistols as they manned checkpoints in an outer protective ring. A public order unit was parked offside on a side street. Dozens of uniformed gardaí and armed detectives were positioned close to the mourners for fear of another attack.

A garda helicopter clattered above as the Hutch family, neighbours and friends walked behind the coffin on the short journey to the church from his sister's home on Portland Place, where Eddie had been waked the night before. The gardaí were determined that there would not be another murderous gangland spectacle at the ceremony.

A similar security operation had been put in place for the funeral of David Byrne – 'Happy Harry' as he was known – four days earlier.

Garda sniffer dogs had searched the St Nicholas of Myra Church on Frances Street across the River Liffey in Dublin's south inner city. It was the heartland of the Kinahan operation in Ireland and was where Christy Kinahan's two sons – Daniel and Christy Junior – had grown up in the Oliver Bond corporation flats. But the heavy police presence and the brutality of the two deaths, along with the intensive media scrutiny, were the only similarities between the two high-profile funerals.

In a tacky, vulgar display of wealth, the Kinahan and Byrne gang members, decked out in expensive matching suits, strode defiantly through the streets behind the €18,000 sky-blue casket. Among them were some of the most dangerous and experienced killers in gangland. They had been well-blooded in a previous Dublin gang war, the Crumlin/Drimnagh feud, which claimed over a dozen lives. Afterwards a convoy of eleven stretch limos had followed the hearse from the church, escorted by a bikers' club.

The sense of menace and intimidation was palpable at the mafia-style funeral – and it was clearly intentional. Daniel Kinahan and his mob had used the event to demonstrate to the world that they were the top tier of organized crime in Ireland. They saw themselves as the meanest, most glamorous bastards on the streets. It represented a contemptuous two-fingered gesture to the media, the police, the public and, of course, the Hutch gang. The cartel relished the huge police presence and the media attention. It was a prime example of the theatrics to be found in what cultural criminologists describe as the 'carnival of crime' – David Byrne's funeral was a ritualized celebration of the gang's oppositional value system.

By comparison there was no display of self-indulgent hubris at the second high-profile gangland funeral of the week. Eddie Hutch's send-off was a traditional north inner-city affair. It was a dignified expression of genuine grief as a close-knit community wrapped its collective arm around his family. The only street theatre was the large police presence. Over the coming months there would be many more such funeral processions through the same streets.

In stark contrast to his enemies, the Monk adopted a low profile at his brother's funeral. The head of the Hutch family was conspicuously absent from the cortege walking behind Eddie's remains. He wore a black baseball hat, pulled down tight over his face to avoid being spotted by the media. When photographers found him in the crowd he was walking in the company of an old childhood friend and criminal associate, Noel 'Duck Egg' Kirwan. Hutch had allowed his once distinctive mop of raven hair to grow so bushy and unkempt that it looked like he was wearing a wig. His dishevelled appearance added to the sense of his dramatic downfall. During the requiem mass he remained in the background, staying away from his family, as his brothers and nephews carried the coffin into the church. Some of them only realized Gerry had been there when they watched the news later that day.

Many there must have wondered what went through Gerry's mind as Fr Richard Ebejer told the congregation that murder 'only degrades the humanity of those who carry it out' and asked, on behalf of the family, that there be no retribution. The priest had made a similar plea at the funeral of Gary Hutch four months earlier. As Fr Ebejer acknowledged it had fallen on deaf ears: 'It was a request that unfortunately has not been respected, with the result that now more families are in bereavement. They [Hutch family] now call on everybody for this cycle of violence to stop, and to stop now.'

Perhaps if he had had time, Gerry Hutch would have pointed out to Fr Ebejer that the Kinahans were the ones who had ignored the plea for peace when they sent their murderers to assassinate him in

Lanzarote. The Monk might have told the priest and the community present that he had been left with no choice – retaliation was the only way he could protect his family.

The attempted massacre at the Regency Hotel had the full support of members of the clan, some of whom also took part in the audacious attack. Gerry Hutch might have been tempted to get up on the altar and apologize for the spectacular miscalculation that had brought so much grief to his family's door and the shadow of fear and danger it had cast over his beloved home turf. But Hutch, a man who preferred silence over eloquence, had more pressing matters to hand. After the funeral he slipped back into the shadows and would later go into hiding outside the jurisdiction, moving between bases and safe houses across the UK and Europe.

The image of Gerry Hutch at the funeral became a metaphor for his catastrophic change in fortune. The once feared godfather had the demeanour of a man on the run, a hunted fugitive with a bounty on his head. The young criminals who had once admired him were now queuing up to take the murder contracts being offered by the Kinahan gang to wipe out his family. A close associate or Hutch family member was worth a reported €10,000 and all the cocaine the killer could shove up his nose. But the biggest prize was reserved for the elusive Monk. Liam Byrne and the Kinahans subsequently offered €1 million to any criminal gang in Europe who could catch the fugitive gangster. The conditions for payment were that the Monk be taken alive and delivered to Byrne who wanted to personally give him a long, slow and agonizing death.

Less than a year earlier Gerry Hutch held an impressive record that bucked the trend in the criminal underworld. His rigid self-discipline and innate cleverness had helped him to navigate into the safe harbour of a comfortable retirement. During his life he had lost a lot of friends and associates, people who had been mentors or business partners at various stages in his career. Some of them had been assassinated, either by rivals or shot by the police during botched robberies. Hutch had attended a lot of funerals in his time and reckoned he had learned from others' mistakes. And now here he was reduced to hiding out, in a nightmare that he could never have dreamt up. As the Monk faced an uncertain, perilous future he must have wondered where it all went wrong.

———————

'As a kid, like I mean, me first conviction was for stealing a bottle of red lemonade. I got a fine and then I was involved in other crime as a kid stealing and breakin' into shops,' Gerry Hutch commented in March 2008. He was being interrogated by RTÉ crime correspondent Paul Reynolds in the only interview the gang boss ever gave for TV.

In the interview the Monk was uncharacteristically open about the criminological roots of his life which ultimately saw him steal his way out of the grinding poverty of the Dublin ghetto that was his birthright. He was recalling his inaugural criminal conviction for larceny on 30 November 1971 when he was a mere eight years old. As he stood beside his mother Julia in the Children's Court, having pleaded guilty, the judge fined him £1 and applied the Probation of Offenders Act which was meant as a caution. It was supposed to encourage young first-time offenders to mend their ways. But the initial warning, and the many others Hutch subsequently received in the same courtroom over the years, did nothing to deflect him from his path. By the time he was eighteen he had amassed another thirty convictions for assault, larceny, car theft, joy riding and malicious damage. He served a total of ten custodial sentences in St Patrick's Institution for young offenders and Mountjoy Prison.

Having had little formal education, prison became the source of his primary, secondary and third-level education. 'I taught myself to read and write, firstly by reading comics and then books,' he once recalled. Prison also completed his criminal education which he passed with flying colours.

The young criminal was born on 12 April 1963, the sixth of eight children – five boys and three girls. Patrick and Julia Hutch and their children, like the majority of their neighbours, were forced to live in squalid poverty. Their home was Corporation Buildings on Foley Street in Dublin's tightly-knit north inner city. The area was bordered on one side by the once thriving docks and on the other by O'Connell Street, the capital's premier boulevard. The area had been blighted by poverty, deprivation and neglect since the poor first colonized the zone in the early nineteenth century. Families were crammed into crumbling tenement hovels that had once been the grand homes of the social elite of the British Empire's second city. By 1936, Dublin was described as having the worst slums in Europe.

A purpose-built flat complex, Corporation Buildings had been constructed in 1900 as part of a slum clearance programme but by the 1960s it had degenerated into a semi-derelict, over-crowded tenement on the brink of being condemned. The eight Hutch children slept in one room in a damp, poky flat that was falling down around them. The electrical supply worked intermittently, and the residents had to share a primitive toilet and water tap in the back yard. Patrick Hutch, who was known as 'Masher', worked as a labourer on the docks unloading coal and slack from the ships. The backbreaking work involved shovelling up to 50 tons of slack or coal in a single shift. For hours of hard graft the labourers who were classified as 'non-button coalies' were paid a meagre wage that was barely enough to feed and clothe the families of workers. Going without the basic essentials of life was common in the neglected socio-economic wasteland of the north inner city.

Long before Gerry Hutch or his siblings were born a criminal subculture had developed in the area which could be traced back to the first tenements in the previous century. The neighbourhood around Corporation Buildings, encompassing the backstreets of Corporation Place, Foley Street and Railway Street, was once the centre of the infamous Monto area, the biggest red light district in Europe. The new Irish Free State with its rigorous adherence to Roman Catholic doctrine shut it down in 1925, forcing the prostitutes out of the brothels and onto the streets. According to a contemporaneous newspaper report, crime 'and all manner of evilness' remained rife in the ghetto. But its geographical location meant it could be kept out of sight of the rest of Dublin society, reinforcing the sense of exclusion felt by its inmates.

The same neighbourhood that was Gerry Hutch's childhood playground also witnessed the era of the notorious Animal gangs. These mobs of unemployed, bored young men, organized along street lines, earned their fearsome name from the bloody street battles fought against rivals from other neighbourhoods. One of the toughest of the gangs came from Corporation Buildings. Knives, potatoes laced with razor blades, knuckledusters and lead-filled batons were the weapons of choice. They wore peaky caps with blades sewn into the brims which they used with devastating effect to slice up their foes – making them the first 'peaky blinders'. But despite their horrendous reputation for violence most of the Animal gangs observed a strict ethos whereby they did not victimize their own people and often came to the aid of their neighbours by distributing stolen food or preventing evictions. To the locals they were Robin Hood figures in an imperfect world, and the community reciprocated by tolerating the gangs' violent behaviour.

In his book *Dublin Tenement Life* Kevin Kearns observed:

> Tenement folk, however, regarded these activities as 'unfortunate' rather than 'evil' realities of life in the impoverished slums. An examination from within the tenement community reveals that these practices were sociologically understandable and socially tolerated under the circumstances of the time… animal gangs were hailed as heroes for their defense of the downtrodden.

The Animal gangs never established lasting criminal empires because in the hungry, jobless thirties, forties and fifties there wasn't very much to rob or extort, and anyone who did was quickly caught and jailed. The last of the street gangs had faded away ten years before the birth of Gerry Hutch but their exploits had gained legendary status in the rich folklore of the area. The former 'Animals' who were still around were objects of fascination for the young Hutch and his friends. They had grown up on a diet of stories about the gangs' violent antics. He was no doubt impressed by the tales of the violent young men protecting the community and not targeting their own, as a means of creating a secure home base from which to operate. In time the community would also view Gerry Hutch through a similarly ambiguous lens – as an iconic Robin Hood figure whose criminality was understood and tolerated.

When Hutch was born Corporation Buildings still carried its criminogenic label. It was seen as the epicentre of criminal activity in the area by the officers attached to the local Garda C District at Store Street garda station, which had the busiest beat in Ireland. The gardaí were a regular sight on the balconies of the dreary flats as they visited the homes of young and not so young offenders.

Gerry Hutch's childhood streets also continued to be the focal point of some of the worst levels of unemployment and poverty in the country. Since the early 1960s the indigenous industries in the inner city, such as brewing, glass works, iron works, textiles and the docks, which traditionally relied on the ready supply of unskilled labour in the area, began closing down. Capital investment in the city centre dropped dramatically as industrial imperatives shifted. In the twenty-year period from 1971 to 1991 when Hutch was growing up the inner city experienced a 50 per cent drop in the availability of industrial jobs which exacerbated an already bleak economic situation. The physical environment turned into a wasteland of dereliction adding to the pervading sense of despair. By the early 1980s the process of disinvestment and urban decay had left Dublin's inner-city landscape pock-marked and scarred, with over 600 derelict sites and buildings.

Outsiders didn't venture into Railway Street and Foley Street for fear of being mugged and the police officers, as the only symbol of State authority, were seen as the enemy. The Hutch family was deeply rooted in the community and they never left. The area was all they knew – the neighbourhood was their world. Michael Finn was assigned as a rookie garda to the C District in the early 1960s. Over the next three decades he developed a strong bond with the local community and understood why some kids got swallowed up in a cycle of crime. He once explained to this writer:

People who initially got involved in crime did so out of need, running into shops and stealing bits and pieces, sometimes out of hunger. As they grew up, they became a part of different gangs and some were

fortunate enough to be weaned away from it. One of the main factors
for young people falling into crime was their family conditions. In a lot
of cases circumstances were not good, families were dysfunctional,
and they had nobody to show them the way. It is an accepted fact that
deprived areas will produce criminals. And it is always those areas
that the police will concentrate on because criminals live there. Crime
is a consequence of how they were reared, where they were reared
and what was available to them during their early times.

Gerry Hutch echoed these sentiments in his interview with RTÉ
years later. He rationalized why he and his peers began thieving, his
words echoing the motives of the generations who preceded him on
the same cobbled streets: 'There was nothin' around, I mean, first
up best dressed, I had no choice. You had to go into crime to feed
yourself, never mind dress yourself.'

In 1971, the same year that the young Gerry recorded his first
scrape with the law, Corporation Buildings were demolished. The
Hutch family moved to Liberty House on Railway Street which was
a slight improvement in their living standards. As the State stepped
up its well-meaning efforts to resolve the housing crisis one of the
unintended consequences was to uproot the bonds that had defined
the inner-city communities. Families were separated from friends and
neighbours and scattered to sprawling new estates on the periphery of
the city. The overall effect of the great migration was a breakdown in
social cohesion. The new working-class suburbs had little to offer apart
from improved accommodation and quickly became unemployment
black spots. Poverty and crime had made the move with the people.

A few years earlier a television programme, *The Flower Pot
Society*, examined the movement of the slum generation and the
commentator had accurately predicted the problems of the future:

'Dublin Corporation are dealing with people all of whom are the same class. It's much easier to treat them like an army and to transplant them from A to B. They have very little choice in the matter. If a child is to improve it will be in spite of their environment – and not because of it.'

Patrick 'Masher' Hutch and his wife had opted to stay put, which would have a profound influence on the young Monk. Anyone who knows him will say that in order to understand the enigmatic gangster you need to understand his attachment to the neighbourhood. He has always expressed a deep affection for the place where he grew up, commenting: 'I love this area. It's my home. My heart is here.' It was a sentiment shared by Ireland's most infamous crime boss, Martin Cahill, the General, who grew up in corporation flats on the southside of Dublin. He always counselled his henchmen and friends: 'Never forget where you come from.'

By the time Gerry Hutch was born in the 1960s, successive generations had developed coping mechanisms to counteract the ingrained misery and constant adversity of life in the slums. They had become a remarkably resilient and cohesive community complete with its own rich and complex customs, traditions, survival strategies and urban folklore. People looked out for one another, sharing their own scarce resources with neighbours when their need was more desperate. The hard-pressed mothers such as Julia Hutch were the real heroes who held it all together and did the best they could for their children. When the boys, Gerry, Eddie, John, Patrick and the youngest Derek, started to get into trouble with the law their mother would go to the garda stations, the holding cells and the court to stand by them. Over the years she spent a lot of time in such places. Her three daughters, Margaret, Tina and Sandra, managed to steer clear of trouble.

Early on Gerry Hutch began hanging out with a gang of tough young tearaways from his neighbourhood – ranging in age from ten up to eighteen – who terrorized businesses in the city centre. The group included his older brothers Patrick, John and Eddie. Of the three, Patrick, who was born in November 1960, was almost as prolific an offender as Gerry. Better known as Patsy, by the time he was twenty-one he had amassed twenty-five criminal convictions with the last one in 1982. After that, as far as his criminal record went, Patsy had gone straight.

In 1972 when Gerry turned nine, he appeared on four separate occasions before the Children's Court on charges of larceny and burglary. While his mother stood alongside him, he was either bound over to the peace or given the benefit of the Probation Act. The following year he was convicted of another three burglaries and was cautioned in each incidence. The young criminal and his associates were making a name for themselves.

On 14 June 1976 Gerry was back in the Children's Court. He pleaded guilty to a burglary and was sent home with his mother. Gardaí who dealt with the youngster would later recall how he was never particularly cheeky or abrasive when they arrested him. Even at the age of thirteen they recalled how he demonstrated a level of astuteness and intelligence that distinguished him from the other kids he hung around with.

Two weeks after his court appearance in June a gangster movie for kids called *Bugsy Malone* was released in Irish and UK cinemas and became an instant hit. Child actors played the adult roles in the spoof about Chicago gangster Al Capone, with the bad guys armed with machine guns that fired cream cakes. The movie release coincided with the increasing notoriety of Hutch and his fellow desperados whose prolific crime rate had made them a regular feature at the Children's Court. A media report compared them to the gang in the movie and the name stuck. The young offenders had found fame and loved it.

Hutch and the other 'Bugsy Malones' became prolific burglars and car thieves, before eventually progressing to armed robberies. Hutch dropped out of school as he was busy acquiring a different type of education. The athletic teenagers would rob banks by doing jump overs where they'd race inside, jump over the counter and grab cash from the tills and dart out before anyone could react. They could be in and out of a bank or post office in minutes before vanishing into the warren of inner-city streets that were their natural habitat. In an interview with journalist Veronica Guerin in 1996 Hutch saw nothing abnormal about his teenage exploits: 'We were kids then, doing jump overs, shoplifting, robberies, burglaries, anything that was going, we did it. That was normal for any inner-city kid then.'

A regular occurrence for the Bugsy Malones was to smash the windows of cars stopped at traffic lights and grab handbags or briefcases from the passenger seats. They were also the first generation of so-called joy riders, dangerously racing stolen cars and jousting with the police during chases. At one stage the joy-riding problem in the north inner city became so acute that officers in the C District were directed not to chase joy riders because of the number of squad cars being rammed and written off. Gardaí were instructed to only give hot pursuit in cases of armed robberies or shootings. Apart from ramming police cars the Bugsy Malones liked to taunt the local officers by sending postcards from sun holidays paid for with stolen money. They would address them to individual officers based in the local garda stations at Store Street and Fitzgibbon Street in central Dublin.

As the Bugsy Malones attracted more media attention a RTÉ radio news programme focused on the gang in a report on the growing problem of juvenile delinquency in Dublin. In a rare display of bravado, the teenage Gerry Hutch bragged about his exploits after leaving the Children's Court. He bragged: 'I can't give up robbin'. If I see money in a car I'm takin' it. I just can't leave it there. If I see a handbag on a seat I'll smash the window and be away before anyone knows what's goin' on. I don't go near people walking along the street... they don't have any money on them. They're not worth robbin'.' And when he was asked what he wanted to be when he grew up, he laughed and replied: 'I'd like to be serving behind the bank – just fill up the bags and jump over the counter.'

The gang became so notorious that in the mid-1970s it prompted the Department of Justice to open a controversial new prison facility at Loughan House in County Cavan to stem the upsurge of juvenile crime. One of the first inmates to be sent there was Hutch's best friend Thomas O'Driscoll, who was seven months younger and from St Mary's Mansions on Railway Street. Another close friend and fellow Bugsy Malone was Eamon Byrne from Sheriff Street.

Gerry Hutch and his compatriots would tell people that they only robbed because living in the north inner-city ghetto they had no job prospects. They weren't lying. In 1978 the communities within the borders of Sean McDermott Street and Sheriff Street had a youth unemployment rate of 50 per cent, which was the worst in Ireland. It was the same year Hutch turned fifteen – but instead of looking for a job he got his first taste of an adult prison. On 11 May 1978 the Children's Court sentenced him to twelve months in Mountjoy Prison in the north inner city, for two counts of attempted burglary and possession of house-breaking implements. Established in 1850, Mountjoy has remained Ireland's biggest committal prison for adult prisoners and it is unclear why the teenage Hutch was sent there.

Two weeks later he got another twelve months for larceny and the unauthorized taking of a car, and four days after that he picked up his third jail term, receiving another year for car theft. The following October the court imposed an additional twelve months on a charge of attempted burglary and malicious damage. Hutch pleaded guilty in each case and the sentences ran concurrently, which meant he spent nine months in Mountjoy.

Even for a cocky youngster the prospect of being locked up with much older criminals was a source of dread. Eddie took steps to protect his little brother while he was inside. Gerry was particularly close to Eddie who mentored him growing up. Eddie organized for a friend of his, a feared gangster serving time for robbery, to protect the fifteen-year-old from bullying or abuse at the hands of the older lags. Eddie's friend used to walk the recreation yard with the Monk and his other young friends. An associate commented to *Magill* magazine on the teenage Hutch's incarceration: 'He was very quiet, really quiet. He kept very much to himself. He worked in the kitchen and the bake room and used to pick his friends.' Apart from learning to read and write on the inside, Hutch also made lasting friendships with other young delinquents from the inner city who would later become members of his crime gang.

In modern times the idea of sending a child to an adult prison is unthinkable. Years later the Monk was still clearly angered by the experience: 'In Mountjoy, fifteen, thrown into it. I have a kid now fifteen and I look at the kid and I say, "My God, when I was fifteen I was in prison." I mean I was in prison with murderers, with rapists, bank robbers, everything, in a male prison full of all them. I mean that's not right. It was like going to college for criminals.'

Hutch's official criminal record shows that the following year, 1979, the sixteen-year-old tearaway received three more sentences, ranging between six and twelve months, which he served in St Patrick's Institution for young offenders. Shortly after being released from a six-month sentence imposed on 21 June for dangerous driving and car theft, he was jailed for another twelve months on 1 November for assaulting a garda which was out of character for him. Hutch was also prosecuted for larceny. He was released on 28 August 1980 and immediately went back to work.

The young villain was gaining a reputation as a serious player on the streets of the inner city. His quiet personality made him stand out from the crowd. Gerry Hutch kept his counsel when everyone around him was mouthing off. He didn't drink and didn't smoke hash which was the main recreational drug of choice in a more innocent time that would soon disappear.

The other members of the Bugsy Malone gang gravitated to him as the natural leader of the pack. The slightly built, small teenager with the head of distinctive raven hair and piercing blue eyes did not swagger or gloat, opting instead to keep a low profile. He was never threatening, and locals remember him as a courteous, respectful kid who made sure he found his victims outside the neighbourhood.

By the time Hutch was sixteen, he was taking part in armed robberies organized by Eddie and his close friend and neighbour Dave 'Myler' Brogan. In fact he was gaining a reputation as one of the youngest of the new breed of criminal appearing in gangland. Brogan, who was eleven years older than the Monk, later described how he 'had serious bottle for a young lad'. The gang's modus operandi was to stick close to the territory that they knew best in the city centre where there was a multitude of banks, payrolls and security vans to be robbed.

Brogan later described one daring robbery which Hutch carried out before his seventeenth birthday in 1980 from a shop on North Earl Street in the city centre. The job was organized by Eddie Hutch who sent Brogan to act as backup for his kid brother in case anything went wrong. Brogan had a spare motorbike parked up to take the young thief away in the event that there was a problem and a weapon had been hidden under a bin outside Clerys department store on O'Connell Street just in case.

The raiders arrived at the shop around 9.30 a.m. on a motorbike driven by sixteen-year-old Gerry Hutch. He and his friend Thomas O'Driscoll were equipped with handguns – a .38 and .45. Hutch drove the motorbike through the front door of the shop as his accomplice grabbed £3,200 in cash (worth €16,000 today). Brogan watched in amazement as the up-and-coming desperadoes then drove the motorbike through the front window and sped away.

It wasn't long before the Monk's unique talents caught the eye of one of the biggest players in Dublin's organized crime world. The mobster spotted the kid's potential and decided to take him under his wing. Gerry Hutch was moving into the big league.

CHAPTER THREE

———

LEARNING THE TRADE

Eamon Kelly was one of the pioneers of Ireland's gangland when the phenomenon of organized crime began to emerge on the coat tails of the outbreak of the Troubles in Northern Ireland in 1969. He was already a hardened criminal by the time Gerry Hutch was caught stealing a bottle of lemonade in 1971. Kelly's status was acknowledged in a garda background report on his activities in the 1970s which stated: 'Eamon Kelly has long been suspected of being concerned in the planning and execution of serious crime. He has a reputation for ruthlessness and is a cunning and vicious individual. He has something of "godfather" status among his associates. He controls his interests through intimidation and the element of fear.'

Born in Summerhill, north inner-city Dublin, in 1947 Eamon Kelly and his older brother Matt, his partner-in-crime, were in trouble with the law from their teens and both quickly earned a formidable reputation as hard men. Kelly's first recorded conviction was at the age of sixteen for burglary. Despite being a habitual thief, he only received another four convictions for burglary, shop breaking and larceny over the following years. He received a few short jail terms but then the convictions stopped, indicating that the career criminal learned from an early age how to avoid getting caught. Matt Kelly, who was three years older, had followed the same predictable route into crime. He was first convicted of larceny in 1956 at the age of twelve. By the time he was nineteen he had accrued another seven convictions for burglary, larceny and assault before he also learned how to stay one step in front of the law. Despite the fact neither brother had a record beyond the incidents in their youth, they were still classified as major criminals.

Like many of his contemporaries who were looking for kicks Eamon Kelly joined the IRA in the 1960s. When the IRA and its political wing Sinn Fein split into two factions, the Official IRA and the Provisional IRA (Provos) in 1970, Kelly remained with the Officials or 'Stickies'. Matt had also been involved in the terror group which soon morphed into an organized criminal group. Their involvement in the republican movement greatly bolstered their already fearsome reputations, a development which the brothers exploited to the full.

The Kelly brothers and their gang specialized in protection rackets, hijacking, fraud, supplying firearms and armed robbery. They ran an extensive protection racket that terrorized legitimate business owners across the north side of Dublin city centre for several years. The Garda's Central Detective Unit (CDU) mounted a long-running, extensive investigation into the racket. However, while business owners across the city had privately admitted that they were paying 'tribute' to Matt and Eamon Kelly, the brothers' reputations as violent hoodlums meant no one would dare testify against them in court. If people didn't pay up, then the Kellys would send their henchmen around to damage the property and rough up the errant owner. If that didn't work the premises would be torched.

The gang also dabbled in the cannabis trade, dealt in forged passports and driving licences, and hired out guns and stolen vehicles to the growing number of armed robbery gangs cropping up across the city. The Kelly brothers also made a lot of money from more legitimate business interests. In 1976 they opened a carpet store, Kelly's Carpetdrome, on the North Circular Road in Dublin which gardaí suspected of being a front for their criminal rackets. By the early 1980s they had opened other carpet and furniture stores on Talbot Street and Mary Street, also in the north inner city. According to one detective at the time, every week business owners would be seen trooping into the Kellys' carpet shops to drop off their protection payments – what the Mafia call 'tribute' – and the police were powerless to do anything about it.

The Kellys commanded a large group of hardened experienced criminals that included a toxic mix of republican sympathizers, IRA members and ordinary villains. By the early 1980s the gang was classified as being in the top three criminal groupings in Dublin, next to the Dunne and Cahill families on the south side of the River Liffey. At the time the capital's criminal community was relatively small in number and they all knew each other and worked together on various robberies or strokes.

It wasn't surprising that the local crime boss first spotted the potential in the precocious de-facto leader of the Bugsy Malones. He knew the Hutch family well as John, Eddie and Patsy Hutch were already part of his wider gang. He provided firearms for robberies organized by Eddie while, officially, John worked for him as a carpet salesman. Kelly was fully aware of Gerry's growing reputation as a prolific robber and liked the way the quiet kid carried himself. He recognized that the teenager was a natural and possessed the ruthless streak necessary to become an accomplished gangster. The godfather had use for a capable young lieutenant and in return found a loyal, able and willing acolyte in Gerry Hutch. It was the beginning of a friendship that would endure for over thirty years.

Hutch had grown up in the shadow of the Kelly brothers, working around the carpet showrooms, running errands and learning the ropes from some of the toughest men in the underworld. When he joined the gang under Eamon Kelly's aegis, being seen as a member of one of the most feared mobs in the city bolstered the teenager's reputation. The gang had plenty of firepower and Hutch was shown how to use a range of guns. Other members of the Bugsy Malones, Hutch's friends Thomas O'Driscoll and Eamon Byrne – the people he trusted most – also began to run in the dodgy circle.

The significance of the alliance between the new kid on the block and the older gangsters wasn't lost on local gardaí. Gerry Hutch wasn't just attracting the attention of older villains: the gardaí had classified him as one of the youngest armed criminals in the city. Such was his reputation that all sightings of Gerry Hutch and his mentors were logged by officers in their collator's intelligence reports as a matter of course. As Kelly's protégé the Monk was ideally placed to take advantage of the explosion of the new world order in Dublin's gangland. When Gerry Hutch joined up, the new generation of armed robbers or blaggers were thriving.

———

By the time the Kellys recruited young Hutch, gangland had been firmly established during the turbulent 1970s. It was a decade which saw an unprecedented, sudden surge in serious crime and violence around Ireland. Only three years earlier, in February 1967, a motley collection of criminals and rebels called Saor Eire (Free

Ireland) had made their mark on Irish history when they robbed a bank in Drumcondra. It was the first armed bank heist in the country since the 1940s and was carried out by an eclectic mix of dissident republicans, socialists, anarchists and hoodlums – idealists, desperados and chancers – who gathered under a flag of political convenience to justify their 'cause' as a struggle on behalf of the downtrodden working classes. Several members of the mob were associates of the Kelly brothers who mixed in the same criminal milieu.

Saor Eire's grandiose pretence of pursuing a legitimate radical political purpose was nothing more than a smokescreen – their purpose was purely criminal. As the country's first professional armed robbery gang they set the bar for scores of would-be blaggers like the Kelly brothers, by showing them how easy it was to rob banks and not get caught.

According to the Garda Commissioner's *Annual Crime Report 1966* there were 'no organized crimes of violence' recorded in Ireland. Such had been the consistently low levels of crime over the previous several decades that the Government at one time considered closing down some prisons where the daily average population was just 300 inmates – today it is over 4,200. The low crime rates were also reflected in the strength of the garda force which had been allowed to fall to less than 6,400 members. The majority of gardaí on the beat had never dealt with anything more serious than break-ins or bike thefts.

Although hardly a footnote in history today Saor Eire succeeded in exposing how the garda force was ill-equipped to take on serious crime, especially well-organized, heavily-armed robbers in fast getaway cars. The gardaí simply didn't have the firepower or the vehicles to confront the new breed of criminals.

The inaugural event was the harbinger of the dramatic descent into chaos that was about to unfold in the Republic. It brought to an abrupt end an age of innocence when crime was traditionally petty in nature and largely confined to Dublin, and often to the streets of deprived communities like the one where Gerry Hutch grew up. This new era of criminality would be remembered affectionately by veteran villains as the halcyon days of crime.

Over the next three years the Saor Eire gang pulled off another eighteen robberies and grew increasingly audacious and reckless. Eventually they went too far on 2 April 1970 and shot dead Garda Dick Fallon during a robbery in Dublin. The gang had set yet another historic milestone in their short existence. Garda Fallon was the first member of the gardaí to be murdered in the line of duty since 1942. The incident deeply shocked the Irish public who turned up in their thousands to line the streets of the capital for the garda's funeral. His murder was the seminal moment that announced the arrival of organized crime in Ireland.

Saor Eire as an organization faded away following the atrocity and was quickly forgotten as its members drifted into other paramilitary and criminal groups, including the Kelly gang. At the same time the conflagration in the North began to spread south of the border with devastating consequences. The dissidents' old comrades in the Official IRA and the Provos had followed the gang's lead and began robbing banks, post offices, business payrolls and security vans with impunity. In particular the Provos unleashed mayhem in the Republic as they pursued a dual objective of funding their 'war' through armed robberies, while at the same time actively working to undermine and corrupt the socio-economic life of the country. They also carried out murders, kidnappings and bombings which placed an impossible strain on the security forces. And in the shadow of the gunmen, a generation of young criminals, many of whom would become household names, were attracted by the new world of limitless opportunity and saw a clear career path.

Between 1970 and 1971 – the first full year of the crime and terror epidemic – Ireland had the fastest-growing crime rate in Europe. In 1967 there had been one armed robbery but by 1976 that figure had soared to 237. By 1986 there were 600. The number of illegal firearms on the streets increased and so did the gangs' willingness to use them. In the days before plastic and online banking there was no end of easy targets in every town and city across Ireland. Every Thursday and Friday, when many people were paid and cash was on the move, businesses, banks and post offices braced themselves for another wave of hold-ups by both the IRA and what the gardaí designated 'crime ordinary' gangs.

There were so many heists taking place that it became something of a national joke. Popular comedian Niall Tóbín even used it for a sketch on a 1970s TV show when his newsreader character presented a robbery report in the form of the weather forecast: 'Today there were robberies in Carlow, Athlone, Navan and Dublin. Tomorrow they will be in Kildare, Tipperary, Cork and Monaghan and next week…'

The unfolding security crisis threatened to engulf the State as the police were stretched to almost breaking point as they tried to regain control of the situation. Dessie O'Malley, Minister for Justice in the early 1970s recalled that it was like being in charge of a fire brigade rushing around trying to put out fires.

The gardaí paid a heavy price in the dangerous new world: in the fourteen years following the murder of Dick Fallon another eleven officers and an Irish soldier were gunned down by the IRA and other renegade republican outfits such as the Irish National Liberation

Army (INLA) and the Official IRA. Most of the killings took place during armed robberies.

The whole focus of the Irish security apparatus and legislature prioritized the terrorist threat over everything else. Human resources were drained as over 1,000 officers – backed up by 2,000 troops from the Irish Army – were assigned to the Border region alone, depleting police numbers everywhere else. The crisis necessitated a major expansion of the security forces and in the space of a few years an additional 2,000 gardaí and 4,000 troops were recruited. The army were called in to escort cash-in-transit vans and all plainclothes garda detectives were armed as new specialist units were formed.

By February 1981, just two months before Gerry Hutch's eighteenth birthday, a group of experienced armed criminals decided that the youngster was good enough to invite on a 'job'. His rite of passage to the big time was to be a baptism of fire – and the closest he ever came to earning a long stretch behind bars. On the morning of the 9 February 1981 the seventeen-year-old was part of a heavily-armed, four-man gang that mounted an audacious raid at the Allied Irish Bank branch on Mary Street in Dublin's city centre. The gang were equipped with two machine guns, two handguns and military grenades. A stolen car rammed through the front of the bank shortly after 9 a.m. as staff were extracting bags of cash from the night safe. The two occupants of the car, armed with handguns, threatened the staff before grabbing the cash. At the same time, a third raider, brandishing a machine gun, stood in the street keeping lookout, while the fourth member of the gang drove the getaway van.

The blaggers ran from the bank with the money bags and the gang piled into the van. As they made their escape in the direction of Dorset Street, a squad car spotted the van and gave chase. The armed gang sped into a side street to discover that it was blocked at one end by bollards. As they abandoned the van, dragging the wallets of cash with them, one of them opened fire with a machine gun, targeting the pursuing squad car. Neither of the officers was injured as they reversed out of the line of fire. The raiders then ran towards Phibsboro Road in north Dublin, where they attempted to hijack a minibus.

The raider with the machine gun stood in the road pointing the weapon at the minibus driver, George Keating, as he was dragged out onto the road. Keating later recalled he heard one of the gang say, 'kill the bastard', and when he looked up there was a handgun pointing at his head. Then he heard a second voice shout, 'Get into the fuckin' van,' and the gang drove off

As armed gardaí began to arrive, the gang only got a short distance before they abandoned the minibus and scattered into the back streets. The leader of the gang, thirty-year-old George Royle, who lived near Gerry Hutch, was arrested at the scene. He was subsequently charged with the armed robbery of £79,000 (worth €314,000 today), the amount which was recovered at the scene.

The fact that detectives quickly nominated the small skinny seventeen-year-old as one of the suspects was recognition of his growing stature in the underworld under the mentorship of the Kelly brothers. Hutch hadn't been seen around his usual haunts that day and later that night gardaí arrested him and brought him in for questioning. The Monk displayed the traits of a hardened, experienced criminal during his detention. He remained silent for over 24 hours and, as gardaí had insufficient evidence to charge him with the robbery, Hutch was released.

The experience had taught him the biggest lesson of his life. Hutch analysed everything that happened that day and realized how the sloppy planning could have had disastrous results. The gang had taken huge risks and hadn't a cent to show for it. It was an operation riddled with mistakes: the stolen getaway van wasn't powerful enough to get away from the cops; the escape route had not been fully checked out; and the gang didn't have an alternative getaway planned either. If it had been more carefully organized, he reasoned, there would not have been a need to fire shots. Shooting at gardaí, especially unarmed members, was something to be avoided at all costs in Hutch's book. The courts and the police were cracking down hard on cop killers as armed confrontations had become commonplace.

The previous year, 1980, had been the bloodiest in the history of An Garda Síochána when three officers were shot dead in the line of duty. Two of the gardaí, John Morley and Henry Byrne, were murdered by an INLA gang in Roscommon after an armed hold-up in Ballaghaderreen, and in Wexford Detective Garda James Quaid was shot dead by an IRA man who was moving a cache of illegal explosives. Two months before the botched robbery in Mary Street, two detectives from Cabinteely garda station, a suburb in south Dublin, were seriously injured when an armed robbery gang led by former Saor Eire member Frank Ward had opened fire with machine guns peppering their squad car with bullets. As Hutch knew in all four incidents the killers and shooters were caught and facing prison sentences of up to forty years. Shooting cops was a dangerous pursuit.

The botched robbery represented a steep learning curve for the Monk who realized the need for planning everything down to the tiniest detail so that the 'job' was mistake-proof and prison-proof. He wouldn't leave it to anyone else either; he'd be in control at all times.

As he fine-tuned his trade, Gerry Hutch took part in several more successful robberies with his brother Eddie, Dave 'Myler'

Brogan, Thomas O'Driscoll and other trusted accomplices. In one robbery a month later, on 4 March 1981, a motorbike pulled up outside the Boyers department store on North Earl Street in central Dublin as security men were about to collect the day's takings. Hutch remained on the bike while O'Driscoll, who was armed with a handgun and wearing a hood, ran inside the store and ordered the security men to hand over the bag of money. They got away with £11,500, a small fortune when the average industrial wage was under £8,000 a year at the time.

Hitting banks and stores in the city centre was part of the gang's modus operandi. Hutch and his compatriots possessed an intimate knowledge of the network of streets and alleyways in the area to make quick getaways. They were often back in their neighbourhood, with the money and guns hidden, within ten minutes of a job.

Another reason why Hutch needed to get his act together and to get money was that his girlfriend and childhood sweetheart, Patricia Fowler, was pregnant with their first child. Hutch would be no use to his new family if he was locked up in Mountjoy Prison. He needed to be on the outside earning a living, however illegally, so that his children would not grow up with the same level of poverty he had experienced. Just two months after the daring raid of Boyers, Gerry Hutch had plenty of time on his hands to contemplate his future when on 8 May 1981 he was jailed for nine months and sent back to St Patrick's Institution for young offenders for larceny of a car.

Hutch's incarceration coincided with the arrival of heroin on the streets of his neighbourhood. The devastating consequences of the availability of the new drug would have a profound influence on his view of the world.

Heroin first appeared on the streets of the south inner city in the late autumn of 1979 when the Dunne crime family switched from robbing banks to selling narcotics. Larry and Shamie Dunne were the first criminals to realize the value of the nascent drug trade. They already controlled a large slice of the hash trade but when the supply was interrupted for a time they got their hands on heroin as an alternative. It was flooding the European market and the glut of the drug coincided with two major international events: the toppling of the Shah of Iran and the Russian invasion of Afghanistan.

Before they fled the country, the ousted Iranian power class converted their gold into cheap heroin. It was coming across the border from Afghanistan, the world's biggest producer of the drug. The Iranians turned drugs into Western currency by selling it to gangs across Europe and North America. At the same time heroin production in Afghanistan soared as the Islamic mujahideen, with the support of the CIA, sold it to raise money to fight the Red Army as part of an amoral geopolitical proxy war. Within a few weeks of first distributing the drug in the south inner city, often free of charge, the Dunnes had established a steady demand. A generation of kids from disadvantaged backgrounds, who knew nothing of its potency, became instantly addicted. As one observer commented at the time: 'The Dunnes did for smack what Henry Ford did for the motor car: made it available to the working man and woman, even the kids on the dole, even the kids at school.'

Just over a year later, in the summer of 1981, the heroin scourge arrived in the streets of Gerry Hutch's neighbourhood where it spread like a bush fire through the desolate landscape, feasting on the ingrained misery of widespread social dysfunction. In a report

on the unfolding crisis a local priest summed up the despair that
was being felt: 'This community has managed to cope with drink
problems, with crime, with unemployment and so on, but I don't
think it is going to be able to cope with this one.'

It was hardly surprising that given its long history of deprivation
and neglect that Hutch's neighbourhood became the epicentre for
the misery. Drug pushers openly plied their trade in the pubs on
Talbot Street, with one notorious boozer, just around the corner
from Store Street garda station, being dubbed the 'Chemist Shop'. A
small park beside Railway Street in the heart of the old Monto where
the Hutch children once played became known as 'Needle Park'.
The scourge heaped more misery on the community as strung-out
addicts broke the old bonds of solidarity and began stealing from
their neighbours and loved ones to buy 'gear'. The new scourge
led to a massive upsurge in street crime and robberies as desperate
junkies tried to get cash to feed their habits.

It also caused problems for criminals like Hutch because
associates who had become heroin addicts could not be trusted.
Their all-consuming need for a fix transcended the moral code of
never ratting on your friends. The ravages of the drug rendered users
veritable zombies who would sell out anyone to feed a habit that
could cost the equivalent of a week's wages in a single day.

A survey conducted on behalf of the Department of Health in
1982 made the alarming discovery that the rates of heroin addiction
in Dublin's north inner city were worse than those among New
York's African-American community in 1970 when the epidemic
was at its height during the Vietnam War. Twelve per cent of
youngsters in Hutch's age range, between fifteen and nineteen, were
heroin abusers. Of the addicts surveyed the majority came from a
background of severe deprivation and had a dysfunctional home

life. They also all had poor levels of education with almost ten per cent unable to read and write and 73 per cent of them involuntarily unemployed.

In the same month that Gerry Hutch was sent back to prison a probation service survey carried out in Mountjoy Prison and St Patrick's Institution for young offenders found that illicit drugs were freely available to the inmates. The survey also found that the majority of abusers were under the age of twenty-five and from the inner city.

The unfolding crisis left a trail of destruction in Hutch's homeland. It led to an unprecedented wave of crime, disease and death, creating a human wasteland strewn with the debris of young broken lives. And when the community thought things could not get any worse, then came the aftershock in the form of HIV/AIDS contracted through the sharing of dirty, blood-filled syringes. While there was a chance of surviving addiction, at the time, AIDS was a death sentence.

Five members of the Dixon family, Gerry Hutch's first cousins, died from a combination of the virus, overdoses and other addiction-related diseases. Members of his future wife's family also perished in the sea of misery. The heroin scourge spelt the end of the Bugsy Malones, claiming the lives of at least five members of the gang. His closest friends and fellow gang members, Eamon Byrne and Thomas O'Driscoll, also became addicts. Following Hutch's imprisonment in May 1981, O'Driscoll was charged with the robbery at Boyers and a second armed hold-up at Pennys Stores on Mary Street on 13 June. In that raid the thieves got away with a whopping £62,000 (worth over €185,000 today).

During his trial for the two robberies gardaí said that O'Driscoll had unexpectedly confessed to the two robberies while being questioned about a separate robbery at Boyers department store which also took place in March 1981. However, O'Driscoll was subsequently acquitted by a jury of both charges. He claimed that he had been 'set up' by gardaí, who he accused of concocting his admissions. He told the Circuit Criminal Court he had become addicted to heroin and had been hospitalized as a result. A year later, in March 1982 O'Driscoll was jailed for five years after pleading guilty to the second armed robbery at the Boyers department store. To Hutch it seemed obvious that heroin had made his friends O'Driscoll and Byrne sloppy and careless as they began doing disorganized robberies to feed their habits. Ultimately Hutch would be proved right to worry.

The fact that Hutch avoided slipping into the heroin or smack trap, at a time when the majority of his peers were experimenting with the drug, before anyone knew how dangerous it actually was, testifies to his self-discipline and intuition. Sickened by the devastation it had caused to his own people and blaming it for the deaths of his best friends, Hutch developed a visceral hatred for the drug and those who sold it. In his eyes dealers were not bona fide criminals but pedlars in death who were to be avoided at all costs. The negative effects of widespread drug addiction reinforced his determination to stay out of prison.

However, when Gerry Hutch was released from prison in October 1981 he went back to robbing. A month later he had another close shave with the law, only this time he narrowly escaped with his life, following a confrontation with armed police. On 23 November 1981 the now eighteen-year-old blagger robbed the Mother's Pride Bakery at Portland Road on the North Circular Road. With him on the job were his brother Eddie and Dave Brogan. Eddie Hutch, who lived close to the bakery, had carried out the surveillance and organized the robbery. He also sourced the weapons for the job – a sawn-off shotgun and two handguns – from Eamon Kelly. The plan was to hit the bakery as the crew of a security van collected the takings. The trio wore balaclavas, anoraks and wigs. Eddie, who was armed with the shotgun, was the driver of the stolen getaway van which pulled up on a side street beside the main office building. Brogan and the Monk, armed with handguns, jumped out and ran into the building seconds after security staff had entered to collect the cash. Brogan stood inside the front door as his teenage accomplice ran into the cash office alone. Hutch threatened the staff at gunpoint before grabbing a bag containing £10,000 (worth €50,000 today). When they returned to the street they found Eddie holding the shotgun to the head of a motorbike garda who had noticed something suspicious and decided to investigate. The unarmed officer was ordered to keep facing the ground as the three jumped into the van and drove off before abandoning it a short distance away. They were quickly swallowed up in the back streets and made their getaway.

But later that day detectives from the Central Detective Unit (CDU) and the local Fitzgibbon Street garda station located the stolen money when they raided a house on Tolka Road, off Clonliffe Road in north Dublin. They also found the Hutches' large cache of weapons which demonstrated the kind of deadly firepower now in the hands of criminal gangs. The haul included a military-spec Stirling submachine gun, three sawn-off pump-action shotguns, a pistol and an assortment of ammunition.

The gardaí decided to lie in wait in the hope of arresting whoever turned up to collect the money and the weapons. They were determined to round up the gang that held such lethal firepower and the Hutches were already the prime suspects. Two officers from the newly-formed Special Task Force (STF) were assigned to stay in the house as backup to a team of detectives who planned to confront the gang when they returned. The STF, which was a forerunner to the Emergency Response Unit (ERU), was established to provide specialist armed support at a time when gardaí were regularly coming under fire during robberies. The STF were issued with Uzi submachine guns and were dubbed the 'Taskies' by the IRA at the time.

One of the STF men was a young garda named Michael O'Sullivan who would become one of the country's most experienced and respected drug crime investigators, rising to the rank of Assistant Commissioner. O'Sullivan currently leads the Maritime Analysis and Operation Centre (MAOC), which co-ordinates operations to prevent trafficking of cocaine into the EU by sea from South America.

During the course of the evening the gardaí arrested four members of the Hutch gang as they arrived at the house at different intervals. Around 1.30 a.m. a distinctive white Datsun sports car with a black roof pulled up outside the house. The car was well known to the gardaí – it belonged to Gerry Hutch. Eddie Hutch got out of the passenger seat and walked towards the house. As he went through the front door he was grabbed by the gardaí who then noticed that the car outside was about to take off. Former Assistant Commissioner O'Sullivan recalled what happened next:

We had been waiting in the house for several hours when the car turned up and we instantly recognized it as Gerry Hutch's because we had often stopped him in it at checkpoints before. Myself and my STF colleague sprinted out the door and stood in front of the car pointing our weapons. Hutch was behind the wheel and we were

shouting at him to stop and show his hands. The adrenaline took over
and we dropped on our knees and aimed the machine guns at him.
He looked like he got a shock when we appeared, but he didn't move.
The window was down and we could not see where his hands were.
We were convinced that he could have a gun and was going to shoot.
I will never forget his cold eyes looking back at me: he seemed to
be in control and the look was one of total contempt. I had my finger
on the trigger and was going to open fire. It was one of the most
frightening moments of my career because in those seconds I came
very close to opening fire. Hutch had no idea just how close he came
to being shot and killed that night. At the time our colleagues were
being shot at regularly and the previous year three gardaí had been
murdered and others seriously injured. We also knew that this crew
had held a gun to the head of an unarmed garda during the robbery.
We then moved in and dragged him out through the window. He didn't
have a gun.

The Hutch brothers were arrested and taken in for questioning
along with other four suspects. However, there was insufficient
evidence to link either of them or Brogan to the haul of money
and guns. An occupant of the house was subsequently convicted in
connection with the find.

Exactly a fortnight after coming so close to being shot Gerry
Hutch had another reason why he didn't want any more run-ins
with the law, threatening either his life or his liberty. On 7 December
he became a father when his future wife Patricia gave birth to a girl
– the first of five children.

From then on everything he did in life revolved around keeping
true to that objective. It was all about control: self-discipline,
discretion and moderation. He developed a sixth sense which

he claimed would alert him if the police had a place staked out just before a job: 'It would be get out of here. Abandon ship. You would get a shiver… like someone dancing on your grave.' Hutch lived a clean life: he stayed fit, rarely drank, didn't take drugs and looked after his wife and kids. He was quiet-spoken, contemplative and unobtrusive as opposed to being impetuous or flamboyant as many of his fellow villains tended to be. He was the quintessential strong silent type which inspired his pals to conceive his famous ecclesiastical moniker – the Monk.

Gerry Hutch stood out from his fellow crooks when it came to his domestic life as well: the marriage remained solid and he ensured that his kids were well educated and didn't follow in his footsteps. In the same month the eighteen-year-old paid £10,000 (€41,000) for a home for his new family on Buckingham Street, in the heart of his old neighbourhood. It was an impressive achievement for someone who had never worked a day in his life. Unlike his fellow gangsters Hutch didn't squander his ill-gotten gains or engage in living a conspicuously high life. One of the first things that went was the flashy, distinctive sports car. Even when he later began pulling off multi-million-pound robberies he did not flash the cash, opting to drive a modest car. His friends ascribe his frugality to an impoverished upbringing. A former associate recalled: 'He was deep – always made the poor mouth about having no money. He was extremely tight with money and would not be flahoolock.'

Despite the young father's new-found responsibilities, he had no intention of giving up his life of crime. Having a baby, not to mention his close shaves with the law, only served to reinforce his determination to avoid getting caught. But as 1982 beckoned organized crime was about to undergo a sinister transformation.

CHAPTER FOUR

———

POWER BASE

On the morning of 6 January 1982 a powerful bomb exploded under a car as it drove onto the Naas dual carriageway in west Dublin. The blast ripped the car apart, lifting it off the road before it landed in a crumpled heap several yards away. The victim of the terror attack was Dr James Donovan, the Director of the Forensic Science Laboratory at Garda HQ in the Phoenix Park, Dublin. He was lucky to survive. The State's most important forensic investigator, whose evidence was crucial in the prosecution of terrorists and criminals, suffered appalling leg injuries which afflicted him for the rest of his life. Initially the finger of suspicion fell on the obvious suspects, the IRA and the INLA, but then the gardaí discovered that it had been the work of Martin Cahill, the General. Organized crime in Ireland had moved to a dangerous new level.

The motive for the attack was pretty straightforward. Cahill wanted the scientist dead so that his forensic evidence could not be used in a forthcoming prosecution against the General and another criminal for an armed robbery. Almost thirty years later it stands out as one of the worst acts of terrorism committed by a gang in the five-decade history of organized crime in Ireland. Despite his injuries, Dr Donovan showed extraordinary courage and returned to work. He gave his damning evidence in Cahill's case which linked him and his accomplice, Christy Dutton, to the robbery of an amusement arcade. In the end they got off on a technicality and the horrific bombing made no difference to the outcome of the trial.

In the aftermath of the horrendous attack garda management realized that years of focusing almost exclusively on the subversive threat had allowed a monster of a different name to evolve amidst the mayhem. The fact that ordinary criminals were prepared to resort to such audacious terrorist-style tactics against a high-profile State official was an ominous development and a wake-up call to the establishment.

The bomb attack on Dr Donovan heralded a brutal intensification of violent crime in the first months of 1982. Two days later an elderly security manager, Gerard Crowley, was shot dead when he tackled robbers who stole the payroll delivery at Clerys department store in O'Connell Street, central Dublin. A month after that, on 20 February, Garda Patrick Reynolds was shot dead when he and colleagues disturbed an INLA gang who were hiding out in a flat in Avonbeg Gardens, in Tallaght. The previous day the gang had robbed a bank in County Limerick. He was the fourth garda officer to be murdered in less than two years.

The continuing crime crisis was placing huge strain on already over-stretched police resources. This was a welcome development for the other gangs who were keeping their heads below the radar. Eamon Kelly didn't have to explain to his young protégé why it was good for business if the gardaí were so distracted. The attempted murder of such a pivotal figure in the prosecution of crime, and the fear his death would instil in other civil servants working in law enforcement, was useful to criminal and terrorist alike. Among

Hutch's criminal fraternity there was also a degree of admiration for Cahill's 'bottle' and how he had shown no fear of the State.

The attack made Martin Cahill 'Public Enemy Number One' as far as the police were concerned and it also confirmed his position as the most powerful figure in the emerging gangland. If Cahill could resort to such violent extremes to attack the all-powerful State, dealing with rivals would be child's play. The General and the Monk would soon have plenty in common as they were destined to become the two best-known names in the Irish underworld.

A team of over sixty detectives was assembled to investigate the Donovan bombing and they launched one of the biggest trawls of the criminal and terrorist communities yet seen. The operation included swarming all over the Kelly brothers and their associates. Their business premises were searched and everyone was pulled over for a chat including the eighteen-year-old Hutch – with good reason. The Dublin criminal community was still small and enduring friendships had been struck up while members of the Kelly gang were serving time in reform schools and prison. As a result the Kelly brothers were closely linked to both the Cahill and Dunne gangs. In the days before inter-gang blood feuds, they were sharing resources such as weapons, false documents and vehicles. As one former Hutch associate recalled:

> There was a lot of crossover between the gangs because it was a small town and everyone knew each other; and there wasn't the same level of paranoia and mistrust you get these days with the drug lads. Gerard got to know Cahill quite well over the years in a professional sort of way and he was friends with individual members of his gang. He admired Cahill's skills as an organizer of big strokes [robberies] but thought he was a mad bastard for doing all the crazy stuff like

blowing up the scientist and putting it up to the cops whenever he could. It wasn't so much that he felt sorry for the scientist because Gerard hated anyone involved with the police; it was bad for business and only give the cops a bigger excuse to come after him. Gerard believed in planning jobs so well that there would be no worries of what a forensic scientist would find at a crime scene.

Among the General's associates listed in garda intelligence reports at the time were two of Hutch's friends, George Royle, still in prison after the botched bank job on Mary Street, and Gerard O'Callaghan, a neighbour from Buckingham Street.

Another link between the two mobs was businessman Niall Mulvihill from Sheriff Street, a close childhood friend and partner in crime of the Kelly brothers. He also had a long business association with Martin Cahill and his sidekick, John Traynor, a smooth-talking fraudster. A few years earlier Mulvihill had sold them a grotty, rundown pub at the North Wall in the Dublin docklands. Called the Jetfoil, it became notorious as the biggest drug-dealing centre in the city during the early days of the heroin epidemic. In 1984 Cahill and Traynor had it burned down so they could collect malicious damage compensation from Dublin Corporation. Some years later they made another killing on the burnt-out property when it became the subject of a compulsory purchase order as part of the process to make way for the International Financial Services Centre (IFSC) and the gentrification of the inner city.

Nicknamed the 'Silver Fox', Mulvihill was not a violent criminal but acted as a 'fixer' for gangs around Dublin. Gardaí suspected his skills included organizing dodgy deals, fraud rackets, handling stolen goods and providing logistics for various crimes. To the rest of the world Mulvihill was a respectable businessman with interests in a number of inner-city pubs, a cafe, a few launderettes and a furniture store. He had no criminal record and was an election agent for political party Fianna Fáil which added gravitas to his role as a front man for the Kelly gang. Mulvihill became a close friend of the young Hutch and was part of his inner circle for almost twenty years.

While Hutch and Mulvihill were cementing their partnership, the heat died down as the investigation team uncovered the identities of the gang who had been involved in the plot with Cahill. Included among them were the Dunne brothers, Christy, Henry and Larry, the heroin dealer. INLA members Gerry Roche, Thomas Healy and Thomas McCarton were also involved. Roche had supplied the explosives while for a fee McCarton made the device. They were amongst those arrested for questioning but there was insufficient evidence to charge any of them. However, most of the conspirators ended up behind bars for other crimes. The three Dunne brothers subsequently received long jail sentences for drug trafficking, kidnapping, armed robbery and shooting at police with intent to endanger life. McCarton was murdered in an internal INLA feud. Healy got twelve years for armed robbery and Roche, who later left the INLA and rejoined the IRA, is still wanted in connection with the murder of Detective Garda Jerry McCabe in Limerick in 1996.

With the investigation concluded, Gerry Hutch and his cronies were back in business. Throughout the rest of the year they carried out robberies on an almost industrial scale. As serious crime increased, official figures showed that Hutch's neighbourhood, the Garda C district, accounted for ten per cent of all crime in Ireland. In 1981 there were forty-eight armed robberies, including the botched raid on Mary Street, and the following year another thirty-four. A garda intelligence report in June 1982 estimated that there were over twenty guns for hire from criminals living in the area. Weapons seized by detectives in Hutch's home base included his mob's machine guns and fragmentation grenades. Around the same time the first gang-related murders started to occur. The teenage Hutch's name would be tied to at least two of them.

On 8 February 1982 an armed robbery took place which was to spark a chain of events that implicated Hutch and his mentor in the shocking murder of a teenage boy. In north Dublin a security man was transferring money from the Allied Irish Bank on Lower Drumcondra Road to a security van when all hell broke loose. A man dressed as a woman, who had been standing at a nearby bus stop, ran forward producing a sawn-off shotgun. He shot and wounded the security man as he grabbed a bag containing £25,000 (over €70,000) and then jumped on the back of a waiting motorbike. It had previously been suspected that Martin Cahill had carried out the shooting but fresh information suggests that it was Gerry Hutch.

Several years later in a statement to gardaí the Monk's former partner-in-crime, Dave 'Myler' Brogan, claimed that Hutch was the raider. He said the Monk asked him to act as his backup, like he had done in the past. Brogan later told detectives:

> I was standing across the road at a hardware store with a stolen motorbike to take Hutch away if anything went wrong. Hutch was wearing a black wig, head scarf and woman's coat. He had the gun under the coat. I saw him shoot the security man as he came out of the bank. He grabbed the bag of money and got on the getaway bike which was driven by a lad from Crumlin. I didn't see him for a few days after that and then he paid me £2,000 (€6,000) for my part.

In the follow-up investigation gardaí only identified one of the suspects involved in the robbery – Michael 'Peggy leg' McDonnell from Crumlin in south Dublin, who according to Brogan was the driver of the motorbike. Some weeks later a fourteen-year-old from Kildare Road in Crumlin discovered a bag of cash hidden in the garden of a house at nearby Saul Road. It was the family home of twenty-one-year-old 'Peggy leg' McDonnell, and the money was his share of the proceeds. McDonnell was part of the wider gang connected to Hutch and Eamon Kelly. The excited fourteen-year-old called his friend Gerard Morgan, who was the same age, and together they counted the cash which came to £5,500 (€14,000) in used notes. The two boys could not believe their luck.

Over the next few days, they managed to burn through £2,000 (€6,000) of the loot. At some stage Gerard Morgan confided in his seventeen-year-old brother, Alan, that his pal had 'a few grand' hidden in his house. Alan Morgan and a friend decided that they would take the money for themselves. The friends broke into the teenager's house and stole the remaining £3,000, dividing it up between them. From his share of the windfall Morgan bought a car, new clothes and a holiday in Spain for himself and his girlfriend. His pal spent his share of the spoils on clothes, drink, drugs and fun.

In the meantime McDonnell discovered that his money had been 'stolen' and began making enquiries. When he discovered what had happened to the loot he blamed Alan Morgan and demanded the return of the money. As an added incentive, on 8 March a number of shots from a .38 revolver were fired through the front door of the Morgan family home on Lismore Road, Crumlin. The following morning McDonnell told Alan Morgan he had fired the shots and that they were just a warning.

When the money wasn't forthcoming from Alan Morgan, 'Peggy leg' McDonnell turned to Eamon Kelly and Gerry Hutch for help.

On 17 May a garda logged a sighting of Kelly, Hutch, Noel 'Duck Egg' Kirwan and McDonnell drinking together in Ryan's Pub on Parnell Street in Dublin city centre. According to garda records, McDonnell had been regularly 'collated in their company' and was classified as a criminal associate of the two men. The following night, 18 May, Gerry Hutch, Eamon Kelly and 'Peggy leg' went looking for Alan Morgan. Hutch and McDonnell sat in the car while Kelly spoke to the teenager on the street. He caught Morgan by the arm and asked if he knew 'Peggy leg' McDonnell. When Morgan acknowledged that he did, Kelly told the teenager: 'There was £6,000 robbed on him and a little bastard like you to come along and rob it from the bloke who went out and did robberies for it. You better have that money at your house tomorrow at 4 p.m.'

At this point Kelly pulled back his suit jacket to reveal a handgun stuck in the waistband of his trousers. 'If you don't pay the money, you're going to get it,' he warned, as he was joined by McDonnell and Hutch to emphasize the point.

The next night Morgan and his girlfriend bumped into McDonnell who had still not received his money. 'Peggy leg' again threatened him, saying: 'You'll get it… there's going to be a lot of killing in Crumlin and it's only the start.'

Around 2 a.m. a few days later, on 26 May, the Morgan household was awoken by loud knocking on the door. As Gerard Morgan went to answer it two shots were fired through the glass door fatally injuring the teenager. Just when it seemed that the gangs could stoop no lower following the Donovan bomb attack and the murders of a garda and a security man, the killing of a teenage boy set a new precedent in depravity. The murder outraged the Irish public and added to the perception that violent crime was spiralling out of control in 1982.

When gardaí launched an investigation into the murder Alan Morgan informed them of the death threats from McDonnell and Kelly. Just under a month later, on 24 June 1982 Kelly and Hutch were arrested at their homes under the provisions of the Offences Against the State Act on suspicion that they had been in possession of firearms at Rathdrum Road in Crumlin on 18 and 19 of May. They were both taken to Crumlin garda station for questioning.

Detectives had managed to trace the car Hutch was driving on the night of the 18 May incident from descriptions given by the dead boy's brother and other witnesses. In the days before CCTV, satnav or automatic number plate recognition technology it had been a painstaking exercise tracking their movements. Kelly had instructed one of his employees in the carpet shop to rent the car using a false driving licence and to then give it to Gerry Hutch. The car was rented on 14 May and returned on 19 May.

'Peggy leg' McDonnell had gone into hiding after the shooting and gardaí were confident that they had enough evidence to charge him with murder. But the investigating team were equally determined that the two major criminals Hutch and Kelly would also face justice. Based on the witness statements and other corroborative evidence, they had a strong prospect of charging Kelly with possession of a firearm with intent to endanger life, and Hutch with being an accessory to the crime.

Eamon Kelly refused to take part in an identity parade so the gardaí improvised and placed nine men of similar age and appearance sitting beside him in a room. When Alan Morgan was asked if he could identify the man who had threatened him on 18 May he did a brave thing – he placed his hand on Kelly's shoulder and said, 'That's the man who threatened me.' When asked to comment Kelly shrugged his shoulders and replied: 'Nothing to say. My solicitor told me not to go on any parade.' Morgan's girlfriend agreed to participate in the same process and also courageously identified the gang boss.

During a later interview Kelly admitted knowing Michael 'Peggy leg' McDonnell but claimed he had only met him 'once or twice'. When he was asked if he knew Gerry Hutch, Kelly answered that his brother John Hutch worked for him. He said he had nothing more to say and that they could charge him if they wanted to.

When Gerry Hutch was formally cautioned and informed of the purpose of his arrest he replied: 'I can't remember that far back. I know me rights and I know that I have the right to remain silent.' After that he said nothing more and stared at the floor for the next four hours. While the cops were well aware of Hutch's reputation as a hardened young criminal, they were still surprised at his ability to handle himself in the intimidating environs of a cramped interview room, sitting across the table from two big policemen. They recognized that he was no ordinary, naive nineteen-year-old thug.

Hutch was a genuine hard case who had learned a lot from the many interrogations he had experienced in his short life. He was what detectives referred to as a 'spot-on-the-wall-merchant', a classification reserved for only the toughest and most experienced criminals and terrorists. The Monk was capable of picking a spot and staring at it for up to 48 hours if necessary. He once explained: 'You just fuckin' did it. You said nothing. You said to yourself, "He wants to put a rope around my neck." You said nothing from start to finish.'

Any questions that he did answer were those he knew he couldn't get out of denying. He confirmed that he had possession of the car and that it was hired for him by Kelly's employee. Hutch admitted he might have been in the Crumlin area with the car but denied driving it on Rathdrum Road.

When Hennessy, the man who hired the car, was brought into the interview room Hutch acknowledged that they knew each other. One of the detectives asked him if he wanted to read Hennessy's statement but the gangster refused, saying that he couldn't read. Nor did he want it read to him. He accepted the employee's account of renting the car and handing it over to him. Later Hutch conceded that he'd had the car in question on 18 and 19 May and that he didn't give it to anyone else. He said he could have been out and about in it up to 9 p.m. but he didn't know where he went.

When he was asked to volunteer for an identification parade Hutch gave the same response as his mentor. Another eight men of similar age and appearance were brought into the room and took up seated positions. When Alan Morgan placed his hand on the Monk's shoulder, Hutch made no reply and lowered his head. Afterwards the detectives asked him for his reaction to being identified by Morgan. 'I wouldn't fuckin' rat on anyone, I wouldn't tell you anything,' he snapped back. After that he looked down at the floor again and remained silent.

The Monk and Kelly were held in separate cells overnight and the following morning Hutch's interview resumed. He was asked if he had been given an opportunity to say anything when he was identified by the victim the previous night. He replied: 'I was but I didn't want to say anything. I was picked out and that chap was going to pick me. He had his mind made up so what's the point in sayin' anything.'

During his detention he was visited by his sister Sandra and his loyal mother Julia who came to see how he was doing. He and Kelly were subsequently released without charge pending the completion of an investigation file for the Director of Public Prosecutions (DPP).

The garda report on the investigation summarized Hutch's growing status in the underworld:

> Since 1971 Hutch has thirty previous convictions for numerous cases of housebreaking, larceny, assault and obstructing police. He has served a number of terms of imprisonment. Gerard Hutch is fulltime involved in the organisation of major crime and is actively involved in the commission of these crimes. It is stated that he has access to a wide range of weaponry and would not hesitate to use it if confronted. Over the years there are many sightings of himself, Kelly and other hardcore criminals together. Although of tender years Gerard Hutch is much respected and feared by the criminal element on account of his previous exploits and violent disposition. He is fulltime involved in the organisation of major crime.

In the file to the DPP, the garda officer in charge of the investigation, Superintendent John Courtney, wrote: 'An unusual feature of this case is the fact that notwithstanding the aura of fear and intimidation which permeates from these suspects, that witnesses have been quite willing to come forward, place their hand on the shoulder of suspects and identify them. This action is of great encouragement to the gardaí in their fight against serious crime.'

Despite the investigation team making a strong case to charge both Eamon Kelly and Gerard Hutch the Director of Public Prosecutions ruled that there was insufficient evidence. The DPP gave instructions to charge McDonnell with the murder of Gerard Morgan. Hutch and Kelly were free men and in gangland terms the young gangster had proved his mettle as a serious player.

'Peggy leg' McDonnell went on the run immediately after the murder and a warrant was issued for his arrest. A year later his friend, twenty-one-year-old Patrick Conroy from Buckingham Street, pleaded guilty to harbouring and assisting McDonnell on the night of the murder. It was a bizarre case given that McDonnell, who had not yet gone on trial, was innocent in the eyes of the law until he was found either guilty or not guilty.

During the hearing before the Central Criminal Court the prosecution read out Conroy's statement in which he described McDonnell coming to his home after the shooting in Crumlin and telling him: 'I think I got the wrong fellah. I think it was a kid. He has to be dead. I hit him in the head and the chest, I think.' Conroy was jailed for seven years which in the circumstances seemed harsh.

The gardaí eventually caught up with McDonnell in April 1985 and he was formally charged with murder. However, the DPP subsequently dropped the charges when the original witnesses refused to testify against him. The passage of time had changed their minds – or perhaps Kelly and Hutch had helped to convince them they had made a mistake.

Gerry Hutch's latest run-in with the gardaí had done nothing to change his implacable hatred for the police. It was hardly a surprising attitude considering the criminogenic environment he came from. Criminals generally hate cops because they are the ones whose job it is to solve the crimes they commit and build the evidence to put them in prison. Criminal psychologists see it as a classic example of cognitive dissonance as offenders tend to hold contradictory values: blaming the police while compartmentalizing and rationalizing the crimes which led to the police coming to their door in the first place. Despite his innate intelligence Hutch was no different. As he told

Magill magazine many years later: 'Growing up in the inner city, you can only have jam on one side of your bread. The police were enemy number one. As a kid, if a police car came up and if you did talk to a cop, you were a fuckin' tout. If a patrol car passed we would throw stones at it.' In November 1982 the gardaí gave Gerry Hutch another big reason to hate them.

At 7 a.m. on 22 November armed officers from the Central Detective Unit mounted a surveillance operation at the B + I Ferry terminal at Alexander Road in Dublin Port. They had received a tip-off that a gang was planning to rob the safe in the purser's office on a ferry that was docked at the terminal. An hour later the gang arrived in a stolen car driven by Hutch's nineteen-year-old friend Eamon Byrne. Byrne and brothers Stephen and David Conroy, wearing balaclavas and overalls, were spotted boarding the ferry. However, one of the gang recognized an undercover garda and they turned to walk away as detectives moved in to arrest them. David Conroy produced a handgun, but he and his brother were overpowered while Byrne made a run for it. As he climbed over a fence Byrne turned and pointed a handgun at two detectives who had caught up with him. In the ensuing scuffle to disarm him Byrne was accidentally shot in the back of the neck. He died from his injuries in hospital three days later.

The Conroy brothers were subsequently jailed for two years each after pleading guilty to conspiring to steal almost £20,000 (over €45,000). A fourth man, Bernard Lennie, who was the driver of a getaway van, also pleaded guilty but received a suspended sentence on the grounds that he had never been in trouble with the law before.

The death of his childhood friend hit Gerry Hutch hard. In his eyes Byrne was set up to be executed by the police and all the other circumstances of the incident were irrelevant, including the fact that his friend was a junkie. The Monk didn't acknowledge that Byrne had been the author of his own destiny. His friend's death gave Hutch another reason to loathe the police.

CHAPTER FIVE

FIRST BLOOD

The black and white photograph taken on 29 April 1983 is dominated by the taciturn-looking young man leaning casually against a wall; his demeanour one of broody detachment, as his eyes look into the distance. Whilst physically present, the picture suggests that his mind is focused elsewhere. To one side of him a huddle of people are talking, and on the other a cluster of decommissioned placards lay against the wall. The atmospheric image by press photographer Derek Speirs proved the idiom that a picture is worth a thousand words.

Twenty-year-old Gerry Hutch was standing on the steps of the Dublin Coroner's Court where the inquest into his friend Eamon Byrne's death was taking place. He was with a crowd of about sixty people who had picketed the court, brandishing placards accusing the gardaí of murder with slogans such as, 'Eamon Byrne Murdered by Gardaí' and 'Gardaí Licenced to KILL?'. The picket was organized by the Prisoners' Rights Organisation (PRO) to demand an independent enquiry into the circumstances of the killing and a review of police firearms training. The bulk of the crowd was made up of the Byrne family's neighbours and friends from the Sheriff Street area in the north inner city. The hearing was adjourned pending the trials of the dead man's accomplices.

After the killing of their pal, Hutch and the remnants of the Bugsy Malones had contemplated taking revenge on the gardaí responsible but pragmatism prevailed and the idea was dropped. Hutch realized how futile it would be. The gardaí were the most powerful gang on the streets and ultimately they would use the full legitimate authority of the State to win any war. Hutch and his cronies, however, did become involved with a ragtag group calling itself the Prisoners Revenge Group (PRG). Set up by Martin Cahill and other senior gangsters, the PRG set about intimidating prison officers who were seen as a soft target. The group later publicly claimed responsibility for a series of six horrific attacks against individual prison officers over the following two years. The young family of a chief officer in Mountjoy Prison were lucky to escape uninjured when their home was engulfed in flames following an arson attack which left them homeless. In another incident the home of a young couple was petrol-bombed just after they'd bought it from an assistant chief officer in the same prison. Although Gerry Hutch was recorded in garda intelligence reports as a PRG member, there was no evidence that he took part in the assaults which ceased when the gardaí successfully convicted individual members of the group. The group disbanded soon afterwards.

When Eamon Byrne's inquest was finally held that July, the coroner's jury heard testimony from the gardaí, medical and civilian witnesses. The court heard that Byrne had been accidentally shot from a range of four inches during a scuffle with gardaí as he tried to get away. Counsel for the Byrne family, the Irish Council of Civil Liberties and the Prisoners' Rights Organisation urged the jury to consider adding a rider to their verdict so that it would include a recommendation for the improvements in garda firearms training and arrest techniques.

After a short deliberation the jury merely reaffirmed the cause of Byrne's death: 'Eamon Byrne died on the 25 November 1982 at the Mater Hospital in Dublin, from cerebral apoxyia and respiratory failure due to a compression injury to the spinal cord caused by a wound to the neck sustained at the B + I terminal on 22 November 1982.'

Case closed.

The fact that the jury refused to include any of the recommendations reflected the public's hardening attitude to the spiralling crime wave and a lack of sympathy for dead armed robbers. Why blame the police if an armed criminal gets shot during a robbery? However, it reinforced the view held by Hutch and Byrne's other friends that it was them versus the rest of the world – particularly as events closer to home were pulling the aspiring gangster deeper into a cycle of violent crime.

———

In his life Gerry Hutch always preferred things to be either black or white, but never grey. It was a more aspirational than realistic philosophy given that the Monk lived in the twilight world of organized crime. Like most serious criminals he compartmentalized problems and issues in order to navigate around a maze of inherent contradictions. The syndrome is most effectively encapsulated in Mario Puzo's *The Godfather*: 'There are things that have to be done and you do them and you never talk about them. You don't try to justify them. They can't be justified. You just do them. Then you forget it.'

On 10 April 1983 some of the Monk's fellow armed robbers identified something that 'had to be done' – the first ever drug-related gangland murder. Their actions would set a new precedent in Irish crime. The apparent contradiction for the twenty-year-old Hutch lay in the fact that many of his associates were also drug dealers and the motive for the killing was a dispute over turf.

The murder represented a major paradigm shift in Dublin's crime milieu. It was a clear signal that the narcotics trade was beginning to transform gangland and undermine the old value system of ordinary decent criminals like Gerry Hutch. The era of the hit man had arrived, and they would not just be operating in the drug trade.

Throughout 1983 Gerry Hutch and other members of the Bugsy Malones were mingling in a pool of armed robbers of all ages and temperaments within the orbit of the Kelly gang including members of republican groups the IRA, the INLA and veterans of Saor Eire. Dave 'Myler' Brogan, the career armed robber who brought Hutch on his first jobs, was one of the gang. Brogan was also one of the first pioneers of the cannabis trade in Ireland. Born in 1952 in the north inner city, Myler had served time as a teenager in the Irish reform schools where he suffered emotional and sexual abuse at the hands of the Christian Brothers. Brogan started his criminal career with Saor Eire before moving to London where he cut his teeth as a professional blagger – and ended up serving a number of prison sentences for his trouble. He returned to Ireland and began robbing with the Hutches in 1980. Over the next six years, by his own admission, Brogan participated in several armed robberies with Gerry Hutch, his brothers and other members of the Bugsy Malones.

The group of armed felons Hutch was now running with also included Brogan's business partners, maverick republicans and hardened criminals Tommy Savage and Mickey Weldon, both from Swords in north County Dublin. Savage, nicknamed the Zombie because of his unpredictable and dangerous personality, was a convicted armed robber and a former member of Saor Eire. The thirty-three-year-old first drifted into the ranks of the Official IRA with Eamon Kelly. In 1974 he was one of the founder members of a new terror gang, the Irish National Liberation Army (INLA) and its political wing, the Irish Republican Socialist Party (IRSP), following an acrimonious split amongst the Stickies. The INLA took over where Saor Eire left off.

The new gang committed some of the worst atrocities during the Troubles. A string of later internecine feuds saw members of the organization murdering more of their own comrades than the supposed real enemy – the British Army. The INLA quickly became a magnet for the dregs of the republican movement – psychopaths, mass murderers, kidnappers and drug dealers – and was never anything more than a vicious, quasi-political organized crime gang.

Mickey Weldon joined the terrorist group in the late 1970s while serving as a corporal in the Irish Army. Corporal Weldon was suspected of stealing a number of weapons from his battalion, including a rifle and machine gun, which he threw over the barrack wall.

Another member of the dangerous clique was thirty-year-old Danny McOwen from the north inner city, a prolific armed robber and Saor Eire alumnus who also joined the INLA. McOwen served time in the 1970s for armed robbery and possession of explosives. In 1980 he and Savage had been jailed for the theft of a getaway car.

Evidence of the unsavoury company Hutch was keeping came to light in 1983 when he was charged with causing malicious damage to a stolen car which was to be used in a robbery organized by the Zombie and McOwen.

Apart from robbing banks and payrolls, by the spring of 1983 Brogan, Savage, McOwen and Weldon were building a major

cannabis distribution network in north Dublin. Money from
the robberies was used as investment capital in the new project.
They sourced their hashish through Brogan's contacts with the
producers in Lebanon's Becka Valley and with international dealers
in Amsterdam. He later recalled:

> I had some big international contacts which could supply good
> quality cannabis. At first when I got involved with Savage and Weldon,
> I thought it was no harm because it wasn't heroin or cocaine. The
> money is easy in drugs but then I got out of it because of the sort
> of reptiles I found myself mixing with. Gerard Hutch avoided the
> business and so did most of his family at that stage.

Despite his 'black and white' loathing for the heroin trade, Gerry
Hutch, like many of his contemporaries, tended to be ambivalent
about the hash trade which was seen as a grey area. By the 1970s
cannabis had been established as the recreational drug of choice in
Ireland. Unlike LSD or smack, people who smoked dope didn't tend
to jump off buildings in the hope of flying, nor did they become
strung-out junkies. It was classified as a soft drug which was enjoyed
by people of all classes in society. Cannabis was first commodified
for the mass-market in the 1960s when UK criminals were
introduced to its charms – and market potential –while on holiday
or hiding from the law on Spain's Costa del Sol or in Morocco. It was
smuggled into UK prisons where inmates found that a quiet joint
was preferable to the dubious effects of hooch fermented in pisspots.
In appreciation of its mellowing effects on their charges, the prison
authorities happily turned a blind eye. Outside the prison walls the
underworld had found a much more profitable source of income.

Gerry Hutch wasn't a convert. He said that he once tried a puff
of a joint while in prison but didn't like it. Many of his associates

on the other hand became major cannabis dealers in the 1980s and 1990s, including Derek, his younger brother, who worked with Tommy Savage.

Criminals, such as the Dunne family, initially moved into the drugs trade by organizing the first big shipments of cannabis into Ireland. They used their extensive network of UK contacts to obtain vast quantities of the drug. The market for hash was much bigger than the demand for heroin and it was hugely lucrative. In the early days the small number of gangs involved tended to observe the equivalent of a verbal agreement when it came to dividing up territory. But over time, as more groups bought in, the prodigious profits made people greedy and turned former friends into enemies.

As part of their operation Myler Brogan ran the gang's patch in the notorious Ballymun tower blocks in north Dublin. Built to commemorate the heroes of the 1916 Rebellion, the huge corporation flat complex on the edge of the city was initially welcomed as a revolutionary new approach to solve the inner-city tenement problems of the 1960s. But with little or no basic amenities and high rates of unemployment, the complex quickly became a downtrodden socio-economic ghetto. Within two years of the arrival of the heroin epidemic there were an estimated 1,000 addicts living in the concrete wasteland. The ingrained misery provided fertile ground for the drug trade.

Gerard Hourigan, a twenty-five-year-old petty crook from nearby Balcurris Road, used a network of local teenagers to distribute the drugs for Brogan and his associates. He operated from a club in the basement of the Joseph Plunkett tower block. But Hourigan had a fatal character flaw – he was greedy. And his brash and ambitious manner made it clear he didn't care whose toes he stood on to get up the ladder. Hourigan got his opportunity in January 1983 when

Myler Brogan was arrested in France as part of an international drug investigation.

The arrest led to a shortage of cannabis in north Dublin so Hourigan made his move. He approached the Dunne family and suggested setting up a partnership selling hash and heroin in the flats. The petty thief had decided to set up his own independent operation. He told associates that he had no fears of old timers like, Savage and Weldon. Hourigan believed that with the backing of the Dunnes he would have no worries taking over. The Dunnes warned Hourigan of the potential folly of crossing swords with the likes of Savage and his INLA comrades, and refused to get involved.

When the French authorities released Brogan without charge a few weeks later the Dunnes tipped him off about his manager's ambitions. Myler informed Hourigan that he was sacked and warned him that 'people' were talking about shooting him because he was 'getting out of his box'. Instead of heeding the warning, the reckless drug dealer upped the ante by raiding the home of Brogan's parents in the inner city looking for the proceeds of drug deals. Then he added insult to injury on 7 April when he robbed his former employer's prized top-of-the-range BMW and rammed it into a wall. Hourigan returned the crumpled motor to its original parking spot outside the Penthouse pub in Ballymun where Myler was drinking and then informed a mutual associate what he had done.

In a subsequent interview with this writer in September 1992, Dave Brogan claimed that he went to 'visit' Hourigan with Gerry Hutch and a close friend of Tommy Savage to teach his errant underling a lesson: 'We went to see him [Hourigan] and gave him a hiding because he was trying to muscle in on our patch. He was getting too big for his boots and he had to have manners put on him. I warned him that he was messing with the wrong people especially Tommy Savage.'

But blinded by hubris, Hourigan let it be known that he was laughing at the INLA hoodlums. He sealed his fate when he went looking for Savage in Swords armed with a handgun and a sawn-off shotgun.

Less than 24 hours later, shortly after midnight on Sunday, 10 April 1983, Hourigan and four friends were returning to the Ballymun flats after spending the day drinking in the city centre. He was still laughing about the death threats he had received and joked that he'd have to get a haircut and wear his best suit so that he looked well when he was shot. As the group reached Plunkett Tower, a motorbike pulled up and the pillion passenger got off, producing a handgun and running towards Hourigan. The ambitious drug dealer ran into the basement club but was cornered by the hit man who shot him in the head at point-blank range. The assassin fired a second shot into Hourigan's head for good measure, before running off into the night. Hourigan's ambitions for the big time had been short lived – and he never got to change his clothes or get a haircut.

Gerard Hourigan was the first of many hundreds who would perish in drug-related disputes over the following decades. Almost a decade later Brogan was adamant that he had not been responsible for the country's first gangland murder, even though he had plenty of motive. He was equally certain that Gerry Hutch had not been involved in the hit either. The two men that he claimed carried out the murder were also identified as the prime suspects during the subsequent garda investigation. No one was ever charged with the killing. Brogan later claimed:

I didn't know they were going to kill him and the first I heard of it was
that Sunday morning when I met Savage and he told me to go home
and lie low. I was one of the prime suspects and I was lifted for it, but
I had absolutely nothing to do with it. I heard about it a few days later.
After that I got out of the hash business and went back to robbing.
When drugs came everything changed. There was no loyalty and
people who had once been friends started turning guns on each
other because one thought the other had ripped him off. Fuck it, it just
wasn't worth the hassle any more.

While the drug trade continued to prosper, Brogan's former partner
Danny McOwen had become embroiled in a bitter dispute between
the Hutch family and an associate who also lived in the north inner
city. The feud arose when the Monk discovered that McOwen's
friend had assaulted his wife Patricia in a local pub while Hutch
was in prison. The offender, who had a reputation as an incorrigible
womanizer, was a member of a new armed robbery team McOwen
had set up called the Gang of Six. The bitter row was threatening
to cause a split between the wider group of inter-connected villains
in the Kelly gang.

The Hutches could depend on the tacit support of Eamon
Kelly, Savage and Brogan. But Tommy Savage and another INLA
associate, who were close to all the parties in the simmering feud,
were anxious to avoid a worsening of hostilities and wanted a
peaceful solution to be found. On the other side, George Royle and
a number of other villains sided with McOwen and the womanizer.
The row escalated as threats were made by both sides. Traditionally
such rows tended to be sorted out with a 'straightener' – a fist
fight – but Gerard Hourigan's murder had shown that times
were changing. Gerry Hutch had made a few efforts to shoot the

offender but missed him. Eamon Kelly agreed with his friend Savage and intervened in an attempt to resolve the simmering feud before it got out of hand. In early June Tommy Savage and Eamon Kelly arranged a sit-down between the feuding criminals. It took place in the Cabra home of one of Savage's closest associates who had been involved in the murder of Hourigan a few months earlier. Brogan later confirmed that he was at the meeting along with Gerry Hutch, his brothers Eddie and Patsy, Kelly, Savage, McOwen, Royle and the offender who had caused the problem in the first place. A garda intelligence report from 1983 also highlighted this meeting taking place. McOwen's associate made it clear that he was anxious to bury the hatchet and move on. According to Brogan the offender apologized to the Monk for his behaviour and he reciprocated by assuring him that the trouble was over between them. But one of the conditions of a truce was that McOwen's associate leave the area. However, McOwen wasn't happy and rounded on the young gangster. According to Brogan's account of what happened next, McOwen was angry that Hutch had made a number of attempts to shoot his pal and said: 'Who the fuck do you think you are at your age making demands of people and then trying to shoot them?' McOwen then threatened Hutch and his brothers with trouble if they took any further action. Gerry Hutch said as far as he was concerned the matter was over and they walked out.

McOwen had made a big mistake. Years later Dave Brogan explained: 'Gerard was a very cold fish and very calculating. He didn't go looking for trouble and minded his own business but if you fucked with him you were walking on thin ice.'

On 7 June McOwen began living away from the home he shared with his wife and children at Clonalvey in County Meath.

Even though he was registered as unemployed he'd paid £25,000 (€65,000) for the house in 1982. Clearly worried for his safety, McOwen began moving between safe houses. He told his wife and trusted associates that Eamon Kelly and Gerry Hutch were going to shoot him. But the former Saor Eire member had a weak spot – he was greedy. Despite having plenty of stolen money the robber never failed to collect his unemployment assistance every week. On the morning of 14 June, he and his friend George Royle turned up at the Cumberland Street labour exchange in Dublin city centre. McOwen was about to collect more than he bargained for.

As he went into the building to collect his dole, his arrival was being monitored from the top balcony of the Avondale House flats. Eyewitnesses later said that a man was sitting on the stairs just where he had a clear view of the labour exchange below. Their description of this surveillance operative bore a striking resemblance to Gerry Hutch – 5' 8" in height, of slight build and in his twenties. The man was wearing a light brown cap, a scarf and gloves, and was 'messing with something under his coat' as he headed down the stairs and across the road towards the dole office. Two teenagers watching him from a balcony laughed at the state of his hair which they told gardaí was 'brown in colour and was bunching up at the end of his cap as if it was a wig'.

As McOwen and Royle walked back out into the street the hit man ran from Avondale House pulling a gun from his jacket. McOwen attempted to run but the assassin opened fire, hitting him four times in the head and chest. The armed robber died instantly. The killer ran back through the flats, jumped a wall into waste ground and disappeared. Royle escaped uninjured.

In his interview with this writer in 1992, and in a subsequent statement he made to gardaí in 1995, Brogan claimed to have witnessed the killing shortly after he met Eddie Hutch that morning:

Eddie was babysitting three children including a baby and he had them in the car with him. He told me he had to drop something down to Gerard and I went with him. He had a gun hidden in the baby's nappy. We drove down to Hill Street and parked on the junction of Parnell Street and Hill Street. I saw Eddie take the gun, a .38 revolver with a short barrel, from the child's nappy and he walked across Hill Street. I saw Gerard coming out of the gate at Avondale House. He was wearing a wig and glasses, but I recognized him straight away. I saw Eddie handing the gun over and Gerard walked back into the flats. I then saw McOwen walking down North Cumberland Street and Gerard came running across the road with the gun in his hand. He fired a shot and McOwen fell. Eddie drove off back to his house but as we left I heard more shots.

In the follow-up investigation gardaí arrested over twenty people from both sides of the feud including Eamon Kelly, Gerry Hutch, Patsy Hutch, Tommy Savage and George Royle. The offender at the centre of the row had gone to ground and could not be located. Hutch followed his by now established technique – he picked out a spot on the wall and refused to speak for 48 hours. Royle later told gardaí that he was in fear that he too might be shot. The suspects were all released without charge due to a lack of evidence.

On 30 June the Hutches discovered McOwen's friend was hiding out with his girlfriend in a flat at Charleville Avenue at nearby North Strand. Around 8.30 a.m. a man armed with a sawn-off shotgun burst in the door of the flat. However, his intended target was ready and waiting, armed with a handgun. The men exchanged shots and their target fled with his girlfriend through a back window. Witnesses saw the gunman running from the flat and the gardaí were called. No one was injured in the incident and it was never officially reported to the police.

Not long after the McOwen murder gardaí received intelligence that Tommy Savage was planning to shoot Gerry Hutch in retaliation. It was understood that the Monk maintained a low profile for a while and there were no more incidents. Officially McOwen's murder was never solved.

When detectives asked Eamon Kelly to give an account of his movements on the day of the McOwen murder he said he was meeting his lawyers in the Law Library at Dublin's Four Courts – and for once he wasn't lying. A fortnight after the McOwen murder Matt and Eamon Kelly were in the High Court to defend an application by the Revenue Commissioners seeking to have them made personally liable for debts of over £1.8 million (€7 million). The proceedings began in 1981 when the Revenue had the Kelly carpet companies placed in liquidation. A year later, in June 1982, Hutch's mentors had their North Circular Road premises burned to the ground so they could collect the insurance money and continue to run other shops in the city centre. It was clear the brothers were not going to go down without a fight.

What should have been a standard bankruptcy case made for unprecedented front page news as the intimidating shadow of the Kelly organized crime gang loomed over the entire proceedings. On the first morning of the hearing there was an arson attack at the home of the senior counsel leading the case on behalf of the official liquidator. In light of the attacks by Martin Cahill on the State's top forensic scientist, Dr James Donovan, it was another indication that the crime bosses considered themselves untouchable. Garda management assigned extra gardaí to provide security in the courtroom and armed police protection was given to the State's legal team, revenue officials, witnesses and the judge himself, Mr Justice Declan Costello, for the duration of the hearing.

The Kellys' former in-house accountant, Brendan McGoldrick, testified that he had been threatened with murder if he opened his mouth. He said Matt Kelly and another underworld associate, Mickey Deighan, had made the threats. The accountant stated that Matt Kelly told him he planned to burn down the carpet warehouse the day before it went up in flames. McGoldrick also admitted falsifying company documentation on the orders of his bosses.

On 27 June the judge ordered the imprisonment of Matt Kelly and Deighan for contempt of court and the accountant was also placed under armed police protection. Such was the gang's reputation for violence that McGoldrick continued to live under armed guard for several years. Matt Kelly had opted to conduct his own defence in the hearing and was entitled to cross-examine the witnesses for the State which added to the sense of intimidation that prevailed. Niall Mulvihill, who fronted a number of businesses for Kelly, acted as his legal assistant and sat beside him on the counsel's bench. But it was of little benefit to them. The court later ruled that the business of the carpet company had been carried on from October 1976 to February 1980 with 'intent to defraud creditors' and for 'other fraudulent purposes' and the Kelly brothers were 'knowingly parties' to the conspiracy. They were held liable for all debts, including the £1.8 million tax bill (€7 million). Matt Kelly was declared a bankrupt which barred him from setting up any business until he had repaid his debts. Under Irish Bankruptcy Law he was obliged to disclose all of the assets he owned to the Official Assignee in Bankruptcy – the legal official who deals with bankruptcy cases. However, despite his problems, the former carpet king secretly became an extremely wealthy property developer. And he would soon be teaching Hutch everything he knew about laundering money and making profitable investments.

The young gangster had plenty to invest after he pulled off his biggest robbery to date. On the evening of Saturday, 10 September 1983, a Securicor van was about to make its final collection of the day from the Superquinn supermarket at Sutton Cross in north Dublin. The van had already collected the day's takings from a number of other stores across the city. The van pulled into the forecourt of the supermarket at 6 p.m. and two security men were about to enter the store when they were suddenly surrounded by three masked robbers armed with two sawn-off shotguns and a pistol. Hutch was dressed in a woman's wig and scarf.

The raiders ordered terrified shoppers out of the way as they forced the security staff to open the back of the van. The Monk and another raider jumped in and he drove the van away while the other blagger held the driver hostage at gunpoint. The third raider followed in a getaway car driven by Dave Brogan. The money was transferred into another car in a laneway near Sutton train station and the driver was released.

The Monk and his crew got away with £100,000 (€309,000). Brogan told this writer and the gardaí that Hutch later brought him to a safe house where he gave him £40,000 (€123,600) as his share of the loot. The robbery bore all the hallmarks of Hutch's careful planning. The day before the robbery he, Brogan and the other gang members rehearsed their getaway route and had drawn up alternative plans if anything went wrong. Happy that he had a nest egg put away to mind his young family, in December 1983 Hutch pleaded guilty to causing malicious damage to a stolen car in the botched robbery 'job' with the Zombie and McOwen. When he went to Mountjoy he got his old job back in the kitchens and hung out with a small circle of friends from his neighbourhood.

As Hutch was acclimatizing to prison life on the other side of the wall there was a bloody postscript to the McOwen murder. On St Stephen's Day heroin dealer Eddie Hayden, who had been arrested as part of the investigation six months earlier, also became a gangland statistic. The former international amateur boxer had grown up in the inner city with the Hutches and had taken part in crimes with them until he became one of the biggest heroin dealers in their homeland. On the night of his execution Hayden was tipped-off that his girlfriend was having an affair with another criminal. It was a trap. When he arrived at her flat in Ballybough in the north inner city, a lone figure emerged from the shadows and opened fire at close range with a sawn-off shotgun. The blast blew half of Hayden's head away. The prime suspects for the murder were members of the Hutch and Kelly gangs. Hayden had been accused of planting heroin in the engine of a car driven by an associate of the Hutches who also worked in the Kellys' carpet store. The gardaí found the drug stashed around the carburettor of the car and arrested the employee for possession with intent to supply. However, it was so obvious to the gardaí that the man had been set up by someone that he was never charged. In the meantime the heroin dealer paid a high price for crossing the mob.

Gangland had become a dangerous place

CHAPTER SIX

———

THE FIRST BIG JOB

On 31 May 1985 Gerry Hutch was released from Mountjoy Prison where he had been classified as a model prisoner. As he passed through the gates to freedom he made a solemn oath to himself never to do time again. It became his *raison d'être* in life. But it had nothing to do with being rehabilitated. Prison had motivated him to single-mindedly set about rectifying an important aspect of his professional life – making sure he was never caught again. At the age of twenty-two his education was complete; he had learned from the mistakes of the past and was determined to put his hard-earned experiences to good use. He had one big ambition for the future – to steal enough money to set him up for life and to get away with it.

Shortly after his release, Gerry Hutch again teamed up with Dave 'Myler' Brogan. The former hash dealer was happy to be back working with the Hutch brothers. He recalled:

> In those days I spent most of the time working with the Hutches. We were all good friends for a long time. Neddie [Eddie] would generally be involved in planning the jobs but left the work to me and Gerard. Whenever they [Hutches] needed a gunman on a job that they could rely on they came to me. During the late seventies and early eighties

I went on several jobs with Gerard Hutch, Thomas O'Driscoll and the other lads he hung around with. I was always the first one in the door of the bank or wherever it was we were robbing.

Brogan specifically recalled a number of 'jobs' they did together. In August 1985 while serving a sentence in Mountjoy Brogan was given day release on compassionate grounds to see his elderly mother. But he and the Hutch brothers had other plans. The gang were planning to hit a security van as it collected cash from Roches Stores in Blackrock in south Dublin. Brogan recalled:

When I got out of prison that morning I went straight to Eddie's house. He knew I was getting out for the day and wanted me to back up Gerard on the job. Thomas O'Driscoll was out of prison and he was going in with Gerard. I discussed the plan with Gerard and Eddie and Gerard told me where to park the getaway car to collect them after the robbery. I did a dry run with Neddie. The job went down around 5.30 p.m.

According to the former blagger Hutch dressed as a teddy boy with a wig while O'Driscoll went as a 'punk rocker'. They robbed £46,000 (over €140,00) at gunpoint from a security man. After the job the guns and money were dropped to another gang member who was waiting beside the Punchbowl Pub, south Dublin, and Brogan then abandoned the getaway car. He commented:

I went back to Neddie's house later and Gerard came in and told me the break down in the money: I was to get £13,000 but I didn't physically get the money as it went to Neddie as a down payment for a shop I was buying from him on Killarney Street. Gerard was laughing about the shock the manager of the centre got as he approached them

to throw them out – they produced the guns and told him to get down
on the floor. Neddie dropped me back to the prison.

Shortly after his permanent release from prison, in December
1985, Brogan went on another robbery organized by the Hutches.
He claimed that Eddie Hutch received inside information about
the movements of a security van which would be carrying over
£1 million (€2.6 million) in cash as it delivered payrolls around
south Dublin. The gang was to include Gerry Hutch, Brogan and
two other well-known freelance robbers. The proceeds were to be
cut five ways to include Eddie. The plan was to hit the security van
as it delivered wages for staff at the Initial Laundry in Rathfarnham,
a suburb in south Dublin. In the week before the planned heist
Brogan and the Monk did the surveillance work and mapped out
the escape route. However, Myler later said that Gerry Hutch pulled
out for some reason and the job went ahead without him. Three
of the thieves lay in wait across the road from the laundry, hiding
in an ESB substation, while a fourth gang member stayed with the
getaway car. But, as Brogan recalled, the plan didn't work out:

> It was supposed to be carrying a £1 million in cash. There were three
> of us waiting for it and I ran over and fired a shot into the van to scare
> the crew and they threw the bags out to us. When we looked inside
> later there was a £1 million alright, but it was in cheques and there
> was just £25,000 in cash. When we went back to Eddie he said, 'We'll
> get them again, don't worry.' That was the nature of the business.

A month later, in January 1986, Brogan, Gerry Hutch and Thomas
O'Driscoll attempted another armed robbery. They targeted the
cash being held at a fuel depot in Ringsend on the southside of
Dublin's dockland. Brogan had received inside information about

the days when large cash amounts were on the premises. The three blaggers had watched the building from a nearby rooftop over a few nights to formulate a plan of attack:

> I drove a BMW that had been stolen and parked up in Ballsbridge. We drove up to the security gates – Gerard was driving and Tomo [O'Driscoll] was the front passenger and I was in the back. Me and Gerard had shotguns and Tomo a pistol. I got out to take out the security guard but I couldn't get him out of his hut. Gerard then came and physically dragged the guard out of the hut and chained him to a railing. As we went into the main office the manager and a staff member ran into the strongroom and locked it. Tomo tried to fire a shot through the door and Gerard fired through a window to make him open the door. When the doors hadn't opened after three minutes we left – we couldn't chance staying any longer than that.

As the raiders were forced to leave empty-handed they began blaming each other for botching the job. Brogan recalled: 'I knew Gerard pretty well and he surprised me that night because he was so furious with the guy in the strongroom that he wanted to go around to his house and blow him away. Gerard was a dangerous man to cross.'

On 29 May 1986 Hutch, Brogan and O'Driscoll were in action again. This time the target was the wages office at the CIE bus depot in Broadstone in the north inner city. That morning Eddie Hutch watched for the arrival of the cash-in-transit van carrying the wages to pay the bus crews while the three raiders waited in a stolen car around the corner. Around 10.30 a.m., just after the money was delivered, the gang hit. Brogan was the driver while Hutch and O'Driscoll, armed with handguns, burst into the office ordering staff to lie on the floor. They grabbed £70,000 (€216,000) in cash and escaped through a window which had been opened the previous night as part of the preparations. Gerry gave Brogan his share of the proceeds a few days later. But the partnership was not to last.

The friendship between Brogan and the Hutches turned sour in a row over money. Brogan claimed that he'd agreed to buy the Killarney Street shop from Eddie Hutch and the problems started when he couldn't come up with the money: 'I was supposed to make the money from a couple of strokes but I didn't get it. When I said I didn't have the cash and wanted out, Eddie told me that I would have to answer to Gerard if I didn't pay up. I knew that meant only one thing – I'd be shot. That was when I decided to leave Dublin. I was sick of it.'

The Hutches probably had a different version of events as confessors tend to craft their admissions to paint themselves in the best possible light. Brogan's instincts for self-preservation, however, prompted him to move back to live in London later that same year.

Brogan's decision to break the code of omerta in 1992 and publicly spill the beans on his former partners-in-crime was unprecedented: professional criminals don't publicly point the finger at former associates or open up about robberies that they weren't charged with. But the former armed robber wanted to expose the Hutch brothers and Tommy Savage. He said it took a lot of soul-searching before he decided to wash the gang's dirty laundry in public: 'I am not doing this because I am some kind of informer. I have never told the police anything in my life. They are detectives and they get paid by the taxpayers to detect. I am just sick knowing the way crime has gone… it has become a very dirty, dangerous business.'

The truth was that even though he had left six years earlier, Brogan was still terrified of the Hutches, especially the Monk who he believed could have him killed on a London street just as easily as on a Dublin one. Brogan had even created an escape route which would enable him to get out through the roof of his home if an unwelcome assassin arrived at his reinforced front door.

While the criminals mentioned were not named for legal reasons in the subsequent article about Brogan that appeared in the *Sunday World* newspaper, the police and criminals knew who was involved. Most of the information Brogan shared was later confirmed by garda intelligence sources familiar with the gang and their crimes. In a pointed reference to Gerry Hutch he said: 'I know the man who will pull the trigger and at least try to kill me… I have been on numerous robberies with him and to tell the truth I actually like him. He is a cold-blooded killer though. If, or when, he comes for me I won't be taking it lying down. I'll go down fighting at the very least.' Brogan's predictions never came to pass.

The Monk meanwhile continued to gather a tight team of robbers around him and managed to stay out of the reach of the police. The same could not be said for his old mentor Eamon Kelly.

Kelly was known as a violent hardman who had managed to evade prosecution for many years. However, on 12 June 1986 his vicious temperament put his criminal career on pause when the Circuit Criminal Court sentenced him to ten years imprisonment for stabbing a man outside the Workers' Party club, also known as the 'IRA club', in Gardiner Place, central Dublin. The incident followed a trivial row over the use of a slot machine between Kelly and his victim, twenty-five-year-old Patrick Quearney, who was a member of the Workers' Party (previously Official Sinn Féin). It had taken place the evening before the knife attack.

On 18 November 1984 Eamon Kelly confronted Quearney for a second time on the street outside the club. Kelly produced a knife and stabbed Quearney several times including twice in the heart. He was rushed to hospital and had it not been for the prompt action of doctors the victim would have died from blood loss. During the three-day trial the gang boss tried to claim that the victim and other eyewitnesses had mistaken him for his brother Matt. Eamon Kelly said he wasn't there when the assault took place and accused a Workers' Party member of instructing prosecution witnesses to finger him. However, the jury saw through the ruse and convicted him of wounding with intent to cause grievous bodily harm and malicious wounding. Giving evidence about Kelly's underworld background Detective Sergeant Michael Diggin told the court that in the seven years he had known Eamon Kelly he had been 'associating with hardened and dangerous Dublin criminals'.

In a plea for leniency Kelly's counsel said the offence was an isolated incident and 'completely out of character'. He said Kelly had nine children to support and that he and his brother had undergone a 'very traumatic experience' when their 'successful' business went to the wall because of 'troubles with the Revenue Commissioners'. The extraordinary claim must have left the judge, legal representatives and witnesses who had received police protection at the bankruptcy hearing in 1983 wondering if they had participated in the same court case.

Judge Gerard Buchanan described the stabbing as a 'vicious assault' and said the evidence revealed a story of 'intimidation and fear' that was abhorrent to the ordinary citizens of Dublin. Kelly, he said, could easily have been facing a murder charge, commenting: 'The maximum sentence for this charge is life. I have searched the evidence for matters in your favour and I find none.'

Eamon Kelly was shocked by the severity of the ten-year sentence. For the gardaí securing a conviction against a gangster who had

successfully protected himself behind a wall of silence, built on fear
and intimidation, was a major victory.

By the time Kelly was on the way to prison, his protégé was
striking out on his own. Hutch had moved away from working
with his brothers and began working with a hardcore group of
the streetwise friends he grew up with and who he could trust
implicitly. Geoffrey Ennis, Paul Boyle, William Scully, Gerard Lee
and Thomas O'Driscoll, who ranged in age between nineteen and
twenty-three, had cut their teeth with Hutch in the Bugsy Malones.
From the time they were children they had robbed, been caught and
been imprisoned together. Like the Monk, the five former Bugsys
stood out from the wider group around them and had all gained
reputations as hardened criminals. One cop who knew them said
they were one of the 'tightest crews' he ever encountered: 'They
shared strong bonds of friendship and were all very capable robbers.
They were airtight because nothing ever got out of their circle which
meant it was hard to get information about what they were up to
until it was too late. Hutch became their natural leader.' The new
kids on the block were to become one of the most successful – and
youngest – armed robbery gangs in Irish criminal history.

In 1986 there were 600 armed robberies in Ireland with the bulk
of them taking place in the Greater Dublin area. From his previous
'jobs' Hutch realized that on average the most a gang could grab was
about £25,000 (€60,000). After being divided up five or six ways, a
few thousand pounds was poor recompense for the risk of running
into armed gardaí and ending up doing a long prison term of about
ten years or more behind bars. Hutch was looking for a bigger
pay out. He was fully aware of how the General pulled off what
was then the biggest robbery in Irish history in July 1983. Cahill's
gang had got away with gold, gems and diamonds worth over

£1.5 million (€3.5 million) from the O'Connor's jewellery factory in Harold's Cross, south Dublin. The Monk viewed that operation as a masterpiece of meticulous planning and execution. As the Hutch gang honed their skills in 1986 the gardaí had classified the Cahill gang as the most prolific armed robbers in the country.

That April Martin Cahill made history when the gang made off with the priceless Beit art collection from Russborough House in County Wicklow. It was one of the biggest art heists in the world. But Hutch and his friends had no interest in such flamboyant expropriations which involved highly risky and complicated efforts to fence the paintings and jewels. They wanted hard cash.

In one sense, however, the Monk's gang did follow the General's lead when it came to detailed planning for bank or security van jobs. They would monitor the movement of money at certain banks or cash-in-transit collections for days and even weeks at a time to figure out the optimum moment to strike – and the best getaway routes. Their planning campaign for robberies went into extraordinary detail and everything was timed to the second. Each member of the team would rehearse the escape route and alternative routes in case anything happened to the getaway driver or they were intercepted by the police. They researched every detail, down to if the doors in the bank opened in or out and the type of security system in operation. Garda patrols were monitored in the area to be hit and Gerry Hutch routinely reported bogus armed robberies to test response times for armed and uniformed units. Soon they were ready for the big one.

On 26 January 1987 a Securicor cash-in-transit van with three crew on board left the main depot at Herberton Road in Rialto, south Dublin. They were starting 'Run Number 2' which followed the same route every week. Over the next three hours they collected cash from fourteen bank branches across north Dublin. At 5.20 p.m. the crew made their final pick up of the day, from the Bank of Ireland at Marino Mart in Fairview. The cash was carried in six sealed bags which the crew pushed through a chute into the van's cash-holding vault. Over the course of the afternoon the security guards had collected over £1.4 million (€3.4 million).

As the front seat observer, Brian Holden, was getting back into the van in Marino a red BMW pulled up behind and three armed and masked men jumped out. One of the raiders, armed with a handgun, pointed it into his face, shouting: 'Get out or I'll blow your fuckin' head off.' A second raider armed with a rifle joined the first and they both pulled Holden from the van and threw him to the ground. The security officer was kicked and warned to stay down or have his head 'blown off'. At the same time a third raider appeared at the opposite door and pointed a gun at the head of the driver, Thomas Kennedy. He was ordered to hand over the keys and get out.

One of the raiders jumped in behind the wheel of the van and drove off while a second hung out the door pointing his gun at the startled security men. The other two robbers got into the BMW and followed. The car had been stolen the previous night from outside an apartment block in Ballsbridge, south Dublin. A short distance up the road the van stopped and a third security officer, Simon Foley, who was in the cash vault, was pushed out. As the van took off again, the passenger in the BMW pointed a rifle at Foley who dived for cover across a garden wall. The armed robbers drove a short distance into the grounds of Coláiste Mhuire school, off Griffith Avenue. They stopped on waste ground behind the school and quickly removed over sixty bags of cash into a number of vehicles they had parked there earlier. The robbers abandoned the car and the van and took off into the night. Twenty minutes later gardaí located the abandoned vehicles. But the cash and thieves had vanished. In many ways the job was a carbon copy of Hutch's earlier robbery at Superquinn in Sutton in November 1983.

Garda intelligence initially nominated a number of possible suspects for the audacious crime. The investigation team was headed up by Detective Chief Superintendent John Murphy and Detective Superintendent Noel Conroy of the Central Detective Unit (CDU) at Harcourt Square in central Dublin. The CDU was an amalgamation of individual specialist squads which were deployed to take on the growing number of organized criminal gangs around the city. It was made up of the Serious Crime Squad, Stolen Car Squad, Drug Squad and Fraud Squad. CDU also had a dedicated armed robbery squad and a small but very effective undercover team which had been trained in surveillance techniques by Scotland Yard and the FBI. The team nominated the General, as a matter of course, on the list of likely perpetrators as were villains such as John Gilligan and republican terrorists. But the investigators quickly established that the culprits were the former burglars and joy riders from the north inner city: Gerry Hutch, Geoffrey Ennis, Paul Boyle, Gerry Lee and Willy Scully. The historic robbery had propelled the five men to the top of the Serious Crime Squad's 'Most Wanted' list where they had given them equal billing with Martin Cahill's outfit.

Later that night, after ensuring they weren't followed, the former Bugsy Malones met in a safe house to divide up what they hoped would be over £100,000 (€244,000). It took them the rest of the night to count and sort the used notes. When they had finished the robbers sat back stunned as they took in the large stack of cash sitting in the middle of the floor – it came to £1,357,106 (over €3.3 million). The Monk's gang had just pulled off the biggest cash robbery in the history of the State. In one 'job' they had suddenly elevated themselves to the senior level in the hierarchy of serious crime.

Gerry Hutch and his gang were aware that having achieved overnight notoriety meant that they would be attracting the undivided attention of the police. This had naturally also been factored into the planning. After years of practice each member of the team was well used to being questioned and was psychologically prepared for an inevitable arrest. Each gang member also had a pre-rehearsed alibi and witnesses to back them up. In the age before the use of DNA testing, the gang had left no fingerprints or other evidence that contemporary forensics could trace to any of them.

The only thing that could link them to the crime was the actual money which had been divided up and moved to safe locations. Gerry Hutch now had to work out how they could launder the loot and it would not be easy.

CHAPTER SEVEN

DIRTY MONEY AND MURDER

The Marino Mart heist proved Gerry Hutch's ability as a criminal mastermind but while he knew how to get the cash he wasn't au fait with the process of laundering it. He turned to the older members of the Kelly gang – Matt Kelly, Niall Mulvihill and Mickey Deighan – for advice on the most effective way of cleaning the loot. Naturally shrewd with money Hutch was determined to use his share of the loot wisely by reinvesting it in a number of property deals being put together by Matt Kelly and his circle of dodgy business partners. The plan was pretty simple: to lodge the money in a number of financial institutions in Northern Ireland. For ease of access they chose Newry in County Down, just over an hour from Dublin.

After the furore had died down, the money could then be withdrawn in the form of legitimate bank drafts from the Northern Irish institutions and used as down payments for the property investments. That was how money laundering worked in a much more innocent time before the creation of Ireland's Criminal Assets Bureau and the passing of the Proceeds of Crime Act in 1996. The 1970s and 1980s were the halcyon days for armed robbers and drug dealers. They had little worries about losing stolen money once it was safely lodged in a bank account as the financial institutions were not subject to anti-money laundering regulations and were not obliged to share account information with the police. Not that it would have made any difference if they did because the police had no powers to chase the money trail or to seize the cash. The fact that the banks Hutch planned to use were in the UK, a different jurisdiction, provided a further layer of protection.

The only problem the Monk faced was the logistics of how to actually get the cash safely lodged in the bank. Gerry Hutch needed two people he could trust to move the money so that he could remain a safe distance removed from it, in case the gardaí decided to search him and got lucky. One of the bagmen would hold the money while the other would physically lodge it across the Border.

Kelly and Mulvihill introduced the Monk to two men who were ideal candidates for the job. Gerry Hutch was assured Francis Joseph Sheridan and Lonan Patrick Hickey would not attract attention as they weren't known to the police and had no criminal records. The two men didn't know each other which was also important to the security of the money laundering plan. Thirty-one-year-old Sheridan, an ex-soldier, was a timber salesman who lived with his wife and three children in Swords, County Dublin. Hickey was the same age as Sheridan and lived at Church Avenue in Drumcondra, north Dublin. Hickey came from a middle-class background and emigrated to Mexico with his family when he was fifteen. He became fluent in French and Spanish and by seventeen was working as a translator for a Mexican television company before moving to live in Chicago, USA, where he worked as a salesman in the carpet business. When he was twenty, Hickey returned to Ireland and continued to work in the carpet business which was how he came to know Matt and Eamon Kelly – a relationship he would bitterly regret. Hickey hit hard times when his business went bust and he broke his back in a car crash which left him mildly disabled. He was unemployed and in serious financial difficulties when the Monk made him an offer he couldn't refuse.

On the Friday morning after the robbery Hutch phoned Sheridan at his work and asked to meet him in the Northside Shopping Centre later that day. The Monk explained to Sheridan that he wanted him to mind a large amount of cash and that there would be a 'a few quid in it' for him. He told Sheridan that over the next two weeks he would be given instructions to deliver quantities of the cash to Church Avenue where he was to hand it over to another man [Hickey]. Hutch warned the ex-soldier not to tell his wife or anyone else about what he was doing.

Hutch arranged to meet Sheridan in the car park of the Halfway House pub on the Navan Road in Dublin at 6 p.m. on Monday, 2 February. Since the Marino heist the Monk and his fellow gang members had been using counter-surveillance techniques to avoid the prying eyes of undercover cops. Sheridan was followed to ensure he didn't have a tail while the gang also monitored the pub car park for any unusual movements. Satisfied that the coast was clear Hutch appeared beside Sheridan and handed over a package containing £320,000 (€786,000) in cash. He also handed the bagman a smaller envelope containing £2,000 (€4,800) for his trouble. Hutch instructed Sheridan to put £30,000 (€73,000), made up of bundles of £20 and £10 notes, into a bag and bring it to Church Avenue in Drumcondra at 8.30 a.m. the following morning. The ex-soldier was told to hand it over to a man who would approach his van.

The next morning when Sheridan pulled up in Church Avenue Hickey was waiting outside his home. He walked to the passenger side of the van and grabbed the bag of cash. Hickey then drove to the Ulster Bank in Newry in a car he had hired on Hutch's instructions. He was to buy a Sterling bank draft with the cash and have it made payable to the Abbey National Building Society. The bank advised Hickey to go directly to the building society, which was just across the road, and open an account there. The building society, however, would not accept the £30,000 as an opening balance until he changed the Irish pounds into Sterling. When this was done, Hickey was all set to open an account in his own name, depositing Stg£26,697.

The following day Hickey met Hutch in the Cat and Cage pub in Drumcondra and explained the problems he had lodging the stolen money. The Monk had also travelled to the Anglia Building Society at Marcus Square, Newry, the day before and opened an account with a lodgement of £1,372 (€3,300) in his own name. The account number 140-1-05795091-0 listed his address at 25 Buckingham Street, Dublin.

On 5 February Hutch contacted Sheridan and told him to deliver £40,000 (€97,470) to the Drumcondra address the following morning. When Hickey had collected the cash he headed for Newry. His first call was to the Abbey National Building Society where he withdrew the Stg£26,000 he had lodged two days earlier in the form of a bank draft made out to Gerry Hutch. Hickey then went to the Anglia Building Society where he converted the £40,000 to sterling and lodged it directly into Hutch's account. He returned to Dublin and delivered the bank draft to the Monk that evening.

Hutch told Sheridan to deliver another £40,000 to Hickey on the following Monday morning, 9 February. When he reached Newry, Hickey converted the cash into sterling and lodged it to Gerry Hutch's building society account. His balance now stood at Stg£75,279 (€237,000). The laundering operation was running like clockwork – but it would not last for much longer.

The Central Detective Unit's (CDU) investigation team had spent hours gathering intelligence and conducting surveillance on the five men involved in the heist. The breakthrough came just over a week into the investigation – about four days before Hickey's latest trip to Newry – when the Serious Crime Squad picked up intelligence that money from the robbery was being moved. The CDU surveillance team was assigned to follow Hutch and his associates, watch their homes and tap phones they were known to use, in order to build a picture of what was going on and who was involved. A former member of the surveillance team commented:

> We got the call that Hutch was personally involved in moving the money out of Dublin but at that stage we didn't know who he was using. It was a fair bet that he wasn't going to be hands-on and that the people he was using wouldn't be known to us. Hutch and the rest of his gang deployed counter-surveillance techniques to get away from us and he wasn't an easy target to watch but we stuck with him.

When Hutch went to meet Hickey to issue new instructions on 6 February the undercover cops were keeping watch. The Monk had used a moped to get through traffic which made it almost impossible to follow him. Then he drove around in circles for well over an hour through the maze of side streets in Dublin's inner city and beyond in a bid to shake off any possible tails. He eventually abandoned the scooter and disguised himself before jogging a long, circuitous route on foot to the scheduled meeting in the Cat and Cage pub.

Despite demonstrating counter-surveillance fieldcraft worthy of a spy, at least two of the undercover officers managed to stick with him. As Hutch eventually sat down with Hickey in the pub one of the CDU surveillance men sidled into the bar and ordered a pint. It was the first time the team had eyes on one of the bagmen.

Surveillance was then placed on Hickey which in turn led them to Sheridan. This was solid progress.

On the evening of 9 February, two weeks to the day since the landmark robbery, Gerry Hutch called Sheridan at his work with new instructions. This time the bagman was told to deliver £81,000 (€197,000) to Hickey the following morning at the usual time and in the same place. By then Sheridan's phone was tapped and the jigsaw fell into place for the listeners. At 8.25 a.m. on 10 February the undercover team tailed Sheridan in his Volkswagen van to Church Avenue. They watched as Hickey walked over to the van and opened the passenger door where Sheridan handed him a large bag with double handles containing clothes to hide the cash. Sheridan drove off as Hickey returned to his hired car.

A few minutes later, as Hickey pulled out to start his journey to Newry, his car was blocked in by unmarked squad cars and armed officers from the Serious Crime Squad. Five minutes later another team moved in to arrest Sheridan on Gracepark Road in Drumcondra. The bagmen were arrested under the provisions of the Offences Against the State Act on suspicion of having committed a scheduled offence, unlawful possession of firearms at Marino Mart, Fairview on 26 January 1987. Hickey was taken to Swords garda station for questioning while Sheridan went to Whitehall station.

Detective Sergeant Willy Ryan showed Sheridan the bag of cash he had seized from Hickey and asked him if the money was from the Marino Mart job. Sheridan replied yes. When asked could he help the investigation any further, the bagman admitted that he had more money at his home in Swords, replying: 'I will bring you there and get it for you… I only want two people to come with me into the house.'

The team drove out to his house and Sheridan showed the officers the rest of the money which he had hidden in the attic. The detectives found two large bags containing a total of £129,361 (€317,000) and an additional £1,600 (€3,600) hidden in Sheridan's sock drawer. They also recovered a box of rubber bands and plastic bags which he had used to pack the money before delivering it to Hickey. He claimed: 'That's all I have out of it, that's all I got...'

When his interrogation resumed back at the station detectives again asked Sheridan where he got the money. 'It's legitimate money, I was minding it for a businessman,' he replied. When he was asked for the name of the businessman he said: 'I can't say.' He was then asked if he was afraid to say who it was and he replied: 'Yes, and I don't want to say any more.' Later Sheridan agreed to tell them how the money came to be in his house but said that he wouldn't name names.

At the same time Hickey's home was also being searched in Drumcondra. Detectives found two building society books, one in Hickey's name, the other in Gerry Hutch's. When he was being questioned Hickey initially claimed he'd lodged the money for a man called 'John' and denied any knowledge that it came from the Marino Mart job. But when the detectives put it to him that 'John' was Gerry Hutch, the holder of the building society account, Hickey said he didn't want to put the name down on paper. When asked if it was Hutch who had given him the instructions to bring the money to Newry Hickey said he wouldn't deny it but that he was afraid of Hutch.

Sheridan and Hickey subsequently both gave statements to the gardaí that they were working for Gerry Hutch but claimed that they were terrified of him.

On 11 February the bagmen were brought before the Dublin District Court where they were formally charged with the Marino Mart robbery and with receiving the proceeds of crime. The charges were later amended to receiving the money traced and recovered by the police.

At the same time the gardaí contacted Securicor, which then obtained an order in the Belfast High Court freezing Gerry Hutch's account in Newry. The sterling bank draft that Hickey had given Hutch was also cancelled.

The arrests of Sheridan and Hickey and the seizure of the money, while an excellent result for the gardaí, was still something of a pyrrhic victory. Hutch and the rest of the gang were arrested for questioning but refused to speak. They were released as there was no evidence to directly link any of them to the actual robbery. Detectives knew Hutch still had the remainder of the stolen money – just over £1 million (€2,457,000) – and it was never recovered.

The Monk wasn't worried that either of the two men would testify against him because they knew better. And in the unlikely event that they did try to finger him the case would have been fraught with legal difficulties. Hutch was no different to other gangsters when it came to the unwritten policy about underlings being caught: it was a risk the bagmen were aware of when signing up for the job so they should just keep their mouths shut and do their time.

A file was subsequently forwarded to the Director of Public Prosecutions recommending that Gerry Hutch be charged with handling the proceeds from the heist but it was decided not to proceed with the case because neither Hickey nor Sheridan were prepared to give evidence against him in court.

The Marino Mart robbery earned the Monk and his crew the widespread respect of the wider criminal community across Ireland for a job well done – and the undivided attentions of the police. Although just twenty-three years old, Gerry Hutch was identified in garda intelligence reports as one of the top gangsters in the country, second only to the General who was fourteen years his senior. The various police assessments of the young Monk were of a feared criminal with a propensity for extreme violence. In a period of less than two years, from 1982 to 1984, Hutch had been connected with four murders. In three of the cases – the killings of fourteen-year-old Gerard Morgan, hash-dealer Gerard Hourigan and international amateur boxer Eddie Hayden – the victims had either directly or indirectly crossed swords with Gerry Hutch, but he had not been the suspected trigger man. He was, however, the prime suspect for the fourth murder, that of Danny McOwen. A few months after the Marino Mart robbery, Hutch consolidated his growing reputation as a gangland killer.

Scrap dealer Mel Cox had a formidable reputation as a street fighter and general bully in the north inner city. The forty-three-year-old was over six feet three inches in height and weighed over 16 stone and local wits nicknamed him 'The Hulk'. Despite being regarded as an outsider – he was originally from Elphin, County Roscommon – Cox was heavily involved in crime and his scrapyard at Mountjoy Square was a meeting place for local villains. His associates included the Kelly and the Hutch brothers. Cox had been nominated by gardaí as being involved in providing logistical support, in the form of stolen cars, for the Marino Mart heist.

The scrap dealer was well known for throwing his substantial weight around during drunken pub brawls and did not differentiate between men or women when it came to landing a punch. On New Year's Eve 1986 he had seriously assaulted a local woman in a fight outside the Sunset House pub in Summerhill, central Dublin. But in June 1987 he finally went too far. On Sunday, 21 June Mel Cox was drinking in O'Neill's pub in Summerhill with his partner Margaret Cashin and her family who were north inner-city natives. Margaret had given birth to twin girls three weeks earlier and the couple were in a celebratory mood.

Around closing time a number of women in Cox's company, including his partner, began trading insults with women from the Burke family and it escalated into a brawl. The situation then deteriorated further when the men on both sides intervened. The row quickly developed into a full-scale riot involving women and men. As it spilled out onto the street members of other local families, including the Hutches, also got involved. By the time the gardaí managed to restore order one local man had been rushed to hospital with serious spinal injuries. A number of the women also suffered injuries including broken teeth. But most significantly a close relative of the Monk had been left with a broken jaw – courtesy of Mel Cox.

Over the following days the word on the streets of the inner city was that The Hulk was in mortal danger and had stepped on the wrong toes. The Hutch family were feared and respected and in order for them to maintain that status Mel Cox would have to pay a price for the broken jaw. Cox, however, was nonchalant about any threat and had supreme confidence in his own physical strength to deal with any problems. The Hulk openly joked in the local pubs that Gerry Hutch would fit in his pocket. The Monk had no intention of letting anyone get away with laughing at him or with breaking a family member's jaw.

On Tuesday, 30 June 1987 Mel Cox was working in the back garden of his home in the sprawling corporation estate at Corduff in Blanchardstown, west Dublin. The Hulk had moved to Corduff Grove with his partner a year earlier. Around 5.15 p.m. a lone gunman, described as being in his twenties, of slight build and wearing a grey tracksuit, walked into the garden and shot Mel Cox three times in the head at point-blank range. The killer who wasn't wearing a mask over his face made his escape across nearby fields. Before Cox's remains were cold, the police and the locals in the north inner city knew the identity of the prime suspect – Gerry Hutch. The Monk was directly connected to his second gangland murder in four years which copper-fastened his reputation amongst the criminal fraternity as someone not to be crossed. Eddie Hutch hadn't been making idle threats when he'd warned Dave 'Myler' Brogan a year earlier that his younger sibling would deal with him.

In the aftermath of the assassination the Monk and his family found themselves sharing the media spotlight with the General, Martin Cahill, for all the wrong reasons. Newspaper reports linked the murder to the pub row ten days earlier when Cox had assaulted Hutch's relative. They also described how the main suspect had been involved in the Marino Mart robbery. The security correspondent in *The Irish Times*, Seán Flynn, highlighted the crime family's links to the Kelly brothers and pointed out, without naming them, that Eddie Hutch and Gerry 'have consolidated their positions as the major criminal figures on the northside' by controlling 'most criminal operations' on that side of the River Liffey. He commented: 'According to gardaí, they enjoy ready access to firearms and they have cultivated extensive underworld contacts since they themselves were petty criminals over a decade ago.'

Cox's grieving partner, who witnessed the murder and had been left with three children under the age of three, was in no doubt as to who carried it out. She was interviewed by the media following the killing and identified Gerry Hutch as the killer although, for legal reasons, he wasn't actually named in the reports. Margaret Cashin had known him all her life as she had grown up in the same area.

In a subsequent interview with the RTÉ *Today Tonight* current affairs programme in early 1988 she said of the Hutches:

> The name of the northside family is well known, well known for crime. Mel was over six foot three. He was well able to take care of himself and he took care of a few people and they couldn't take it, so they had to come out and do that. Mel used his hands; he didn't use a gun on anybody. It wasn't a bad fight it was just that Mel was well able to take care of himself and these people they had to have guns. They'd do the same thing to me as they did to Mel. It's just a coward's way out because they will have to answer to God. That's one being they won't be able to run from. They mightn't care now but they will when the time comes. I don't know how they can sleep at night.

Hutch was subsequently arrested for questioning about the Cox murder. But yet again there was no forensic evidence and there were no witnesses, apart from Cox's partner whose testimony alone was not deemed strong enough to support a murder charge against the now notorious hit man. All garda intelligence files relating to Gerry Hutch since 1987 have identified him as the murder suspect.

For his part Hutch has consistently and vehemently denied murdering Mel Cox. One of the reasons why he has been particularly touchy about the accusation is that it damaged his relationship with his local community, many of whom were sympathetic to the plight of Margaret Cashin who was one of their own. In reality there was little sympathy for Cox in the eyes of those he had crossed – he was a bully and a blow-in – but there was for his partner and her family.

Two months after the Cox murder the Monk experienced some bad karma of his own when a robbery went terribly wrong for two of his fellow gang members. On 1 September 1987 Thomas O'Driscoll and Geoffrey Ennis joined up with a third robber from Crumlin, south Dublin, to hit the North Cumberland Street labour exchange where they collected their weekly unemployment assistance. Shortly after 10 a.m. O'Driscoll and the Crumlin hood burst into the building while Ennis waited nearby in a getaway car. Armed with a sawn-off shotgun, O'Driscoll covered his partner who smashed the glass partition at Hatch 33 with a sledgehammer. He vaulted the counter and began scooping cash into a bag. At the same time Detective Garda Dominick Hutchin from Fitzgibbon Street garda station who was on protection duty in the building heard the commotion.

The detective ran out into the public area and pointed his .38 revolver at O'Driscoll ordering him to drop the gun. The raider pointed the shotgun at the policeman who again ordered him to surrender it. Instead, O'Driscoll grabbed a pistol from his accomplice and handed him back the shotgun. He moved towards the detective and fired twice, narrowly missing him. At the same time the Crumlin raider, who had jumped back out into the public area with a bag of money, also fired at Detective Garda Hutchin, hitting him in the face and body with buckshot pellets. The injured detective fired all six rounds in his revolver at O'Driscoll, hitting him five times. The robber fell back into a sitting position, still pointing the handgun at Hutchin who retreated back inside the staff area to reload his gun and raise the alarm.

The second robber pulled the seriously injured O'Driscoll outside to the waiting getaway car. O'Driscoll, who was still clutching the bag of money, leaned against a parked car while his partner, armed with the handgun, took up a covering position in the middle of the street and signalled to Ennis who was parked down the road. At the same time a squad car, responding to the alarm, screeched around the corner at the bottom of Cumberland Street and drove towards the raiders. The Crumlin robber pointed his gun at the squad car forcing the unarmed officers inside to duck. At the same time the getaway car drove up behind them.

The gunman pushed O'Driscoll into the car which then sped off. As it went towards Hill Street and then on towards Mountjoy Square another uniformed officer tried to smash the windshield with his baton. The squad car gave chase but lost the raiders whose car was much more powerful. After driving through a few more streets to ensure they'd lost the gardaí, the three robbers abandoned the car. They dragged O'Driscoll to a second car, a Toyota Starlet, that Ennis had borrowed that morning from a friend.

At Roseglen Avenue in Kilbarrack, a suburb in north Dublin, O'Driscoll's partners realized that he was critically injured. They decided to push him out onto the side of the road so that he would get medical attention when the police found him. O'Driscoll was moaning and calling for help when he died from his gunshot wounds a few minutes later. Gerard Hutch had lost another close friend.

Gardaí subsequently arrested thirty-seven-year-old Crumlin criminal Martin Leonard in connection with the robbery. Geoffrey Ennis went into hiding but Laurence Alford, a thirty-four-year-old dock worker from East Wall was also charged with the robbery. He had loaned the Toyota Starlet Ennis used to make their getaway. He was subsequently acquitted following a trial. The £25,000 (€60,000) taken in the raid was never recovered.

Detective Garda Hutchin had a lucky escape and recovered from his injuries. He was subsequently awarded the Scott Medal for bravery, the highest honour the force can bestow for courage in the line of duty.

O'Driscoll's death had a profound effect on the Monk. His friends described how he became more introspective after it happened. Hutch would not have approved of such a reckless operation. The Cumberland Street labour exchange, like others in the city, had been regularly targeted in armed robberies and it was well known that armed officers had been assigned to protect them. It was speculated that O'Driscoll's heroin addiction was one of the reasons for the desperate raid, but Hutch disagreed, saying that his best friend was clean at the time of the robbery. A friend later told *Magill* magazine: 'The only time I ever saw Gerard cry was at Thomas O'Driscoll's funeral. He was inconsolable, the tears were streaming out of him.'

CHAPTER EIGHT

A MAN OF PROPERTY

By the end of 1987 Lonan Hickey and Francis Sheridan were paying a hefty price for accepting Gerry Hutch's offer of 'a few quid'. To add to their sense of injury they were the only people ever to be convicted in connection with the Marino Mart robbery. Sheridan pleaded guilty at the earliest opportunity to a charge of receiving some of the proceeds from the robbery and was sentenced to twenty-one months imprisonment in November 1987. On 16 February 1988 it was Hickey's turn to face the music when he too entered a plea of guilty. The Circuit Criminal Court heard that he had been threatened by a 'notorious criminal godfather' to launder nearly £200,000 of the loot.

Hutch was identified in the proceedings as 'Mr X' on the grounds that to name him might be prejudicial to any future prosecution for the robbery. In a plea for leniency Hickey's counsel said that the carpet salesman was in fear of the unnamed Monk who he alleged had forced him to take part in moving the stolen cash. His counsel claimed Hickey was the victim of 'ruthless and dangerous men'.

Adjourning the case, Mr Justice Frank Roe said that the matter 'illustrates the old adage that there would be no thieves if there were no receivers'. He commented: 'I can see no way in which Hickey can expect to walk out of this court with a suspended sentence.'

A month later the judge also sentenced Hickey to twenty-one months inside. Since the heist had been the biggest cash robbery in the history of the State the sentences were a favourable result for the bagmen. With remission for good behaviour they served no more than fifteen months each. From Hutch's perspective it wasn't a bad result either.

The Marino Mart job and the murder of Mel Cox had earned Hutch considerable notoriety already. With the convictions of Hickey and Sheridan the media had another opportunity to highlight the young godfather's rise to gangland prominence. Up to that time the Irish media had not given the growing problem of organized crime in Dublin the coverage that it merited. The nearest thing to an exposé was a short profile piece headed 'Mr X – A Top Criminal' which accompanied the court report in the *Irish Press* newspaper. The article went as far as it could without actually naming Gerry Hutch for fear he might sue for defamation. It described how 'Mr X' was from a 'family with a long history of crime' and that he was known to gardaí as 'one of the city's two most successful armed criminals'. Fergal Keane, the newspaper's security correspondent wrote: 'Mr X is the most successful of them [the Hutch brothers] and has a reputation for viciousness and violence almost unparalleled among top Dublin criminals.'

But the media attention on Gerry Hutch was a one-day wonder as the organized crime spotlight had already shifted elsewhere. The Monk got a reprieve of sorts thanks to the activities of Ireland's undisputed 'Most Wanted' criminal at the time – Martin Cahill, the General.

Less than a week before Hickey's court appearance in February, RTÉ's *Today Tonight* current affairs programme had broadcast an hour-long documentary that placed organized crime front and centre in the public debate. It was a ground-breaking, riveting exposé of the extraordinary illegal activities of Cahill and his gang. It was watched by over a million viewers around Ireland and made the armed robber a household name overnight.

The programme briefly listed the activities of the two other big gangs operating at the time. The first one referenced was the Monk's mob. Reporter Brendan O'Brien said it included members of a 'notorious family and its associates led by a man in his twenties'. The programme referred to the Marino Mart robbery and the murder of Mel Cox. His widow, Margaret Cashin, was interviewed and described how the man who had shot her husband was from a well-known criminal family from the north inner city.

The other gang referenced was the 'Factory Gang' led by John Gilligan, which specialized in the systematic plundering of millions of pounds worth of goods from warehouses and factories across the country. The programme name-checked two members of Gilligan's gang who had been convicted for robbing a truck load of bovine medicine – George 'the Penguin' Mitchell and Gerard Hopkins. Mitchell went on to become a major international drug trafficker and Hopkins, who was related to Gerry Hutch through marriage, remains the Penguin's partner-in-crime. Hutch, by far the youngest gang leader on the scene, hadn't yet done enough damage to merit any more airtime and much to his relief he was merely a forgettable footnote in the story. He was the warm-up act for the star of the show – Martin Cahill. In reality, there was no serious competition to his top billing.

The award-winning investigation caused public and political uproar when Cahill was filmed collecting his unemployment assistance despite living in a private house he'd bought for £85,000

(€213,000) in cash a few years earlier. The documentary was prompted after Garda HQ decided to go to war with the General, whose prolific high-profile crimes could no longer be tolerated. Apart from carrying out armed robberies and aggravated burglaries on an industrial scale, the psychotic godfather took the fight to the State and the gardaí at every opportunity. In his sub-cultural world they were the root of all evil.

By 1988 the list of Cahill's serious crimes was a national outrage. He'd blown-up the State forensic scientist, plotted to murder a senior garda, burned court offices and equipped his gang's arsenal with weapons stolen from a facility where gardaí stored confiscated firearms. In August 1987 he had targeted the heart of the Irish criminal justice system when he broke into the offices of the Director of Public Prosecutions and stole 150 of the most sensitive crime investigation files in the country. A month later Cahill had added the final insult to injury when he slipped the net after initially taking the bait in an elaborate garda sting operation after he met an undercover Dutch cop who was posing as a criminal art fence who wanted to buy the Beit paintings. It was the first time Cahill had taken the bait and on 27 September 1987 he came tantalizingly close to being nabbed red-handed in possession of the priceless paintings. However, it all went terribly wrong. The police's radio network broke down, causing utter confusion, while Cahill's survival instincts kicked in and he became suspicious of the bogus 'art dealer'. The undercover cop was promptly pushed into a car and brought back to the city while Cahill, another associate and the paintings took a different route. Instead of keeping his head down after the botched operation, Cahill taunted the gardaí at every opportunity. For the police it was the final humiliation at the hands of their hated enemy.

On 1 January 1988 Cahill and six of his top lieutenants awoke to find teams of smiling cops sitting outside their homes. They were members of the Special Surveillance Unit (SSU) which had been hastily mobilized a month earlier. The unit was made up of seventy young gardaí, many of whom had only been in the force a short time and had been hand-picked for the operation. The plan was to use overt, close-up surveillance to harass and antagonize the targeted gangsters as much as possible. It was unprecedented in the history of the gardaí. Each of the seven initial targets was followed by up to six officers at a time and was given a codename. Cahill was T (target) One or in radio phonetics Tango One.

The mobsters were well used to police surveillance but had never seen anything like this before. Seamus 'Shavo' Hogan, one of the seven targets, later recalled: 'The first week it started we thought this is great craic. But it became a nightmare: beeping horns and shining torches into the house at night. It really fucked-up everything. You could not go out for a drink without a cop sitting beside you.'

As he did in every other aspect of his life, Gerry Hutch watched and learned from the extraordinary spectacle playing out in full public view. And while they may have come from strikingly similar socio-economic backgrounds and were both accomplished criminal masterminds, the Monk and the General could not have been more different. Gerry Hutch kept out of sight while Cahill and his henchmen tried to intimidate the T Squad, openly threatening them in the street. At the height of the surveillance operation the General's underlings even dug up the greens at the garda golf course. It was a move the Monk would never have contemplated as it would inevitably lead to even more garda attention.

Within six months the Tango operation had effectively smashed Cahill's gang as one by one his trusted lieutenants slipped up.

Within a year they were incarcerated in Ireland's maximum-security Portlaoise Prison, serving long sentences for possession of firearms, attempted armed robberies and assault. But Tango One himself, the General, escaped.

While the other gang members had tried to shake off the intense media scrutiny Cahill embraced it. He seemed to enjoy playing the fool in front of the cameras while at the same time maintaining a level of mystique by hiding his face behind a balaclava. Whenever the media pack descended on the eccentric villain, he made sure to put on a spectacle for them to report.

On one occasion he appeared outside a court wearing a white nightshirt with the words 'One Flew Over the Cuckoo's Nest' handwritten on his chest and back, and a bird's nest strapped to his head. When the reporters asked was he the General, Cahill responded by blowing a duck decoy, asking a photographer if he was a chicken and pointing to a bicycle asking if it was a boat. When he got on the bike, he asked a bemused pedestrian if the road was the River Liffey before cycling off. At another court appearance for a breach of the peace he began singing 'I'm Gonna Sit Right Down and Write Myself a Letter' in a direct reference to the most valuable of the stolen Beit paintings, Vermeer's *Woman Writing a Letter with her Maid*. Then he dropped his trousers to reveal Mickey Mouse shorts and for good measure shouted: 'Mickey Mouse!'

According to former associates Gerry Hutch could not get his head around the General's clownish antics and wondered whether he was genuinely mad or if this was just him playing his legendary mind games. By contrast, the Monk prided himself on his Zelig-like ability to merge into the shadows and avoid attention. Keeping a low profile was the only way the twenty-four-year-old knew how to survive.

Hutch despised the gardaí, possibly even more than Cahill did, but common sense told him that there was nothing to be gained by blatantly trying to antagonize or humiliate them. If he was halted by the police, Cahill would turn the 'stop and search' into a provocative spectacle, taking off his clothes or lying down in the road screaming that the cops had beaten him. Whenever Hutch was stopped, he would remain cool and calm avoiding confrontation. If the cops tried to rile him he wouldn't take the bait. One detective who had stopped and searched Gerry Hutch many times commented: 'Most criminals are full of bravado and testosterone and they'll give you abuse but you never got that from Hutch. He was courteous in a businesslike sort of way but you still knew that he despised you. The other lads in his inner circle were the same.'

The Monk was a student of life who tried to learn something useful from every experience. He had no intention of making such a nuisance of himself as to prompt an unprecedented backlash from the gardaí. Hutch didn't want the T Squad to descend on him and his mob. He would tell friends that Ireland was a police state and prison was its means of exacting revenge. In his philosophy those who fought the law found that the law won in the end – no matter how long it took. As a former associate told this writer:

> Gerard was a very sharp guy who knew his limitations; he knew how far to go and had the discipline to stay within the limits. He hated the cops every bit as much as Cahill, but Cahill had drawn a lot of unnecessary heat on himself from all sides – the police, media and politicians. Gerard said that Cahill had lost all credibility because it was his loyal gang members who paid the price for his bullshit and theatrics. His rule in life was to only pick the fights that you can win – or fights that didn't mean you ended up in jail if you lost. As far as

he was concerned the General was a madman on a one-way trip
to disaster.

It was a sentiment which many of the General's most loyal associates were beginning to share. They blamed Cahill's buffoonery and pathological hatred of the State for their loss of liberty, while he was still free to act the clown in the streets. Gerry Hutch wouldn't go near him as just being seen talking to Cahill was enough to have someone arrested or investigated. The T Squad had made the gang boss a pariah and former close associates began to move away from him. One of them was Paddy Shanahan who decided that working with the Monk and his associates would be a safer option.

A successful businessman Paddy Shanahan was one of the most unlikely gangsters ever encountered by either Martin Cahill or Gerry Hutch. He had a promising career until he made the choice of getting involved in serious crime. The decision was not made because of deprivation or life's hard knocks. Shanahan embraced organized crime because he loved the glamour, the buzz and the easy money.

Born in 1946 in the village of Kill, County Kildare, he came from a respectable family with no criminal background of any kind. Compared to his future partners he had an idyllic childhood; he was good at sport and a star pupil in school. Shanahan studied English and History in university but dropped out after a year. He then worked in various jobs and set up a few businesses before he made his life-altering career change.

Shanahan's natural talent was for armed robbery which, unlike Gerry Hutch, he saw as a glamorous lifestyle choice. In Dublin he began looking for a start in his chosen profession, rubbing shoulders with criminals who initially viewed the well-spoken 'culchie' with suspicion. He eventually convinced the clannish city villains that he was serious and not a garda plant. Shanahan began working with the Dunnes and then later with Martin Cahill. Henry Dunne, who brought Shanahan on his first job, recalled:

> He loved crime; he was fascinated by the whole thing. He wasn't like the rest of us. We did it for a living; he did it for the sheer buzz. When we went on a stroke it was like he was acting in a movie. He was a complete Walter Mitty character. He loved dressing up and handling guns. We often had to warn him that the shooters were only being used to frighten the people in the bank and prevent any heroics. He was the type who seemed like he wanted to blow someone away – fortunately he didn't get the chance.

Shanahan later moved to England where he began specializing in the theft of antiques. In 1980 he was arrested with two accomplices after raiding the Staffordshire home of an elderly collector of antiquities. The old man suffered a heart attack and would have died if Shanahan had not administered first aid. The gang stole antique clocks, watches, Japanese ivory figures, jade, gems and cash valued at Stg£361,000 (Stg£1.56 million). The police traced Shanahan after forensics uncovered his UK address indented on a receipt book he'd left at the scene. For his trouble Shanahan received a six-year jail sentence. He was released in 1984 and returned to Ireland.

The former businessman's experience in England did nothing to dampen his enthusiasm for stolen art and antiques. He began to burgle Irish stately homes and would offload the loot through his contacts in London, tapping into the lucrative black market for stolen heirlooms across Europe. Shanahan's partner in the operation was Jim Mansfield, a major figure in the emerging Irish crime scene. Mansfield specialized in laundering dirty money while fronting as a legitimate high-profile businessman, a pretence he maintained until his death many years later.

Born in 1939 in Brittas, County Dublin, Mansfield started out as a haulage contractor before moving into the property business. The cover provided him with a protective blanket of respectability and kept him beyond the reach of gardaí. In the early 1980s Shanahan and Mansfield were involved in a successful business venture involving machinery, vehicles and scrap that had been abandoned following the Falklands War in 1982. Mansfield bought up the war materiel and later auctioned it off in the UK for a huge profit.

It was Shanahan and Mansfield who had identified Russborough House in County Wicklow as a likely target. But they had been more interested in the valuable antiques in the stately home than the priceless Beit paintings. Shanahan took advantage of the daily guided tours to identify the artefacts, including furniture and Ming porcelain, for which he had buyers in the UK. In 1985 he'd gone to Martin Cahill with a plan to rob the place. The General loved the idea but decided to cut the businessmen out. Shanahan severed his ties to Cahill after that. The circus around the T Squad investigation convinced him he had made the right decision. He realized that armed robbery was no longer such a glamorous calling and decided to go legitimate. He set up a construction company and began buying property around Dublin with Mansfield. By 1987 he was ideally placed to go into business with Gerry Hutch and Matt Kelly to launder the proceeds of the Marino Mart job.

Apart from the money recovered in Dublin and Newry the remaining £1 million (€2,457,000) was never traced. However, garda intelligence sources were reporting that Matt Kelly and Gerry Hutch had become involved in a number of major property deals in central Dublin. Within a few months of the Marino Mart job Mansfield agreed to sell a large premises he owned in Talbot Street, central Dublin, to Kelly and Hutch, with Shanahan acting as the front man. Mansfield established a business relationship with Gerry Hutch who he viewed as a 'pretty smart guy'.

An investigation conducted by the Criminal Assets Bureau years later proved that Shanahan had fronted the deal and that Hutch and Kelly were the real owners. At the time Hutch and Kelly used another businessman to set up a furniture company on the premises. Garda intelligence was fully aware of where the funds to finance the clandestine arrangements were coming from but were powerless to do anything about it.

The Talbot Street property was to become the first stage of a large-scale money laundering operation that enabled Gerry Hutch and Matt Kelly to acquire an extensive property portfolio which included shops, pubs, apartments and vacant sites earmarked for development. In time they began to secretly invest in the UK property market where they bought nursing homes, pubs and apartments. It was also later established that Gerry Hutch was a silent partner in two hotels owned by Mansfield in west Dublin. According to a secret garda report a decade later the two premises were being used for 'large-scale criminality' including laundering the proceeds of crime.

Some of the properties in their portfolio were registered in the names of various associates such as Niall Mulvihill and Charlie Duffy, a long-time friend of the Kellys who owned a scrap business in the Smithfield area of the north inner city. Duffy had a corrupt business relationship with George Redmond, the assistant city and county council manager for Dublin. Born in 1924, Redmond began working as a clerk in Dublin Corporation in 1942 and advanced to become one of the most powerful local authority officials in the capital. As the person with ultimate responsibility for granting planning permission for building projects Redmond took huge bribes from developers and criminals. By the time he retired in 1989 he had helped to make a lot of people wealthy, including Gerry Hutch.

One major project the corrupt public official took a backhander to rubber stamp was the redevelopment of Buckingham Buildings, a disused tenement complex on Buckingham Street, in the heart of Hutch's beloved neighbourhood. It was bought by Paddy Shanahan and in October 1987 his construction company, Manito Enterprises, began refurbishment work to turn it into modern apartments. Matt Kelly supervised the gutting of the old building and Gerry, Eddie and Patsy Hutch were also regular visitors to the site. On 13 October gardaí spotted Patsy Hutch and Gerry's brother-in-law loading rubbish into a large skip. It was an open secret that the mob was behind the development.

While Shanahan, Hutch and Kelly were the primary investors it was later discovered that the project was also used to launder money on behalf of a number of other criminals including George 'the Penguin' Mitchell. The second stage of the development included in the planning permission granted by Redmond involved the erection of a new block of apartments on a vacant site next door. The renamed Buckingham Village contained 100 apartments that were largely rented by the recipients of Eastern Health Board rental support and subsequently by foreign immigrants and asylum seekers.

Even though Buckingham Village was built on the proceeds of drug trafficking and armed robbery, the development qualified for tax incentives designed to encourage investment in the inner-city areas which had fallen into dereliction due to many decades of neglect. It was ironic that the criminal fraternity were behind the first major investments in the depressed inner city before Ireland's construction boom took off in the mid-nineties.

Hutch continued to grow his portfolio and in August 1989 he paid £20,000 (€46,000) for two more houses on Buckingham Street, on either side of the one he already owned. He converted the houses into rented accommodation for the Eastern Health Board and went on to purchase another house on the street in 1993.

Several years later Hutch was still protesting the provenance of his wealth when he told an RTÉ interviewer: 'I bought property. I bought a couple of properties in my neighbourhood which were very cheap at the time and done them up. I rented them out, re-mortgaged them, went onto another one and another one... I done a lot of business in property. It was a good time and that's where I made me money. If people say armed robberies so be it.'

It would later be discovered that Hutch and Kelly owned at least seventeen apartments between them in Buckingham Village. The Monk also secretly owned another eight properties on Talbot Street and three more around the corner on Foley Street. The property in the area was cheaper than in the rest of Dublin. Outside investors were reluctant to put their money into an area that was so run down and plagued by drug addiction and street crime.

The Monk's decision to plough the illegal proceeds of the Marino Mart job into his old neighbourhood proved to be fortuitously prescient. In 1987 Dublin's International Financial Services Centre (IFSC) was established on the derelict port authority lands at the

North Wall and George's Dock where the Monk's father once eked out a living as a labourer. It heralded the beginning of a property development bonanza – and Gerry Hutch was well positioned to cash in. Within a few years he was one of the biggest landlords in the north inner city. When the Celtic Tiger era arrived it turned his investments into pure gold. It was a dramatic change of fortune for the young tearaway whose goal was to rob his way out of poverty. But the Monk had no intention of giving up his illegal activities.

———

CHAPTER NINE

A NEW RECORD

Throughout the late eighties the Monk continued to expand his property interests. To fund his investments Gerry Hutch and his team were actively on the lookout for other potential targets to rob. However, they had agreed that there would be no more reckless escapades like the ones which had claimed the lives of Hutch's close friends Thomas O'Driscoll and Eamon Byrne.

Unlike many of his contemporaries at the time the Monk could foresee that the days of robbing banks were coming to an end. By 1990, following the crackdown on the General's gang, the cops had seriously upped their game in terms of surveillance and armed response times. As a result, more gangs were being confronted and caught. Gerry Hutch was well aware that their previous successes had placed them on the Serious Crime Squad's 'Most Wanted' list. They could safely assume that they would be under regular surveillance, so Hutch reasoned that they had to be fastidious in their choice of target. One meticulously planned high-end million-pound job every few years was a much more effective, less risky approach than a string of low-earning bank heists.

Detectives who monitored the gang commented that the former Bugsy Malones were still one of the most secretive, impenetrable crews operating in gangland. This rare trait was attributed to the unique personality of the gang leader. Everything they planned was hermetically sealed and no information leaked out. The gang members were always careful. They did not discuss business with people outside their group, even wives, and they never said anything incriminating on the phone. The aftermath of the Marino Mart robbery had also taught them a few valuable lessons about garda surveillance.

Long periods of inactivity between heists also meant that the detectives would get fed up watching and listening. They would end up moving on to other less conscientious villains, giving the gang the freedom to plot another big expropriation. It was a game of patience and meticulous strategic planning. It was about not getting caught. But in October 1990 Hutch's gang found themselves in the garda spotlight again.

It began when an amateur radio enthusiast in Waterford city picked up two men relaying messages to each other on a walkie-talkie. What immediately caught the person's attention was that the men, with strong Dublin accents, were discussing the movements of security personnel and gardaí at a bank in the area. The radio enthusiast decided to tape the exchange and he called the police. When detectives heard the recorded conversations they quickly established that the gang was watching the Allied Irish Banks cash holding centre at Lisduggan in the city.

The centre was one of four depots in Ireland where millions of pounds were stored on behalf of the Central Bank by the two main banking groups Allied Irish Banks (AIB) and Bank of Ireland. The premises had been purpose-built to be robbery-proof. It was equipped with state-of-the-art CCTV cameras, infra-red detectors to pick up body heat and inertia sensors to pick up unusual vibrations, such as hammering in the walls. The high-tech alarm system was also directly connected to the Waterford Garda HQ. There were regular garda patrols in the area and an armed detective was on duty in the building 24/7. On an almost daily basis gardaí and Irish Army personnel arrived with deliveries of cash collected from banks in the region. The building was considered impregnable and any attempt to raid it was viewed as complete folly.

When the tape was played to detectives in Dublin, they identified the voice of Geoffrey Ennis. He was Hutch's right-hand man in the planning and execution of the gang's robberies. The second voice was never identified.

The discovery sparked a major security operation. Garda chiefs hoped it would lead to catching one of the country's most successful crime gangs in the act. Detectives also discovered another link back to the Hutch gang. Earlier in 1990 Ennis had rented three properties in Dublin, Waterford and Wicklow which the gang used as bases from which to carry out surveillance for armed heists. He rented an apartment in Monkstown, south Dublin under the alias Gerard Brown and two houses, one in Waterford city and another in the Wicklow countryside, using the aliases Gerard Brown and Gerard O'Brien.

Security was stepped up at the Lisduggan cash holding centre and teams of armed officers were deployed to intercept the gang in the event that a robbery took place. A review of the security arrangements at the premises found that the regime was adequate and effective. The operation continued for a number of months but was stood down after Geoffrey Ennis was arrested following an armed robbery in Kilkenny on 14 December 1990. Detectives investigating the hold-up of a Securicor employee at Ballybough Street in Kilkenny later found two stolen sawn-off shotguns when they raided Ennis's hideout in Wicklow. Hutch's partner-in-crime was charged in connection with the robbery but was subsequently acquitted.

During interrogations detectives had played the recording of his intercepted radio chat and the gang discovered that their surveillance operation in Waterford had been rumbled. Ennis denied it was him on the tape and said nothing more. The now high-risk robbery plan was shelved. The Monk and his mob had been relatively lucky, unlike several of his gangland associates.

The same year, 1990, is remembered with universal affection as the one when Ireland made it to the quarter-finals of the FIFA World Cup in Italy. But it is also remembered with less enthusiasm in Ireland's gangland as the year that armed robbery became a decidedly hazardous occupation. A new paramilitary-style special weapons and tactics force called the Emergency Response Unit (ERU) was deployed on the streets with devastating results. In the first six months of 1990 the ERU shot dead three blaggers and seriously injured three more, following armed hold-ups in Athy, Enniscorthy and Dublin.

In January, Austin Higgins from Dublin's northside was killed while holding a gun to the head of a hostage after the ERU surrounded his gang at the Bank of Ireland in Emily Square in Athy, County Kildare. What would be remembered in gangland folklore as the 'Athy Gang' was a potent, deadly mixture of criminals and republican paramilitaries, some of whom had previously taken part in robberies with the Hutch mob. Thomas Tynan, Brendan 'Wetty' Walsh, P. J. Loughran and William Gardiner formed the nucleus of an overall team of ten who came from all over Dublin. During 1989 they had been responsible for thirty-two of the forty-nine armed bank robberies carried out across the country. But in Athy the gang came to a sticky end following a major operation led by the CDU's Serious Crime Squad in Dublin. Two robbers, Tynan and Loughran, were also shot and seriously injured during the stand-off. Loughran was left semi-paralysed as a result. The violent encounter reinforced Gerry Hutch's penchant for meticulous planning and internal security. The Athy incident had showed the other gangs that the cops were using much more sophisticated methods including tracking devices and planting bugs on getaway cars which recorded the gang's conversations.

On May Day the gardaí scored another major victory over the crime gangs. A seven-member IRA gang was captured when they were confronted by local gardaí during an armed hold-up at the Allied Irish Banks branch in Enniscorthy, County Wexford. One of the robbers, Kenneth Bolger, was seriously injured in an exchange of gunfire. A month later, in June, William 'Blinkey' Doyle and Thomas Wilson, members of Hutch associate Tommy Savage's gang, were shot dead when a high-speed chase across north-west Dublin ended in a shoot-out with the ERU. The two violent armed robbers were members of the grandly named Irish People's Liberation Organization (IPLO) which was formed in 1987 by Mickey Weldon and Savage following a bloody split in the INLA. The Monk's associates had been involved in the internal feud which resulted in a string of murders.

Patrick Pearse McDonald from Newry was another member of the motley IPLO rabble. He was released from Portlaoise Prison in 1989 after serving a sentence for kidnapping and firearms offences. A barber by profession, he was the second in command of the IPLO next to Savage. He set up a hair-dressing salon in Marino in north Dublin, earning the sobriquet, 'Teasy Weasy'.

On 20 December 1991 McDonald was executed by a lone gunman as he fixed the hair of an elderly female customer in his salon. He was shot six times: once in the head and five times in the body. One possible motive for the hit was a shooting incident in St Joseph's Mansions where Gerry Hutch's good friend Noel 'Duck Egg' Kirwan lived. In the previous July, McDonald was suspected of entering the flat complex with two other men and firing a shotgun blast which injured four women.

In the follow-up investigation Gerry Hutch was identified as one of the suspects for the murder. It was discovered that Teasy Weasy had fallen out with Hutch and his deadly IPLO comrades. Weldon and Savage were also nominated as suspects and a line of enquiry that detectives investigated was that Hutch had organized the hit on their behalf. Garda background intelligence reports identified Hutch as the prime suspect for the murder. One such report states: 'Gerry Hutch sprang to prominence in the 1980s and was regarded as the main suspect in the murder of three men namely: Danny McOwen in June 1983, Mel Cox in July 1987 and Patrick "Teasy Weasy" McDonald in December 1992.'

Hutch has always denied involvement in any of the murders connected to him. The garda investigation of the McDonald murder was noteworthy in that their enquiries were met with a wall of silence and they made no progress. Hutch was not arrested for questioning on the grounds that there wasn't enough evidence to connect him to the crime.

After McDonald's murder Savage and Weldon moved their operation to Amsterdam where they felt safe from old comrades and the police. The volatile Zombie later claimed that he was forced to 'emigrate' because the gardaí and the media had made it known that he was a suspect in the case. He said that an IRA hit team from south Armagh had agreed to assassinate him in revenge for McDonald's murder – for 'old times' sake'.

Meanwhile the Monk had other things on his mind as he was busy planning his next spectacular heist. Hutch and his gang were going back to Waterford.

At 4.15 p.m. on Monday, 6 January 1992, two men armed with AK-47 rifles crashed through the ceiling of the AIB Lisduggan cash holding centre as staff were about to place a consignment of £2.5 million (€5.2 million)in a safe. In the first week after the Christmas and New Year holidays the thieves knew that there would be more cash available than at any other time of the year. Sometime earlier, possibly the previous night, the two men had cut through a perimeter fence at the complex and made their way onto the flat concrete roof of the single-storey building. They then broke through the roof into the void between the roof and suspended ceiling inside the building. Somehow, they were not picked up by the CCTV system or the sensor alarms in the roof. Their information was axiomatic. A short time earlier a cash van escorted by the gardaí and Irish army officers had delivered the cash, the final load of the day. The gang made their move after the escort left the area.

The two raiders fired a number of shots to subdue the staff and ensure that there were no heroics. At the same time a third armed raider appeared at the window of a security office, having climbed over an outer wall into the yard at the back of the facility. Again, he knew exactly where he was going. He pointed an automatic rifle at the armed detective inside, ordering him to drop his weapon and lie on the floor. Two members of the AIB staff were also held at gunpoint.

The raiders in the vault wheeled a trolley loaded with bags of cash out of the building and into a waiting van, which had been driven into the compound by two more armed robbers. The gang jumped into the van and made their escape. The operation had taken less than five minutes. The cash-holding depot was in an ideal location for a quick getaway as it was close to a number of routes out of the city.

As emergency garda units were dispatched to intercept the raiders, the gang took a back road into south Kilkenny. At Fiddown Bridge, about 12 miles from Waterford City they drove through a checkpoint manned by two unarmed gardaí. When the officers went to give chase, the gang fired a burst of automatic fire at their squad car.

The getaway van was later found abandoned on a country lane close to the village of Mullinavat. The gang and the huge cash haul vanished. Hutch and his crew had achieved a new record – the biggest cash heist in the history of Ireland. In just two jobs, exactly five years apart, they had got away with a cool £3.9 million (€8 million). Apart from the amounts seized from Hutch's bagmen following the Marino Mart job none of the rest of the loot was ever recovered.

The fact that the heist was executed with military precision and the raiders were armed with AK-47 assault rifles initially pointed the finger of suspicion at the IRA. Two months earlier the security services had discovered that the IRA had taken delivery of two huge arms shipments from Libya including hundreds of AK-47s. Gerry Hutch was known to have forged close links to senior members of the IRA living in the north inner city. There were a lot of crossovers between the two groups as they helped each other out in the organization of robberies and the movement of stolen goods.

The recording of Ennis staking out the cash holding centre fifteen months earlier provided a direct link to the Hutch gang.

But investigators discovered that when the robbery was taking place Ennis had a cast-iron alibi – he was in prison serving a sentence for the theft of a van. On 24 October 1991 he had escaped from the open prison at Shelton Abbey in Wicklow. He was rearrested on 5 November and served the remainder of his sentence until his release on 5 May 1992.

Ennis's crucial role in organizing robberies with Gerry Hutch made detectives suspect that the Monk may have sold on the information to the IRA for a portion of the money. However, it was later discovered that the IRA had broken with their own rules and loaned AK-47s to Hutch in return for a fee. It underlined the nexus between organized crime and the republican groups. The use of the powerful military-spec weapons would become a feature of Hutch's future crimes, including the attack on the Regency Hotel.

———————

Despite his near miss following the arrests of Lonan Hickey and Francis Sheridan after the Marino Mart heist, and the fact that he already had plenty of money, the Monk was not prepared to give up the remainder of his 'hard-earned' cash which had been frozen by the Belfast High Court. According to former associates Hutch was extremely tight with money which was probably a consequence of his underprivileged upbringing.

A total of Stg£103,000 (€238,000) had been frozen in two building society accounts, one in Hutch's name and the other in Hickey's, and the cancelled bank draft in the injunction granted to Securicor by the Belfast High Court in February 1987. In an extraordinary display of chutzpah the Monk decided to fight the injunction and seek the return of the money. Hutch and Hickey mounted a joint legal challenge arguing that there was insufficient evidence to connect the money frozen in the accounts with that stolen at Marino Mart. Hutch attended the various hearings in the company of his advisers Matt Kelly and Mickey Deighan.

While it may seem an astonishingly brazen-faced stunt the case illustrated how, in the absence of money laundering legislation, criminals like Hutch were untouchable by the law much to the utter frustration of the gardaí. Apart from the legal costs he had nothing to lose. The case finally came to a full hearing in the Belfast High Court in July 1992. Hutch's counsel claimed that Hickey had been acting as his agent when he lodged the money to the account in his name in the Anglia Building Society. However, neither of the two men could offer a credible explanation about the origins of the cash. The court heard how Hickey had been jailed after pleading guilty to receiving £191,000 of the stolen money.

On 30 July 1992 the Right Honourable Lord Justice Murray ruled that the money was the proceeds of the Marino Mart heist and ordered the cash be returned to Securicor. But Hutch still wasn't prepared to throw in the towel and appealed the case to the Appeal Court of Northern Ireland. On 22 November 1992 the Lord Chief Justice upheld the High Court decision. The defiant Gerry Hutch then appealed the case to the House of Lords in London. On 23 February 1994 the Lords' Appeal Committee unanimously refused the Monk leave to appeal the case and ordered that the criminal mastermind pay all costs in the various actions. After that Hutch threatened to bring the case to the European Court but he later dropped the appeal. The extraordinary case was cited as justification for EU-wide anti-money laundering legislation which was introduced in 1994. When he was asked about the Securicor case by RTÉ's Paul Reynolds several years later Hutch still clung to the absurd line that the money belonged to him: 'In the end of the day they [Belfast High Court] weren't happy that I had proper title to it and they didn't give it back to me... I did claim that that was my money, yeah. It was my money and I lost me case. It wasn't their money.'

Over the years the Monk had better luck in the Dublin courts where he lodged a number of personal injury compensation claims. It was another income source for the entrepreneurial Hutch. In the late 1980s he received a total of £25,000 (€60,000) from the Department of Justice for falling and breaking his ankle while working in the kitchens at Mountjoy Prison. He would later comment: 'In prison I had an accident and I broke me ankle. I have three screws still in my ankle today and I was awarded £25,000. I went out and I used that wisely.'

In another case – in an example of supreme irony – Hutch received £8,000 (€19,000) for a 'whiplash' injury after a Securicor van shunted into the back of his car. Hutch had also shown that he was prepared to sue for libel if the media wrote about him. He settled a claim against the *Sunday Tribune* newspaper for £2,000.

Gerry Hutch would later claim that the source of his wealth came from investing the money in property. While he was still appealing the decision of the Belfast High Court, a new business venture involving Hutch's old mentor Eamon Kelly was about to go disastrously wrong.

———

On 3 September 1992 John Francis Conlon arrived in Dublin on a flight from London. As he walked through the arrivals hall he spotted Eamon Kelly who was waiting for him. Neither man spoke as they walked separately to the car park where Kelly had parked a van. A surveillance team from the Central Detective Unit had also been waiting for the flight and tailed Kelly as he drove into the city with his passenger.

Originally from Westport, County Mayo, fifty-two-year-old Conlon was a quintessential international man of mystery who dabbled in the high stakes' world of spying and gun-running. He had documented links with several agencies, including the Israeli secret service Mossad, the CIA and MI5. He had supplied huge arms shipments to Iraq during the Iran-Iraq war and to the Afghan rebels in the 1980s on behalf of his spy handlers. Conlon also had contacts with the American Drug Enforcement Agency (DEA) and Colombian drug cartels – he played both sides of the tracks in the world of state-sponsored subterfuge.

The purpose of his visit to Dublin was to organize the delivery of a shipment of high-quality cocaine to Eamon Kelly. Hutch's mentor had become involved in the cannabis trade with Tommy Savage, Mickey Weldon and Dave Myler Brogan but moving into cocaine distribution was a significant step up. At the time cocaine was the preferred drug of the social elite who could afford it. The Colombians began targeting the European market as a new outlet for their product, partly as a result of a huge crackdown on the South American cartels by the US government through its much hyped 'war on drugs'. Conlon, who had met Kelly through mutual criminal acquaintances, had sourced a kilo of the drug from his Colombian contacts. The delivery was a trial run for a series of shipments which the hoodlums planned to import. But someone had tipped off the Drug Squad and they had been secretly monitoring Kelly and his associates for over six months. There was never any evidence that the Monk was one of the investors although it could not be ruled out.

Despite his opposition to the heroin trade he would have no problem making a profit on the back of the bad habits of high society snobs.

On the south side of the city Conlon went to a bank and withdrew £2,000 (€4,000) and then drove to Jurys Hotel in Ballsbridge, south Dublin. A short time earlier Elizabeth Yamanoha, a Cuban woman, had checked into the hotel. She had just arrived on a flight from Miami where Conlon had recruited her to courier the drugs. The portly forty-year-old had smuggled the kilo of cocaine in the folds of her body fat. She handed the drugs to Conlon who paid her the £2,000. He then left with Kelly, driving towards the north inner city. The Serious Crime Squad swooped on the pair as they crossed the River Liffey at the East Link Toll Bridge. Detectives seized the cocaine and arrested Kelly and Conlon.

Catching one of the city's top crime lords red-handed was a huge victory for the gardaí. The cocaine, which was 85 per cent pure, was the biggest seizure of the drug yet recorded in Ireland. It had a street value of £500,000 (approx. €1 million) and had a profit margin of over 90 per cent. Kelly, Conlon and the Cuban courier were arrested and charged. Four months later an arrest warrant was issued for Conlon when he absconded after being released on a £140,000 (€230,000) bail bond.

Following a three-week trial in May 1993 Kelly and Yamanoha were convicted by a jury on charges of possession of drugs with intent to supply. Kelly claimed that another Irish criminal based in the UK, James 'Danger' Byrne, had asked him to pick up Conlon at Dublin Airport and that he had no knowledge of a drug deal. He also accused Conlon of setting him up to be arrested which was by no means inaccurate.

There was plenty of circumstantial evidence to show that Conlon had been an agent provocateur but nevertheless on 27

May Kelly was sentenced to thirteen years imprisonment. The Mayo man was subsequently rearrested and in 1998 pleaded guilty to his 'peripheral' role in the failed drug smuggling operation. Members of a number of international security agencies were in court to monitor the proceedings. Conlon got a five-year sentence. He was spirited away from court following the hearing and vanished.

Kelly wasn't the only one of Hutch's associates to run into trouble. Niall Mulvihill, the Silver Fox, had become comfortably wealthy from his involvement in organizing drug deals, logistics and money laundering services for different crime gangs. He fronted numerous property deals for Gerry Hutch over the years and was also registered as the owner of businesses on his friend's behalf. In 1990 Mulvihill paid £150,000 (€335,000) for a house in upmarket Shrewsbury Park in Ballsbridge, one of Dublin's most affluent neighbourhoods. Around the same time he began putting together a deal to sell part of the stolen Beit art collection which had brought the General nothing but bad luck. Members of Cahill's gang said the paintings were 'cursed' as anyone who tried to sell them got caught.

In October 1992 Mulvihill concluded a deal with Martin Cahill on behalf of a syndicate of Irish and Belgian criminals. He paid Cahill £500,000 (€1 million) as a down payment of £1 million (€2 million) for eight of the paintings. Cahill handed over the works of art to two of Mulvihill's associates in Rathfarnham, south Dublin. The paintings were later smuggled out of the country by trucker and gangland operator Liam Judge from Allenwood, County Kildare. Judge, however, was also a garda informant. Mulvihill and a Belgian underworld art dealer intended to sell the artwork to a German national for £1.5 million (€3 million). However, the art deal fell through when Mulvihill's Belgian partner became suspicious that the German buyer was an undercover cop. It turned out he was right.

As part of the same deal Cahill loaned Mulvihill back £100,000 (€203,000) to buy 125 kilos of cannabis in Spain which was to be driven back to Ireland via London. Mulvihill and Cahill agreed to split the profits and the deal was done in Malaga. When Cahill couldn't find someone to transport the consignment back to Ireland the Silver Fox turned to Gerry Hutch. At a meeting in the Coachman's Inn near Dublin Airport the Monk introduced his friend to a criminal called 'Oxo' who agreed to transport the cannabis haul to Dublin from Spain via London.

According to garda intelligence sources Mulvihill waited in London for 'Oxo' to arrive with the drugs. When he failed to turn up at a prearranged location Mulvihill phoned an associate and told him to ask Hutch what had happened to his precious cargo. The Monk told Mulvihill's man that he knew nothing about the whereabouts of the drugs and all he had done was procure a driver for the operation. The hash haul never materialized and Martin Cahill was out of pocket by £100,000. The General suspected that the Silver Fox had ripped him off.

Cahill demanded the return of the paintings from Mulvihill. He agreed on the condition that the General returned the down payment for the botched art deal. In the end a compromise was reached whereby Mulvihill held onto four paintings and returned the rest to Cahill. The criminal fixer and his Belgian partners had negotiated a new deal to sell the remainder of the paintings, this time to two criminals from Belgium and England. The Silver Fox and his associates were to be paid £1.5 million (€3 million) in cash and high-quality heroin which was to be shipped into the UK by a Turkish gang.

On 23 July 1993 Mulvihill met one of the prospective buyers on the outskirts of Antwerp. He opened the boot of a Mercedes car and showed them the *Woman Writing a Letter with her Maid* by Johannes Vermeer. Just over a month later, a second meeting took place between Mulvihill and another individual to check the financial credibility of the buyer. Satisfied that everything was in order, it was agreed to do the handover at Deurne Airport in Antwerp on 1 September.

That morning Mulvihill and two other London-based Irish criminals arrived at the airport in a hired Opel Vectra. Some time later the buyer arrived and one of Mulvihill's associates brought him to the car and showed him eight paintings including the £3 million (€6.7 million) Vermeer. As he did so the art fences were surrounded by the police and arrested. The two buyers turned out to be cops – one from the Belgian national police and the other from Scotland Yard. Mulvihill's two Belgian criminal partners were also arrested.

Four of the eight paintings were the ones from the Beit collection and the rest, which included two works by Picasso, had been stolen from European art galleries. The curse of the paintings had struck again. Mulvihill and his co-conspirators were held for three months but were released without charge by the Belgian prosecutor on a legal technicality. The Silver Fox returned home immediately.

———

While his old friend was running around Europe doing deals with undercover police officers Gerry Hutch was making efforts to go legitimate, setting himself up as a landlord. In 1993 he availed himself of a controversial tax amnesty which was designed to give Irish tax dodgers a clean slate and bring them into the tax net.

Hutch, like all the other applicants, did not have to disclose how he'd made the money in the first place.

The Monk's only recorded employment was a brief stint working as a motorbike courier. His social welfare record showed that he had only claimed unemployment assistance for eight months in his life. On his application for the amnesty the godfather claimed to have earned just over £30,000 (€61,000) in rental income between 1991 and 1994. He paid a total of £9,000 in back tax after stating his name and address and signing a declaration that his statement of affairs was true and accurate. There was no mention of Marino Mart or the cash holding centre in Waterford. As far as the law and Gerry Hutch were concerned, he was now a legitimate tax-paying Irish citizen.

Although the north inner city was his spiritual home the Monk moved his family to more upmarket Clontarf. While it was geographically only two miles to the north it was a world away from his old neighbourhood. Hutch paid £100,000 (€203,000), £70,000 of it in the form of a mortgage, for a comfortable four-bedroom house in a quiet cul-de-sac in the leafy, coastal suburb. It was the only mortgage registered in his name. By this time his fifth child, a girl, had just been born. He wanted his kids to have the opportunities he did not have and enrolled them in private fee-paying schools on the south side of the city.

Meanwhile in 1993 Hutch's property partner Paddy Shanahan commenced construction of a shop and apartment complex called Drury Hall in Stephen Street, in central Dublin. The project was a partnership between the former armed robber and a legitimate businessman from the Midlands who had no connection with crime. Hutch and Matt Kelly secretly invested in the project through Shanahan. Hutch made a number of payments to

Shanahan which came from bank accounts held in fictitious names in Northern Ireland and the UK. Among the payments were two sterling bank drafts worth Stg£130,000 (€289,000). They were withdrawn from an account held in the name of his wife, Patricia Fowler, at the First Trust Bank at Queen's Square in Belfast. The lodgements were made to Shanahan's company account on 28 October and 3 November 1993.

While Shanahan was working on his latest construction project the murder of his old friend Martin Cahill sent shockwaves through gangland. On 18 August 1994 Martin Cahill was assassinated and members of the Cahill gang accused Gerry Hutch of ordering the hit because the General had threatened his friend Mulvihill. A month before the assassination Cahill had cornered the Silver Fox on a street and told him that if he didn't come up with the money from the Beit deal he would be shot dead. The Cahill gang members were also aware that a few years earlier in an interview with an English magazine Cahill had referred to the prospect of a power struggle with Gerry Hutch and his gang. The General said that if it ever came to a confrontation between him and the Monk: 'It will be either him or me, one of us will have to go.'

Hutch was furious when some media reports in the immediate aftermath of the landmark killing speculated that he had some involvement in the plot to murder Cahill. The Monk was particularly concerned that he could be pulled into a feud if some of the General's hot-headed associates, hell-bent on revenge, lashed out at him. Hutch told associates that the General's death had been 'long overdue' because he crossed too many people including the INLA and the IRA. He had no interest or reason to take on the General, particularly as there was already a queue of people with an interest in killing Cahill.

The Monk was proved right when the IRA claimed responsibility for the attack which was carried out by two members from Finglas in north-west Dublin. In justifying the last murder the organization carried out before the 1994 ceasefire, they accused Cahill of collaborating with the hated loyalist terror group, the Ulster Volunteer Force (UVF). A few months earlier the terror gang had attempted to bomb a Sinn Féin function at the Widow Scallans pub in Dublin city centre. They falsely blamed Cahill for providing logistical support for the gang who shot dead an IRA member in the attack.

However, this was not the case. The only tangible link between Cahill and the UVF concerned the sale of one of the Beit paintings, *Woman Reading a Letter* by Gabriël Metsu, to the terrorist group. As far as Cahill was concerned it was purely a business transaction and he hated the loyalists as much as he did the republicans. The UVF planned to swap the painting for a consignment of weapons from South Africa. But the 'curse' struck yet again when the Turkish dealer who agreed to buy the painting turned out to be an undercover police officer. The arrests that followed and the attendant publicity had cast Cahill in a dangerous light. And it was not the first time he'd appeared on the IRA's radar. Years earlier Cahill's mob almost went to war with the Provos when they tried to extort some of the proceeds of the O'Connor's jewellery heist and the General refused to pay up. The Provos had long memories.

The day after Cahill's murder Sinn Féin/IRA boss Martin Ferris, the so-called officer commanding of the IRA inmates in Ireland's maximum security Portlaoise Prison, sent one of his men with a message for the General's associates. Most of the murdered godfather's henchmen were incarcerated on a separate wing, E1, which was reserved for members of organized crime gangs. The IRA emissary had a stark warning for the mobsters who were baying for blood. They were told that if there was any revenge against the IRA there would be a war in which there would be just one winner. The gang members got the message and there was no retribution for Cahill's murder.

Outside the prison the IRA exploited the power vacuum created by the high-profile killing to muscle in on Dublin's crime scene which was already undergoing a dramatic change in direction. At the time most of the criminal fraternity were moving wholesale into the drug trade. Gangsters such as George Mitchell, John Traynor and John Gilligan were in the process of building new empires the likes of which had not been seen in Ireland before. When the General's men were eventually released, they too became drug traffickers. Gerry Hutch had decided not to get involved in the trade because he considered it too dirty and treacherous. At the same time gangland assassinations were growing steadily. One of them was going to have a major impact on the Monk.

In the weeks following the murder of his former partner-in-crime, Paddy Shanahan was clearly anxious and distressed. He was making genuine efforts to go straight and cut business ties with one of his gangland investors in the Buckingham Village project. The investor wasn't satisfied with the return he'd received from Shanahan, about £1 million (€2 million) and he'd been exerting pressure on Shanahan for more money. Shanahan confided in his wife and close friends that the criminal figure had threatened to kill him when he announced he was ending the partnership. Shanahan told his wife that he wanted to 'walk away and walk away clean' from the criminal. In late September the criminal arrived at the Stephen Street site and was 'ranting and raving' at Shanahan. The builder ejected the furious criminal from the site and told him never to come back.

On 14 October Shanahan was walking into his gym in Crumlin, south Dublin, when a gunman emerged from the shadows. The assassin shot his former business partner once in the face at point-blank range. The shooter then calmly walked out to the nearby roadway and jogged off, disappearing into the busy traffic and the gathering gloom of an autumn dusk. A friend who was accompanying Shanahan, identified the furious investor as being the gunman.

Detectives later met with Gerry Hutch to ascertain what he knew about the killing and Shanahan's falling-out with the former investor. At the time police sources revealed to this writer that Hutch was more talkative than he had ever been. One detective recalled:

> Hutch never co-operated or talked to us but that time he did because he was obviously very upset about Shanahan's murder. You could see that he was angry about it. We were pretty happy that he had played no part in the murder but he knew the person who had organized the killing. We heard that he had confronted the man responsible but nothing more came of it.

Matt Kelly was one of several people arrested and questioned about the crime. He too was uncharacteristically co-operative and gave detectives a full account of his involvement with the Buckingham Village project. Kelly said that he had been 'very happy' as a result of his dealings with Shanahan.

Gardaí later sent a file to the Director of Public Prosecutions recommending that the prime suspect be charged with murder. They had one eyewitness who could identify the shooter and statements from the people Shanahan had shared his concerns with before he was killed. However, the DPP decided that there was insufficient concrete evidence with which to proceed and the case was dropped.

Apart from Shanahan being a trusted conduit for laundering stolen money, he was also a friend of Gerry Hutch. It was well known in Dublin gangland circles that the Monk was deeply angry at the prime suspect and that he cut ties with him after that.

The Monk soon had other matters to occupy his active mind – an operation that involved a fresh injection of cash. Hutch was planning to make history for a third time.

———

CHAPTER TEN

THE BRINKS-ALLIED JOB

When Paddy Shanahan met his ignominious end Gerry Hutch and his crew were already in the process of preparing for their next major robbery. Despite being already linked to two of the biggest heists in gangland history he had no intention of retiring just yet. The target was the Brinks-Allied cash holding depot in Clonshaugh Industrial Estate in Coolock, north Dublin. On the surface it seemed like it would be an almost impossible nut to crack. But Hutch and Ennis had an advantage. They had sensitive inside information which revealed glaring weaknesses in the depot's security infrastructure.

The Brinks-Allied depot had been relocated in a specially converted warehouse in 1993, situated at the northern perimeter of the industrial estate. The building backed onto two large fields which had been earmarked for industrial development. The fields were bordered to the north by Turnapin Lane and to the west by the M50 motorway extension which was under construction. Turnapin Lane had been blocked off due to the road works. It was unlit and there was no traffic in the area.

The circumstances provided perfect cover for the gangsters to approach the depot from the rear where it was most vulnerable. The

inside information revealed that the boundary fence surrounding
the compound was not alarmed or covered by CCTV cameras.
Hutch and his team reckoned they could pull off a robbery after
secretly surveying the area. But like the Waterford job it would
require detailed methodical planning that left nothing to chance. It
didn't matter how long it took – they were prepared to work months
or even a year on it if necessary. The plan for the job would have to
be foolproof to minimize the risk of getting caught. The Monk was
in no rush because the prize was worth waiting for. If everything
went to plan, they stood to earn even more millions than on the
Waterford job.

On 16 October, two days after the Shanahan hit, Geoffrey Ennis
rented a disused shed from a farmer at Oldtown, County Meath.
They planned to use it to store stolen vehicles for the heist. The gang
would need four-wheel-drive jeeps to negotiate the muddy ground
leading to the depot. Identifying himself as 'John', the blagger told
the farmer he worked for a finance company and required a discreet
location to store repossessed cars. Two days later 'John' met the
owner in the Big Tree pub in Swords, north Dublin, and paid £600
(€1,200) for three months' rent in advance.

After a few weeks the farmer became concerned about the
comings and goings at the shed as they took place mostly at night
under cover of darkness. On one occasion he noticed that the
door locks were broken on two cars in the shed. He phoned 'John'
to voice his concerns that the cars may have been stolen. The
following day Ennis introduced the farmer to his 'boss', 'David
Ryan'. It was the alias used by a well-spoken businessman from
Shankill, south County Dublin, who had been involved in dodgy
deals with the criminal for about three years. 'Ryan' successfully
convinced the shed owner that everything was above board. He

explained that the damage to the cars had occurred while they were being repossessed. Over the following weeks the farmer noticed up to eight vehicles were stored in the shed at different times.

On Saturday, 26 November 1994, a major alert was issued after gardaí spotted Hutch apparently monitoring a security van at the Northside Shopping Centre in Coolock. The van was on the same route as the one targeted in the Marino Mart job seven years earlier. Gardaí reasonably suspected that the gang was preparing for a repeat performance. But hitting a security van for the second time would be a lot riskier than the gang's first escapade.

A review of security in the wake of the Marino Mart job had resulted in the provision of armed garda escorts to all cash-in-transit vans carrying more than a million pounds in the greater Dublin area. It was the officers escorting the van who had identified the gangster. In the rest of the country the gardaí and army had been escorting cash-in-transit operations since the 1970s. Each escort had up to ten heavily armed soldiers in two jeeps. No gang had ever attempted to take them on – not even the Monk's.

A top-level security conference was held at the Central Detective Unit (CDU) at Harcourt Square in response to the intelligence. It was decided to launch an investigation codenamed Operation Liffey to catch the gang in the act. The Hutch gang was top of the unit's 'Most Wanted' list and senior gardaí were determined to put them out of business. For almost two months surveillance teams, backed up by the Emergency Response Unit (ERU) and the Serious Crime Squad, shadowed the main suspects and security vans but with negative results. The operation was stood down in the days leading up to Christmas. The Monk and his men had confounded their watchers yet again as they gave no indication that they were planning another job. Despite the garda attention, the gang members had often slipped their watchers and continued with their preparations for the Brinks-Allied job undetected.

On the night of 1 December, two Mitsubishi Pajero jeeps had been stolen from a garage compound at Castletroy in Limerick for use in the upcoming job. The jeeps were then stored in the rented shed in north Dublin. On 8 December an associate of the gang, John Good, who owned a motorbike and jet ski company in central Dublin, had ordered four sets of false number plates from a motor parts company. The registration numbers for the stolen jeeps, were copied from similar vehicles randomly spotted in the street. If gardaí checked the numbers of any of the stolen vehicles they would come back as not being stolen or suspect. It later transpired that one set of number plates had been copied from a vehicle owned by the world-renowned musician Phil Coulter.

The fake registration plates were collected the following day. Gardaí were later told that Good had been asked to order the plates by Paul Boyle, a member of Hutch's crew.

Hutch decided that the best time to make their move on the Brinks depot would be in January. It seemed to be his favourite month for big heists – the Marino Mart and Waterford robberies had also taken place at the start of the year. On the night of 11 January, two more jeeps were stolen in Ballsbridge and Sandycove in south Dublin. They were fitted with the false plates and driven to the storage shed. In a bizarre twist of fate one of the jeeps, a Pajero, had previously belonged to Paddy Shanahan and had been sold to a legitimate customer a few weeks before his murder. The jeep had been repossessed by a finance company when the builder stopped paying his car loan. It was either a total coincidence or intended as a symbolic gesture by someone who planned everything down to the flimsiest of details. The Monk's associates would later say that he used the jeep in the robbery as a tribute to his slain friend.

On 17 January 1995 a second urgent garda circular was issued to all stations and units warning that Hutch and his gang were planning a major armed robbery. The document again named Gerry Hutch and eleven other suspected members of the gang from the north inner city including the main players, Gerry Lee, Geoffrey Ennis, Paul Boyle, Willy Scully and Noel Murphy. The document stated: 'Information to hand suggests that a number of prominent criminals are planning a major armed robbery. The likely target is money in transit by a security company.'

The circular included photographs of the notorious team of villains and listed their physical descriptions, ages, addresses and modes of transport. The gardaí had correctly nominated the members of the gang Hutch had assembled for the job but that was about all the information they had. The Monk and his crew had made sure nothing leaked out.

On Monday, 23 January the gang took the four jeeps and a car from the shed in Oldtown. The following morning a security van with call sign 'Yankee 29' left the Brinks-Allied depot at Clonshaugh and drove to the main AIB Bank Centre in Ballsbridge. Yankee 29 rendezvoused with its garda and army escort and set off on Run 16, collecting cash from AIB branches in the south-east of Ireland. The cash would then be taken back to the security depot and deposited in the vaults. Before the day was over the Run 16 team had collected almost £3 million (€5.6 million).

At 6.25 p.m. Yankee 29 returned to its base in Clonshaugh Industrial Estate. The security van drove through the front gate of the Brinks-Allied complex, which was operated electronically from a control room, and round to the rear of the building where the loading bays were located. Once the security van was safely inside the compound the garda and army escort withdrew. The gang were working on detailed intelligence: they knew that Yankee 29 was carrying a large amount of cash and would be the last van returning to the depot that evening. That information was vital because it reduced the risk of the gang running into the army. A member of the gang had been keeping watch on the depot. As the escort left the estate, he fired three flares into the night sky. It was the gang's signal to move.

Just under an hour earlier, at 5.30 p.m., five men had been spotted driving in a jeep up Turnapin Lane towards the section of the road closed off for the ongoing road works. The gang had meticulously prepared their route into the depot. A section of the perimeter fence that bordered the fields between the industrial estate and the motorway construction site had been removed. Further on the gang had breached a dividing ditch between the two fields. The jeep drove through the hole in the fence and into the first field where a second jeep was waiting.

The two jeeps then drove in darkness through the breach in the ditch. It was marked by a reflective road sign from the motorway construction site. When they reached the second field the jeeps drove to the boundary fence at the rear of the Brinks-Allied depot which was floodlit at night.

The next obstacle was a trench six feet deep which bordered the boundary fence of the industrial estate. It was covered by shrubbery and small trees. During the previous weekend the gang had cleared a section of the undergrowth and built a makeshift bridge across the trench using railway sleepers and sheets of fibreboard. Strips of timber were fastened to the sheets to give the jeeps extra traction. The sheets had been painted green to camouflage the structure. Nothing had been left to chance.

Once across the bridge the jeeps were at the perimeter fence at the rear of a warehouse next door to the security depot. The retaining bolts in the palisade fence had also been pre-loosened and it took only seconds to remove a section which gave the vehicles access to the warehouse yard. As the flares erupted in the night sky all that separated the gang from the cash-loading bay was the simple steel fence between the two yards. It too had been weakened when the supporting transverse bars were cut some time before. The extensive preparatory work had been carried out without attracting attention or activating any of the depot's security systems. From their inside information the gang knew that the warehouse yard and boundary fence were not covered by the Brinks-Allied's CCTV cameras.

As Yankee 29 drove into loading bay number 3 the staff got ready to transfer the money to the depot's armour-plated vaults. The roller-shutter door on the loading bay was being lowered when the first jeep – previously owned by Paddy Shanahan – smashed through the weakened fence. It rammed the roller-shutter door pushing it inwards and up, leaving a gap large enough on either side for the raiders to rush in. The door was hit with such force that it shunted the security van forward. Three of the raiders wearing balaclavas and overalls and armed with handguns ran in through the gap. They fired four shots in the air to subdue the staff and take total control of the situation.

Another raider, carrying an AK-47 rifle, stood guard outside as the others began grabbing the cash bags and carrying them to the second jeep which had been reversed up to the dividing fence between the warehouse and the cash depot. The unfolding drama in the loading bay was being watched live on the cameras in the control room and the staff immediately alerted the gardaí at 6.30 p.m. The thieves jumped into the second jeep and drove in darkness back through the hole in the warehouse fence, across the makeshift bridge, down through the adjoining field and through the breached ditch. When the first squad cars arrived at the scene eight minutes later the raid was already over – the gang had been in and out in just over five minutes.

Two eyewitnesses saw the jeep driving at speed back down Turnapin Lane and across the newly constructed M50 motorway flyover towards an industrial estate on the Swords Road. The jeep then drove into another field, off Barberstown Lane, where the second pair of stolen jeeps had been parked earlier. Other members of the gang were waiting for them there. The loot was transferred into the two jeeps and driven off in different directions – while the gang went straight into the history books.

Hutch and his gang had got away with £2.8 million in cash (€5.55 million) which beat their previous historic milestone. In the course of three major January heists the Monk's crew had stolen a total of £6.7 million (€13.5 million). They were the most successful armed gang in the history of organized crime in Ireland. Hutch had earned his place in the pantheon of criminal masterminds. Like an artist, the Monk was quite proud of his dubious achievements. Even when he was denying any involvement in the robbery years later he could not help but praise his efforts. When he was interviewed by RTÉ in 2008 Hutch claimed he had no knowledge of the Brinks job but then added smugly: 'I think it was a good job, best of luck to whoever got the few quid.'

The Brinks-Allied loot was later sub-divided and stashed in a number of safe houses around the north side of the city where it was counted, packaged and hidden away until it was safe to move it on. Hutch had learned that important detail after the Marino Mart robbery. Impatient criminals anxious to spend their stolen cash inevitably ended up in prison. The remaining getaway jeeps which had taken the money away were later hidden in the back of a 40-foot articulated lorry. Late one night they were driven into the River Liffey near the 3Arena in the old docklands. They were discovered by commercial divers on the bed of the river six months later.

As soon as the Brinks-Allied robbery was reported the gardaí launched a major investigation. It would later transpire that on the day of the robbery Hutch was being watched by a surveillance team but he had given them the slip. They thought that he was in his home the whole time. The gardaí knew who they were looking for – and headed to the north inner city. Most of the suspects had returned to their homes but gardaí stopped Geoffrey Ennis in a car on Strandville Place, just over an hour after the heist. When detectives searched his car, they found a number of traffic cones along with overalls and boots that were wet and muddy. Ennis was arrested under Section 30 of the Offences Against the State Act for unlawful possession of firearms at the Brinks-Allied depot. He was taken to Store Street garda station where he was questioned for 48 hours. The former Bugsy Malone refused to speak and was released without charge.

The Brinks gang as it quickly became known had exposed glaring weaknesses in the security at the depot. Apart from the perimeter fences not being alarmed or covered by security cameras, it was found that the shutter doors on the loading bays were not strong enough to withstand being rammed. When detectives reviewed the security video footage they hoped to find images that could match the overalls and boots found in Ennis's car. But they found that the CCTV footage was of such poor quality that they could not even make out a vague description of the raiders. The tapes had been rendered illegible after being used continuously over a long period.

In the days before digital technology CCTV footage was recorded on VHS cassette tapes which were susceptible to wear and tear. The Hutch gang had been well informed.

In terms of successful armed robberies, the Brinks job was a masterpiece of precision planning and execution. In the follow-up investigation gardaí could find no forensic evidence to link any member of the gang to the crime. And like the Waterford cash holding depot robbery, none of the money was ever recovered. It was suspected that four legitimate businessmen from Dublin, Northern Ireland and the UK had been recruited separately to help launder the cash. The gang's adherence to a strict code of omerta also meant that no useful information leaked out about the robbery or the whereabouts of the loot.

An internal garda report on the robbery which was subsequently sent to the DPP confirmed this point. It stated:

> The investigation team are satisfied that the main suspects as outlined [Hutch and his associates] were involved in the commission of this crime. It has not been possible to gather sufficient evidence to support charges against any of these culprits. All are hardened, ruthless and experienced criminals who plan and execute their crimes within a tight circle. The lack of feedback from informants reflects this.

When the Monk tried to catch a flight for the Canary Islands two days after the robbery, he encountered a problem due to an uncharacteristic oversight. On Thursday, 26 January he was prevented from boarding the flight after it was noticed that the name on the ticket did not match the name on his legitimate passport. Hutch promptly left the airport. The next morning he returned with a ticket that matched his name. The heat of the sun was a welcome alternative from the sort of heat he was suddenly attracting back in Ireland. Garda intelligence later discovered through Interpol that the trip had been akin to a busman's holiday for Hutch. He was meeting contacts to discuss the laundering of the Brinks cash. Tommy Savage, the Zombie, had flown in from Amsterdam to meet his former partner-in-crime.

While the Monk could handle whatever the police threw at him, the historic robbery had other unforeseen, long-term consequences. Hutch lost his cherished anonymity as he became the media's new criminal celebrity – an ideal figure to fill the void left by the General. Much to Hutch's intense annoyance the glare of the spotlight that Martin Cahill had hogged for several years suddenly shifted onto him. Hutch had unwittingly provided a new gangland bogeyman to occupy the public's fascination.

Although he wasn't named and no pictures of him were published, the public was informed about his past, the origins of his nickname and his unusual lifestyle as a clean-living criminal godfather. In an attempt to describe him, society's latest bête noire was compared to the TV comedy character Mr Bean. Hutch's previous exploits were reported on in detail, including the suspected murders, which added to his new-found notoriety. The faceless criminal mastermind with the ecclesiastic sobriquet became a household name overnight. His celebrity would soon make life very uncomfortable for him.

The robbery also propelled him into the political sphere. The huge heist caused sparks to fly in Parliament. In the Dáil the opposition benches seized on a chance to accuse the Government of losing control over criminal gangs. On the same day that Hutch got on the flight to Spain the front page splash in the *Irish Independent* revealed how gardaí had been in possession of intelligence that the Monk was planning a major crime. The newspaper corroborated the story by reproducing the internal garda bulletins. The story was a political bombshell that caused intense embarrassment for the Government and garda management.

In the farce that followed the only person ever convicted in connection with the biggest robbery in Irish history was the journalist who broke the story. In a classic example of shooting the messenger Liz Allen and the paper were charged under the Official Secrets Act for publishing the documents. The journalist and the *Irish Independent* were convicted and fined £380 (€750) for having the temerity to do their job.

On the following Sunday, 29 January, crime journalist Veronica Guerin added fuel to the political fire when she revealed in the *Sunday Independent* that the Monk had availed himself of the infamous tax amnesty a few years earlier. Although she had only been working as a journalist for two years Veronica was already well known for her campaigning newspaper work.

In the aftermath of Martin Cahill's murder she'd run a speculative story, based on information from underworld sources, that the head of a notorious crime family from north Dublin [Hutch] had been responsible for the murder and not the IRA. She later wrote another story about how she had been warned that she was under threat from the same elusive gangster. She was told by her informant that the reason for the threat was that Hutch felt he had been singled out for retribution from the General's acolytes. In October 1994 a shot was fired through a window at the journalist's home. It was seen as a warning that she was getting too close to the criminal underworld for comfort.

Around 7 p.m. on 30 January there was a knock on the front door of Veronica's home in north County Dublin. Her husband and son were out at the time and she was getting ready to go to a staff party.

When she answered the door a man wearing a motorcycle helmet pushed her inside, knocking her to the ground.

He produced a handgun and pointed it at Veronica's head. The thug then lowered the weapon and shot her in the thigh narrowly missing a major artery. Veronica later underwent emergency surgery and was lucky to escape with her life. The shooting reinforced the public's perception that crime in Ireland was out of control. Veronica was a hero in the eyes of ordinary citizens. The journalist made a full recovery and courageously vowed to continue her work. She was given armed police protection for a time but asked the authorities to take it off because it interfered with her work. A year later she was assassinated on the orders of drug trafficker John Gilligan.

In the immediate aftermath of the near fatal shooting the Monk was nominated as the obvious suspect. He was in the eye of a storm of political uproar following the Brinks robbery and the revelations about his tax affairs. Politicians were calling for his tax affairs to be investigated and the amnesty rescinded which would create a world of financial trouble for him. The shooting at Veronica's house took place while the godfather was in Spain which could be interpreted as him ensuring he had a cast-iron alibi. When Veronica was discharged from hospital she was determined to get to the bottom of her own story. Still using crutches, she hand-delivered a letter to the Monk's home demanding to know if he had been responsible for the attack. When she received no reply she confronted Hutch on the street and asked him the question in person.

Hutch told the journalist that he had nothing to do with her shooting and politely told her to 'fuck off'. The exchange was accurately recreated several years later in the 2003 Hollywood movie, *Veronica Guerin* produced by Joel Schumacher. Cate Blanchett played the role of the eponymous heroine. Hutch was also portrayed in an earlier movie version of the same story, *Though the Sky Falls* where Veronica was played by actor Joan Allen. The box office treatment bolstered Hutch's image as a gangland celebrity. But it was not of the same scale as that which the General posthumously received when he was immortalized in a book and no less than three movies. The real-life, publicity-shy Gerry Hutch, however, would have preferred to have been ignored.

While the Monk was seriously angered by the stories, he had absolutely nothing to do with the gun attack on Veronica Guerin or the previous shooting incident at her home. Nor had he anything to do with the threats which followed on from her story about the Cahill murder. The truth was that despite his annoyance and anger with media coverage over the years Hutch never made threats against journalists. He accepted that reporters were as much an occupational hazard as the police. It was part of his moral code as an Ordinary Decent Criminal.

It was revealed in subsequent investigations that the man who orchestrated the threats and the shootings was John Traynor, the Coach, Martin Cahill's former sidekick and John Gilligan's partner in a multi-million drug trafficking empire. Even though he was one of Veronica's primary sources, Traynor wanted to show Gilligan that he had the 'bottle' to shoot a meddling reporter. Traynor had deliberately utilized the cover of Veronica's stories seeing an opportunity to implicate Hutch.

In his unofficial role as a police informant the Coach helpfully tipped them off that the Monk was considering retaliation following the Cahill murder story. Traynor survived by hunting with the hounds and running with the foxes. He also fed Veronica the same line and then sent a thug to fire a shot at her house for good measure. The story about Hutch's tax amnesty, less than a week after the

Brink's heist, provided him with a perfect opportunity to finger the Monk for her shooting. It typified Traynor's perfidious nature.

But Veronica and the gardaí had already realized that the Monk was innocent. She subsequently wrote about the false connection between her shooting and the Brinks job: 'The Monk was immediately identified by gardaí and the media as the man responsible for both crimes. He denies both and, although I am still convinced he was responsible for the Brinks-Allied raid, I know he was not connected to my own shooting.'

Traynor was subsequently arrested and questioned about the shooting but there was no evidence to link him with the crime. In May 1995 she warned this writer about having dealings with Traynor: 'He is a dangerous two-faced bastard. He would have no problem setting you up.'

Incredibly however, despite Veronica's obvious suspicions she continued to talk to the Coach until she threatened to expose him in the *Sunday Independent* in May 1996. Traynor was complicit in her murder a month later.

With the benefit of hindsight it is reasonable to speculate that were it not for Veronica's murder and Traynor fleeing Ireland afterwards, he would have been the victim of a gangland assassination. In such a counter-factual scenario the prime suspect would almost certainly have been the arch-robber and Mr Bean lookalike.

Meanwhile, as the dust settled on the Brinks furore, back in the real world Gerry Hutch's loyalty to his family was about to bring him precariously close to a bloody gangland feud.

CHAPTER ELEVEN

———

FAMILY BUSINESS

In Dublin in the 1990s League of Ireland soccer star Derek 'Maradona' Dunne from the north inner-city was a sporting hero to thousands of children. But off the field the twenty-eight-year-old semi-professional football player with St Patrick's Athletic augmented his income by being one of the biggest heroin traffickers in the city. He was a ruthless drug dealer who had no appreciation for the young fans who followed his exploits on the field. One of his partners in the smack trade was another local sporting icon from the north inner city, Thomas 'Boxer' Mullen, who had represented Ireland as a light middleweight champion fighter.

The two sports stars were typical of the new breed of heroin traffickers who emerged in Ireland in the nineties. Having witnessed from childhood the devastation inflicted by heroin on their peers and communities, these guys consciously avoided being sucked into the vortex of addiction. They focused their teenage energies on excelling in their chosen sports. But somewhere along the line they made a strategic choice to profit on the misery, becoming narcotics entrepreneurs and poisoning the same kids who looked up to them.

Sporting role models who doubled as venal smack peddlers and openly displayed their illicit wealth sent out a deeply confusing message to impressionable, socially vulnerable teens. For some of these youths the contradiction validated the heroin trade as acceptable and normative. It added to the general sense of betrayal and hopelessness that pervaded Hutch's home turf.

The Monk was a fan and a friend of the two young sportsmen before their change of career. Their friendship with the gang boss had given them a degree of street credibility in the community. Mullen, who was seven years Hutch's junior, even claimed to be a member of his gang – until it emerged how the boxer really earned his money. The Monk was still highly regarded in the north inner city where the majority of people saw him as a local hero and ODC. Hutch despised the heroin scourge and those who plied its trade. The Monk's opinions hadn't changed. In his view heroin dealers were not real criminals: they had no ethics, no loyalty and no bottle. All they did was to make life more miserable for their own people. In the Monk's book Dunne and Mullen were pariahs and loathsome parasites.

Gerry Hutch worked as a volunteer in the operation and management of the local Corinthians Boxing Club which was tucked away down an alleyway off Rutland Street in the north inner city. Founded in 1928, the club had traditionally been one of the few outlets for local kids like Hutch and his friends growing up. Corinthians had produced its fair share of boxing heroes across the generations and symbolized the resilience of the local people. Over the years Hutch immersed himself in the club. Working with the kids was his way of doing what he could to prevent them falling into the clutches of smack.

Hutch tended to be hyper-sensitive, even paranoid, about being linked in any way to the heroin trade. On the few occasions that he gave media interviews it was to refute coverage where he perceived that such a link had been made. The Monk made no secret of his contempt for the likes of Derek Dunne but the politics of Dublin gangland meant that it went no further than that – for as long as the soccer star or other heroin dealers didn't cross Hutch or anyone belonging to him.

In May 1995, however, Dunne found himself on a one-way collision course with the Monk after becoming embroiled in a feud with members of his family. The drug dealer lived close to Eddie Hutch in Portland Place where there had been numerous altercations between the footballer and local kids, including Hutch's nephews who were involved in a range of street crimes such as burglary and car theft. One Sunday night the animosity came to a head when Eddie Hutch's eighteen-year-old son, Eddie Junior, was accused of throwing a brick through the window of Dunne's car. Minutes later the footballer attacked the young vandal, beating him so badly that his face was left unrecognizable. Hutch's nephew had to be rushed to intensive care with serious head injuries.

While doctors fought to save the teen's life, the Monk and Eddie Hutch immediately went looking for Dunne. The drug dealer had already fled with his girlfriend and daughter in anticipation of the inevitable backlash. Gerry Hutch was well known to be staunchly loyal to his own blood and held the view that if anyone hurt one of them, they also hurt him. He was particularly close to his nephews many of whom were beginning to follow in the family business.

While Hutch was not given to parading his influence, in the past he had shown that crossing his family would not be tolerated. The same fealty to his kin would be the prime motivation for the Regency Hotel attack over two decades later. Within the criminal hierarchy the Monk's stature dictated that disrespect could not be allowed in case it was interpreted as weakness. In the gangland jungle only the fittest and strongest survive.

Hutch let it be known that Dunne was a dead man walking. That night a group of men armed with iron bars smashed their way into his lavishly decorated house and set it on fire. The closely knit community was firmly on the Hutch family's side. At the same time Hutch's associates were sent to comb the city in search of the drug dealer. The former footballer began moving between safe houses on the southside. When he ventured back to the northside Dunne had a lucky escape as he was spotted by one of Hutch's gunmen. The footballer's fitness saved him as he vaulted several garden walls in Drumcondra and got away.

The situation was threatening to escalate out of control as Dunne had plenty of clout in gangland. He sought the protection of George 'the Penguin' Mitchell. Rachel Mitchell, the Penguin's cherished only daughter, was Dunne's partner and the mother of his child. Dunne had abandoned his wife and children for Rachel and left them in penury. Such was his callous disregard for his own children that he did nothing when they were evicted from their home. Mitchell was furious that his daughter and grandchild had been put in harm's way by the Hutches and he made it known that he would protect Dunne. It was an ominous development.

By 1995 the Penguin, a former member of the Gilligan and Cahill gangs, had become a major international drug trafficker and one of the most powerful figures in Ireland's underworld. Mitchell was the leader of a large extended gang of robbers and drug traffickers. The group included many of Hutch's old associates and one of the most feared assassins operating at the time, a thug from County Wicklow called Mickey Boyle. Mitchell's international partners encompassed powerful crime cartels in London and Amsterdam. Through them he organized the importation of all classes of narcotics and large quantities of sophisticated, military-spec firearms which he supplied to other gangs and the IRA. Mitchell and Hutch were acquaintances since the days of the Prisoners Revenge Group (PRG). Even though the Penguin was thirteen years senior to the Monk they shared a mutual 'respect' – in other words an understanding of each other's capacity for violence. Mitchell had been involved in armed robberies with Paddy Shanahan in the early years and was one of the secret investors in the Buckingham Village development.

Garda intelligence sources reported that Mitchell told Hutch of his concerns for the safety of his daughter and grandchild and warned that if anything happened to them there would be all out war. The Monk assured the Penguin that he had no interest in hurting innocent women and children but insisted that Dunne would be shot, especially if he returned to the Hutch's north inner-city domain. The attack on his young nephew, however, was unforgivable and would have to be avenged.

Over the following weeks, as Hutch's nephew recovered in hospital, the stand-off continued. Gangland was a powder keg and concerns of a further escalation were raised when Mitchell was seen visiting Dunne's fire-damaged home. Hutch saw it as a public act of defiance and a declaration of support for Dunne.

As gardaí attempted to prevent a bloodbath, intelligence sources revealed that Mitchell's associates in London, the Daly crime family, had offered him two hit men. The Penguin had a large group of loyal felons around him who weren't afraid of the Monk. There was also a risk that other gang bosses would take sides. But Hutch also had plenty of weapons and the men willing to use them. He had no problem fighting fire with fire but only as a last resort.

Pragmatism and common sense, however, were traits Hutch and Mitchell both shared. They realized that a conflagration was bad for business. In the end people from both sides would be dead and the real winners would be the police. Instead, a sit-down was arranged in a city centre pub between the two godfathers. Mitchell was sympathetic about the attack on Eddie's son and said that Dunne would pay compensation of £20,000 (€39,500). Hutch agreed not to have 'Maradona' shot as long as he never returned to the north inner city. Mitchell concurred and a war was averted as the two godfathers shook hands.

True to the agreement, Dunne sold his house in the north inner city and was never seen in the area again. The following year he was tried in a UK court for conspiracy to ship heroin to Ireland but was acquitted. After that the footballer moved to live in Amsterdam with his partner and child, where he continued his drug business. In 2000 he was shot dead in front of Rachel Mitchell by former Eastern European partners who had accused him of ripping them off.

As the two sides stepped back from the precipice the Monk was again pulled into a potential altercation when he had to come to the aid of his brother Derek, who was a year younger than Gerry. Derek was described as highly volatile and given to bouts of violence. A heavy drinker, he had also struggled with drug abuse issues. Derek had followed the same route into crime as his brothers and received his first criminal conviction at the age of ten for being carried in a stolen car. A garda who dealt with the youngest of the Hutch boys commented that he was 'a disturbed young lad'. When he was fifteen, Derek was convicted of rape and sentenced to five years detention.

Unknown to his infamous brother, a few years earlier in 1991 Derek Hutch had murdered another criminal from Dundrum in south Dublin and then buried his body in an unmarked grave. Derek accused the criminal of stealing part of a cannabis haul and replacing it with turf. It later emerged Hutch had forced the man to dig his own grave before shooting him, but the body was never found. It was assumed that the victim had left the country and lost contact with his family. The victim was never reported as a missing person and gardaí knew nothing of the incident. Derek Hutch kept it a closely guarded secret and told no one. The case only came to light when he walked into a garda station several years later and confessed to the murder. However, gardaí searched the location he gave them and found nothing.

On this occasion, however, there was a living body and Derek was facing a charge of attempted murder. On 18 August 1994, just hours after Martin Cahill's assassination, Derek Hutch gunned down a nightclub security man in Ballybrack, south County Dublin. The victim had beaten up Hutch's close friend and he wanted revenge. Hutch shot the thirty-nine-year-old doorman three times with a handgun at close range, hitting him in the stomach, back and shoulder. As his victim lay seriously injured on the ground Hutch then placed the revolver under his left ear and delivered a fatal single shot. It was a classic example of a cold-blooded mafia-style assassination carried out by someone who had experience in killing. Derek Hutch ran off to a waiting getaway car confident that his victim was dead. The bullet from the powerful magnum revolver, however, had ricocheted around the doorman's head, lodging in the front of his skull. Incredibly he confounded neurosurgeons and made a full recovery from his injuries.

By June 1995 the doorman was well enough to give the gardaí a full account of the shooting and to identify his attacker. Derek Hutch was arrested and taken to Shankill garda station where he was questioned for 48 hours. The victim formally identified his attacker in a line-up. Gardaí had enough good evidence to charge the would-be assassin with attempted murder and possession of a firearm with intent.

After his release from custody Derek went to the Monk for help. The cops had a strong case and he was facing at least fifteen years behind bars and possibly longer given the cold-blooded nature of the shooting. It was decided that the only way the case would be dropped was if the witness didn't testify. The Monk sent a message back to the doorman that if he didn't withdraw his testimony he would be shot again and this time he wouldn't be as lucky.

Around the same time this writer interviewed the doorman who gave a detailed account of the shooting and how Derek Hutch had threatened him previously. The doorman said that he was determined to testify and had no doubts about his attacker's identity. He was placed under police protection but when he was told that Gerry Hutch had personally issued the message the doorman retracted his statement. It left the gardaí with no choice but to drop the case. The Monk had saved his family again.

Around the same time the gardaí investigating the Brinks-Allied robbery decided to make their move. On 26 September 1995 Gerry Hutch, Willy Scully, Noel Murphy, Gerry Lee and Paul Boyle were arrested at their homes and taken in for questioning. The gang had been expecting the knock on the door for months. Arrest was all part of the game – an inevitable inconvenience that came with the job. They knew the cops had no evidence to charge them with anything.

A week earlier Geoffrey Ennis had been arrested for a second time in connection with the Brinks job when he was questioned about the theft of the two jeeps in Limerick which had ended up in the River Liffey. The gardaí had also previously arrested John Good and another man who was involved in renting the storage shed.

None of them answered any questions about the robbery. The Monk picked out a spot on the wall and didn't open his mouth for the entire time. Two days later they were all released without charge. According to members of the gang they later regrouped in an inner-city pub. Hutch ordered a round of drinks for his pals and declared with a grin: 'The Brinks are on me, lads.'

A month after the arrests detectives from the Central Detective Unit travelled to London to meet with Dave Brogan. He agreed to tell them what he knew about Hutch and his operation. On 23 October 1995 their lengthy interview with Brogan provided the details of the numerous robberies he had been on with the Monk and his brother Eddie. Brogan, who was still living in fear of retribution from the Hutches, said that he was prepared to testify in court. But the passage of time – Brogan last worked with the Hutch brothers in 1986 – meant that there was no evidence to corroborate his claims and the gardaí could not advance the case any further.

In the intervening months thirty-two-year-old Gerry Hutch had begun to ponder retiring from 'the life'. It was time to quit while he was ahead. But he still liked to indulge in occasional mind games with the police. In the final months of 1995 gardaí launched a major surveillance operation at Securicor's main cash-holding depot on Herberton Road in Rialto, south Dublin. Hutch had been spotted acting suspiciously near the building and it was reasonably assumed that he might be planning yet another spectacular heist. When the operation was stood down after three months some of the Monk's associates claimed he had deliberately allowed himself to be seen in the area purely to get the cops in a panic. The local detectives who enjoyed plenty of overtime in the run-up to Christmas weren't complaining. They were glad of the extra cash.

A few months later Hutch was back in the spotlight again when he lost another friend at the business end of an assassin's gun. On 9 March 1996 Gerry Lee and his wife Lynda were celebrating their joint 31st birthday at a house party in Ferrycarraig Park in Coolock, north Dublin. Apart from his armed robbery activities Lee was also involved in the cannabis trade, as were several other members of the Monk's gang. As far as Hutch was concerned it didn't bother him as long as it wasn't heroin. In the middle of the party a gunman burst into the house and shot Lee twice in the chest. The Monk's friend died instantly. At first it was thought that Lee had been hit because of his involvement in the drug business. But detectives later discovered that the assassination had been ordered after Lee violently assaulted a woman.

The Monk's attendance at the funeral of his childhood friend provided a unique opportunity for this writer and his colleagues to finally get a picture of the elusive gang boss. The following weekend the *Sunday World* published a picture of the Monk on the front page under the headline: 'Public Enemy No. 1'. A thin black strip was placed over his eyes and he wasn't named. It was the first time the notorious godfather's face had been seen by the Irish public. Everyone suddenly understood why the mysterious godfather had been likened to Mr Bean.

The story that accompanied the picture was the first comprehensive exposé ever printed about the enigmatic gangster. It revealed his involvement in armed crime and his connections to gangland murders. The article also focused on his controversial tax affairs and his links to other well-known criminals, including drug dealers. Even though the article nowhere suggested that the Monk was involved in the heroin trade Hutch went into defensive mode. He claimed the coverage was an attempt to portray him as a drug dealer.

Hutch was so angry that he broke his vow of never speaking to the media. He wanted to clear his name so through his friend Niall Mulvihill he accepted a long-standing invitation from *Sunday Independent* journalist Veronica Guerin to do an interview. Mulvihill had started as one of Veronica's sources before they forged a genuine friendship.

The Monk admired the journalist for the courage she had shown by confronting him. He called by appointment to Veronica's home one afternoon which he had no problem finding – the Brinks-Allied depot was less than a mile away. They talked for several hours over cups of tea and she later described him as: 'intelligent, chatty, well informed, surprisingly personable and a man motivated by meeting his family's needs'.

The following weekend Veronica's scoop was published in the *Sunday Independent* under the headline: 'Crime, drugs and the Monk's creed'. Hutch complained bitterly that claims about him were exaggerated or scandalously wrong. But he was in no mood for making confessions or shining a light on the darker corners of his life. He blamed a garda dirty tricks department for spreading false stories about him to the media: 'I think they do it to make themselves important. No matter what crime happens, I'm blamed.' His main gripe was with the *Sunday World* coverage, particularly with its headline. He asked the journalist:

What's public enemy number one? Public enemy number one is drugs. I've nothing to do with drugs and I never have. Naming me as public enemy number one is linking me to drugs. I don't do them, sell them, finance them, nothing – I hate drugs. The drug trade has robbed me of family and friends. To see people you love dying week in, week out is hell. When the media try to connect me to drugs it's like connecting me to their deaths.

Hutch claimed that the 'misinformation' circulating about him had caused him to be more security conscious in the context of escalating gang violence. 'I'm conscious that some ill-informed begrudger could do something on me.' But he didn't elaborate as to why somebody would want to kill him. He also flatly denied being involved in the Brinks job but couldn't allow the issue to go by without giving a nod to his proudest achievement: 'The Brinks was a brilliant job. The best of luck to whoever done it.'

When Veronica asked him where he got his money from Hutch replied: 'I don't think it's your business where I get me money from. The guards know where I got it and they know it's legal.' He said that he had moved into property in the late 1980s and was therefore entitled to the tax amnesty: 'I came into the tax net in 1993. If there was an amnesty going I'm entitled to avail of it, like thousands of others. I don't see their statements blasted all over the papers.'

Hutch articulated his insistence on loyalty among friends and associates which had kept him on the right side of a prison fence. 'My philosophy in life is simple enough. No betrayal. That means you don't talk about others, you don't grass and you never let people down.' He also claimed that other criminals had used his name to intimidate people: 'It happens all the time. If I have a problem with somebody I talk to them myself. I don't do other people's work, so if anyone is being threatened by the Monk, disregard it. It's crap.' If it wasn't for his genuine terror, perhaps the doorman with the bullet lodged in his head would have challenged Gerry Hutch on that assertion.

The normally laconic gang boss had taken a major step coming out from the shadows and talking to a journalist to set the record straight. It was another example of his strategic approach to dealing with problems. Although still not named, the Monk was satisfied that he had successfully put down an unequivocal marker in the eyes of the only public that mattered to him – the people of the north inner city. He hoped that the interview would be an end to his fame, and he could resume his Zelig-like pose in the background. But three months later a brutal twist of fate would throw his plans into disarray.

On 26 June 1996 John Gilligan became Ireland's undisputed public enemy number one when his hit men executed Veronica Guerin as she sat in her car on the Naas Road in Dublin. One of the most feared professional hit men in gangland, Patrick 'Dutchy' Holland – a suspect for the murder of Paddy Shanahan – shot the courageous journalist five times at point-blank range. The outrage represented a terrifying paradigm shift in the twenty-six-year history of organized crime in Ireland.

The fact that a drug trafficker considered himself to be so untouchable as to stage such a high-profile atrocity was a chilling wake-up call for society. Anyone who crossed Gilligan, no matter who they were – cop, journalist, judge – was now fair game. He had taken on Martin Cahill's legacy and thrown down the gauntlet, once again challenging the legitimacy of the Irish State.

Less than three weeks earlier the IRA had sent a chilling message that they had not gone away either. On 7 June, a Provo gang murdered Detective Garda Jerry McCabe in Limerick and critically injured his partner, Detective Garda Ben O'Sullivan. The two officers had been gunned down without mercy and the savagery of the cold-blooded attack shocked the entire nation. Now the State had to face two major enemies: the criminals had followed the Provos' lead and become narco-terrorists.

The motive for Veronica Guerin's murder was greed, pure and simple. No one was going to disrupt Gilligan's multi-million-pound cannabis empire. He was facing serious charges for savagely assaulting the defenceless journalist after she arrived at his luxury home and equestrian centre in County Kildare. The gang boss launched a ferocious attack, punching her about the head and body and repeatedly threatening to kill her. Veronica later made an official complaint to the gardaí and a major investigation was launched. Given his criminal record, the diminutive thug was facing at least three years behind bars if Veronica testified against him. They had a strong case as her lawyer had also witnessed a call Gilligan made to the journalist the day after the assault in which he threatened to kill her and sexually assault her son if she didn't back off. In a calm menacing tone Gilligan had warned: 'If you do one thing on me, or write about me, I am going to kidnap your son and ride him. I am going to shoot you. Do you understand what I am sayin'? I am going to kidnap your fucking son and ride him, and I am going to fucking shoot you. I will kill you.'

The reason for Gilligan's fury was Guerin's temerity in posing the question which the State was failing in its duty to ask: considering that he was officially unemployed, where did he get his new-found wealth? That, in Gilligan's eyes, was no one's business – especially not that of a nosy journalist. He also cherished his privacy and didn't want details about his life appearing in any newspaper. Having ignored his threats and offers of money, Gilligan and his cronies decided that Veronica Guerin would have to die. The former thief was supremely confident that he could get away with one of the highest-profile murders in Irish history. However, that arrogant assumption would prove to be a grave miscalculation.

The wall of flowers that built up outside the gates of Dáil Eireann within 24 hours of the murder of Veronica Guerin symbolized the unprecedented outpouring of public shock, anger and revulsion. Thousands of notes and prayers pinned to the bouquets expressed sorrow, demanded action and asked God to mind the woman who overnight had become a martyr in the eyes of the people of Ireland.

Such a depth of feeling over a murder had not been witnessed in the seventy-four years since the foundation of the State. Coming so soon after the killing of Detective Garda Jerry McCabe in Limerick, it sent a shudder of fear through the entire establishment. Politicians, judges, prosecutors, civil servants, media, anyone who could interfere with the workings of organized crime were justified in believing they could be the next target.

The politicians inside the railings of Leinster House did not need the messages on the cards to realize they had to act decisively. Decades of neglect and inaction had created an underworld monster that now threatened the security of the State with the equivalent of a criminal coup. For once political posturing was put aside and the parliament worked in unison to take urgent legislative action.

The Dáil achieved an historic record when, in the space of just four weeks in July 1996, it passed a tough raft of anti-crime legislation. The *Irish Bar Review* described it as '…the most wide-ranging proposals for change in Irish criminal law and procedure since the foundation of the State'. Six new Acts of Parliament were passed on the night of 25 July 1996, the eve of exactly one month after the brutal murder galvanized the nation. The package of laws was tailor-made to provide statutory mechanisms for identifying the proceeds of criminal activity and empower officers of the State to ask the question that had cost Veronica Guerin her life: 'Where did the crime lords get their money?' The law laid the legislative framework for a new agency to trace and seize the proceeds of crime.

Hutch was appalled when he heard about the murder of a wife and mother. It went against everything that a self-confessed ODC stood for. He had no real love for journalists, but he did have considerable respect and admiration for Veronica Guerin. Hutch knew Gilligan and Traynor well and was also friendly with two of the gang's senior lieutenants, Brian 'the Tosser' Meehan, who rode the motorbike used in the assassination, and Peter Fatso Mitchell. During the ensuing murder investigation gangland was turned upside down and gardaí received an unprecedented level of co-operation as criminals strove to distance themselves from Gilligan and his gang. Even Hutch spoke to detectives to tell them what he knew. He also made a public gesture of sympathy for the fallen journalist.

A few days after the murder, Gerry Hutch and three associates joined the queue of law-abiding citizens waiting to sign a book of condolences in the offices of Independent Newspapers where Veronica had worked. The line stretched from the lobby of the busy newspaper building halfway down the street in Dublin city centre and the sympathizers were oblivious to the presence of a gangland celebrity amongst them. The leaders of church and state, the captains of industry and various celebrities had also come to sign their names. For a change the criminal underworld was coming out of the shadows to pay its respects in a rare example of solidarity with normal society. As Hutch and his friends shuffled slowly towards the door two detectives also joined the queue making no secret of the fact that they were following him.

The scene descended into near farce as the entourage of villains and gardaí piled into the front lobby. The detectives watched over

Hutch's shoulder as he signed the book of condolences. When he finished the cops quickly signed their names and hurried out the door after him.

As the aftermath of Veronica's murder continued to cause complications, thanks to his family, Hutch had another problem with the law which was not of his making.

Hutch's nephews were emerging as up-and-coming villains following in the family tradition. Eddie's second son, nineteen-year-old Christopher 'Bouncer' Hutch and his fifteen-year-old cousin Gary, Patsy's son, were members of a fledgling gang which would form the nucleus of the Kinahan crime cartel. Apart from robberies and car theft rackets, Gary and Bouncer were beginning to dabble in the cannabis trade as part of the group led by nineteen-year-old Daniel Kinahan. Kinahan and his younger brother, Christy Junior, from Oliver Bond flats in the south inner city, had been introduced to the Hutch family through mutual friends like twenty-year-old Gary Finnegan from the Hardwicke Street flats. Finnegan was Bouncer's best friend and was close to Eddie Hutch. Finnegan's fifteen-year-old cousin Barry was another member of the menacing group, as was Matthew Dunne. The youngsters also began hanging around with a group of thugs from the south Dublin suburbs Crumlin and Drimnagh, who had close family ties in the north inner city. Their families had migrated from the tenements to the new estates on the periphery of the city in the 1950s and 1960s.

The gang's main supplier was Daniel Kinahan's father, Christy Senior, nicknamed the 'Dapper Don', who would later build the international organization known as the cartel. Born in 1957, Kinahan was a friend and criminal acquaintance of Eddie, Patsy and Gerry Hutch over the years. Unlike the Hutch family, Kinahan's upbringing in Phibsboro was comfortable and he came from a middle-class background. Yet he opted to take a different direction and dropped out of school for a life of crime.

The suave fraudster, who taught himself to speak several languages, was one of the first criminals who realized the value of the heroin trade in the 1980s. But his initial foray into the business came to an end when the Drug Squad nabbed him with over £100,000 (€253,000) of heroin in 1986 for which he subsequently received a six-year jail sentence. It was the biggest seizure of the drug that year. One of the undercover officers involved in Kinahan's arrest was Michael O'Sullivan, the young detective who had come close to shooting the Monk a few years before. Soon after his release, Kinahan and Eddie Hutch were involved in an attempt to offload a large consignment of travellers' cheques in 1993. They had been stolen in an armed bank robbery. Following an undercover surveillance operation Kinahan was arrested after handing over £16,000 (€33,000) worth of the cheques to another villain. The Dapper Don was charged but while out on bail he absconded to Holland where he began building the Dutch side of his drug empire. Back in Dublin his son Daniel, Gary and Christopher Hutch and their friends were making a name for themselves.

The group of young hoods had become a major source of crime in the inner city under the mentorship of Eddie Hutch who saw himself as their leader. Neddie Hutch liked the idea of being a godfather. Inevitably they began attracting the attentions of the local gardaí. Three dedicated young detectives based at Fitzgibbon Street garda station took a keen interest in the gang and arrested the young villains on a number of occasions for questioning about robberies. From their investigations the cops knew that this was a serious up-and-coming mob and deliberately increased the pressure by stopping and searching the Hutches and their pals on an almost daily basis.

Eddie and Gerry had taught the younger criminals the importance of avoiding unnecessary aggravation by being courteous to the gardaí no matter how hard that was to do. But the constant police attention began to grate on the more volatile teenage Hutches' nerves and they attempted to turn the tables on the cops. The three officers were followed to their homes and members of the gang began turning up in the pubs where the officers socialized. Bouncer Hutch and Gary Finnegan were spotted watching the family of one of the officers in County Meath.

In the weeks leading up to the Guerin murder gardaí received information through a reliable intelligence source that the Hutches were planning to attack the named detectives. They were to be shot on their way home from work by Geoffrey Ennis on the orders of Gerry Hutch. Rather bizarrely the same intelligence source had 'suggested' that the threat would be lifted if the three gardaí were transferred to another part of the city.

It later transpired that the information had come from 'godfather' Eddie Hutch who was playing both sides of the fence. Local gardaí used to call him the 'collator' because the affable villain always knew what was going on and was often happy to share the information with them – as long as it didn't affect his family. Eddie was the Hutch family's conduit to the gardaí if they wanted to pass on information or get a message across.

Considering the criminal records of the individuals involved, the threats were taken seriously. Each of the officers concerned wore personal issue firearms and received armed escorts to and from work from their colleagues. Extra garda patrols were mounted in the vicinity of their family homes. In the febrile atmosphere that existed in Dublin in the summer of 1996 the gardaí were not going to tolerate any more intimidation from organized crime gangs.

On 1 August the gardaí arrested the five conspirators for questioning: the Monk, Eddie Hutch, Bouncer Hutch, Gary Finnegan and their friend Matthew Dunne. Over the 48 hours that he was held in Fitzgibbon Street garda station Gerry Hutch's only comment was a complaint about the state of his holding cell. They were all released without charge. Gardaí were later satisfied that the Monk had nothing to do with the plot. Eddie had used his brother's name to deliberately escalate the threat in the hope that it would scare off the enthusiastic young cops and force garda management to transfer them. It had been a classic bluff that backfired.

Not even Gerry's friends know what he said to Eddie afterwards, but it can be assumed that it was not pleasant. Words exchanged amongst family members were hermetically sealed and never leaked out. Those who know them best say that the eight Hutch siblings were an exceptionally close family unit and any internal rows were kept strictly *en famille*. In any event Eddie didn't use his brother's name in vain after that. Nor were there any more threats from the Hutch nephews. The three gardaí stayed put and kept up the good work.

Meanwhile, in the tension-filled summer that followed the murder of Veronica Guerin the people of working-class communities across inner-city Dublin renewed a campaign against the heroin dealers in their areas. Hutch threw his support behind one such initiative by the Inner City Organizations Network (ICON) of which his friend Noel Kirwan was a leading member. So too were several of his associates in the IRA which had traditionally attempted to infiltrate such groups for political gain.

On 22 August, Hutch and some of his friends attended a public meeting organized by ICON in Rutland Street School in Summerhill. Times had changed dramatically in the few months since Hutch's first foray into the media limelight: he had learned the value of playing the public relations game. This was an opportunity for him to affirm his image as an ethical villain in the eyes of the public.

The media were invited to cover the 500-strong meeting and Hutch made no attempt to keep his head down, sitting with his entourage near the front. The Monk was happy to be photographed for the first time in his life and the opportunity gave the newspapers the opening to identify Gerry Hutch as the mystery man behind the religious moniker.

In the new world order to be labelled a bank robber was a lot better than being called a hated drug dealer. Hutch told a reporter that he was there because he wanted to put something back into the community. During the highly charged meeting he clapped his approval for the various suggested proposals on how to deal with the heroin problem which included forcibly evicting junkies and even beating them up.

But he remained impassive when Tony Gregory the local independent TD suggested that instead of targeting the unfortunate addicts they should go after the big players who controlled the supply chain, men such as Derek Dunne and Thomas Mullen. Strangely Hutch didn't seem to support such a move. When Detective Sergeant John O'Driscoll, the head of the local drug unit, got up to speak Hutch made a point of folding his arms in a gesture of contempt. O'Driscoll was a hard-working cop who had made the drug unit one of the most successful in the country. Fate would have it that two decades later O'Driscoll would be the officer in charge of the investigation of the Kinahan and Hutch feud. The Monk wanted the community to know he didn't support the police and that they should sort the problem in their own way. When it was proposed that demolishing flat complexes was one possible solution, Hutch

October 18, 2000. Gerry Hutch reading the newspaper on Buckingham Street   ©Photo by Derek Speirs

2: Hutch at a Prisoners' Rights Organisation protest in Dublin city centre ©Photo by Derek Speirs

3: A young Gerry Hutch playing as a kid around Corporation Buildings

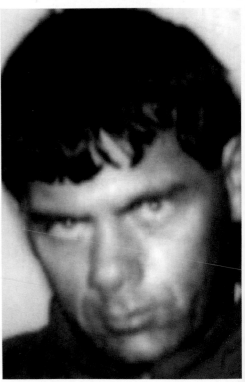

4: An early garda mugshot of Gerry Hutch

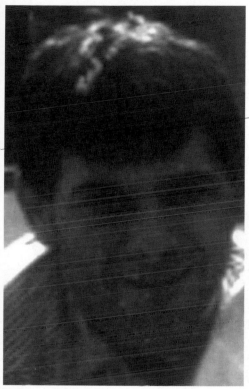

5: Gerry during his rise to fame

6. Gerry at the funeral of his brother Eddie

7: The once abstemious Monk outside his favourite pub

8: Former US heavyweight champion boxer Mike Tyson with Hutch, his driver, in chauffeur's uniform

SUNDAY WORLD

Vol. 25 No. 14 June 29, 1997 £1.00 incl. VAT (UK 75p)

IRELAND'S No.1

ANOTHER BRUTAL GANGLAND HIT

JACK GAMBLE
BOOKMAKER

SHOT IN THE HEAD IN BOOKIE'S SHOP

FULL STORY ON PAGES 2&3

MEET THE MONK

ANOTHER SUNDAY WORLD EXCLUSIVE

'Businessman' Gerry Hutch is named as top gangland boss

By PAUL WILLIAMS

THIS is Gerry Hutch, the criminal mastermind who has earned notoriety behind his nickname, the Monk.

The 33-year-old 'businessman' from Dublin's North inner city is the latest target of the secretive Criminal Assets Bureau.

CAB believe that Hutch has made

millions of pounds from his activities as a major-league armed robber.

And they have hit him with a tax bill for almost £400,000 — money which it is alleged he made from crime.

But it has been estimated that the bill could be as high as £750,000.

Hutch, who has 20 criminal convictions, the last of which was 13 years

ago, is probably the only gangland figure in Ireland who has not been involved in the drug trade.

Instead he prefers "decent" criminal activities like armed robbery. In the past 10 years he has been named as the prime suspect for masterminding heists worth over £3 MILLION.

■FULL STORY: Pages 4&5

EXPOSED: We name top gangland boss Gerry Hutch as The Monk.

9: The *Sunday World* first exposed Gerry 'the Monk' Hutch as a top gangland boss in 1997

10: November 13, 1998. Hutch (centre) at the Corinthians Boxing Club in inner-city Dublin, with coaches, committee members and young boxing enthusiasts. ©Photo by Derek Speirs.

11: From crime czar to oil sheik

12: Gerry with nephew Derek 'Del Boy' Hutch

13: The bundles of cash Hutch lodged to pay part of his CAB tax bill

Bank Draft **Bank of Ireland**

ACCOUNT PAYEE ONLY

48 TALBOT STREET DUBLIN 1

90-07-11

y C. A. B.

DATE 23 MAR 2

IR£ 500,000

IR£ 500,010 — Not Over

For Bank of Ireland

251199

Number 2772

Signature Numb 2942

14: A copy of the draft issued to the CAB after the bank took possession of the Monk's cash deposit

15: August 22, 1996. Dublin. The Monk attending an ICON (Inner City Organizations Network) anti-drugs public meeting to address the heroin problem in Dublin   ©Photo by Derek Speirs.

16: Eddie Hutch

17: Patsy Hutch

18: John Hutch

19: Derek Hutch

20: Gareth Hutch

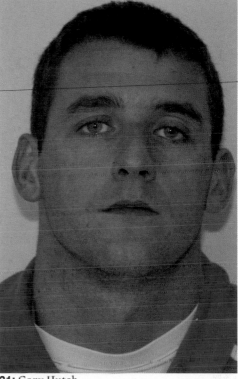

21: Gary Hutch

22: Christopher 'Bouncer' Hutch

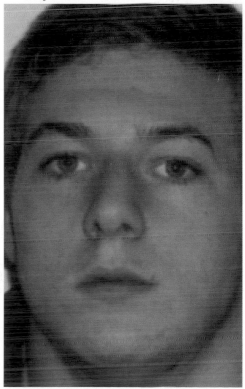

23: Patrick Hutch Junior

24: Noel 'Kingsize' Duggan

25: Geoffrey Ennis

26: Eamon Kelly, the Monk's mentor

27: Niall Mulvihill

28: Willy Scully

29: Martin 'the General' Cahill

30: George 'the Penguin' Mitchell

31: Eamon 'the Don' Dunne

32: A young Christy Kinahan Senior before his rise in the criminal world

33: Christy Kinahan at a family wedding

34: Daniel Kinahan and cartel member Gary Finnegan (right), who is wanted in connection with the murder of Eddie Hutch

35: A Hutch mugshot

36: Gerry leaves the High Court after a tax battle

Irish Independent

IRELAND'S BEST-SELLING DAILY NEWSPAPER — www.independent.ie **Saturday 6 February 2016** €2.30 (£1.50 in Northern Ireland) C

CENTENARY PAPERS

PART FOUR
FREE INSIDE
REVIEW

Daylight murder

Two men dressed as gardaí and carrying AK-47s enter the Regency Hotel in Dublin, where they opened fire, killing a man

(C) Independent Newspapers

■ Exclusive picture shows moment assassins struck

■ Gangland killers dressed as gardaí to carry out murder

■ Crime hits election agenda; hotel was used by Fine Gael

HOTEL TERROR: SPECIAL REPORT, PAGES 2-7

Recommended retail price of the Irish Independent in ROI is €2.30 (£1.50 in Northern Ireland)
Vol. 125 No. 31 Irish Independent

37: Coverage in the *Irish Independent* the morning after the Regency Hotel shooting

SUNDAY, FEBRUARY 7, 2016 €2.45

SUNDAY WORLD
THE PEOPLE'S PAPER

WORLD EXCLUSIVE

KILLED: David Byrne

MEETING: Daniel Kinahan (left) and 'Fat' Freddie Thompson (right) arrive at the Byrne house yesterday

DRESS TO KILL

● **Gunman in drag and pal on the run after hotel bloodbath**

● **Cartel chief Daniel Kinahan was No.1 target in €350k hit**

● **Costa mob holds council of war to hit back at Hutch army**

Picture © **SUNDAY WORLD** THE PEOPLE'S PAPER

ON THE RUN: A man wearing a flat cap and another man dressed in women's clothes, both carrying guns, flee the scene of Friday's hotel weigh-in bloodbath

OUR MAN'S BRUSH WITH THE HITMEN — PAGES 6&7

9 770791 676876 05

38: The *Sunday World* captured two of the Regency gunmen fleeing the scene

39: Members of the Hutch gang dressed as a police SWAT team storm the Regency Hotel in February 2016. It sparked an unprecedented cycle of bloodshed and violence

was applauded loudly when he questioned the notion, declaring: 'The problem is not the buildings. It's the dealers who live in them. They're the people who need to be got out.'

Sounding like the fictional Don Corleone in *The Godfather*, Hutch said that no one had come looking for his help to rid the area of the heroin pushers or for money for treatment. Then he used his new platform to take a swipe at his perceived enemies in the media including this writer: 'I don't see Williams here. Why isn't he down here doing a real story about drugs? The media aren't interested in the real story.'

As part of the charm offensive Gerry O'Callaghan, Hutch's long-time friend, spoke up on his behalf to the *Star* newspaper, declaring:

> He has lost some of his closest friends to drugs. As bad as people brand him, he has a conscience. He hates drugs, and I've known him since he was a child. No matter what you might say about him he is one good father. He idolizes his kids and moved out of the area to try and better himself and the kids. He got money and sent them to private schools.

O'Callaghan trotted out Hutch's old trope that the media were guilty of wrongly accusing him: 'If you put him in front of a jury tomorrow for murdering Cock Robin, they'd find him guilty.'

The Monk's issues with his portrayal in the media would soon pale to insignificance as he found himself doing battle with a powerful new enemy – the Criminal Assets Bureau (CAB). He had never encountered a foe like this one before. The new law enforcement entity would erase the traditional way of doing things and rewrite the rule book. The CAB was about to smash open Gerry Hutch's secret life and it would cost him dearly.

_____

CHAPTER TWELVE

OPERATION ALPHA

A month after Hutch signed the Book of Condolence for the murder of Veronica Guerin, the Proceeds of Crime (POC) Act was passed into law. What came to be seen as a fitting tribute to the journalist's courage, it was the most potent weapon in the new arsenal of anti-crime legislation. The Act empowered a revolutionary new approach to tackling organized crime with the establishment of a multi-agency unit, the Criminal Assets Bureau. Consisting of garda, customs, tax and social welfare officers using their combined powers, the CAB's raison d'être is to relieve criminals of their illegal wealth. As the implications of the new unit dawned on the godfathers there was a rush to move money out of the country. For the first time in Europe an agency had the power to seize assets and money from any individual suspected of criminal activity, but only if they couldn't prove the legitimate provenance of the wealth. The criteria for an individual to become a CAB target are that they possess identifiable and traceable assets – cash and property – which could be linked to criminal activity.

Significantly the new legislation recognized what gardaí had known for many years: that money laundering would not be possible without the use of the skills of white-collar professionals. Under

Section 14 of the Criminal Assets Bureau Act, which complemented the POC Act, CAB officers were given the unprecedented power to search anywhere they suspected there was evidence of involvement in creating a false money trail including the offices of solicitors and accountants. Traditionally, in a more deferential age, white-collar professionals were considered off limits. The Section 14 warrant meant that CAB teams could raid such offices unannounced and that their occupants had no choice but to co-operate. The new laws also imposed a statutory obligation on financial institutions to report suspicious transactions and to provide an individual's account details on demand.

The Proceeds of Crime legislation was unprecedented in that it shifted the onus of proof onto the criminal using Irish civil law, which requires a lower standard of proof than criminal law. In civil law proof is established on the balance of probabilities instead of the criminal law requirement of beyond all reasonable doubt. Making criminals pay, even if they had never been convicted was counter-intuitive to the prevailing legal orthodoxy in Ireland. It took the judiciary and the legal profession some time to absorb the new dispensation. Lawyers for the crime bosses challenged the legislation arguing that it was draconian and went against the principles of the law. However, the High Court ruled that it was a proportionate response to an increasingly sophisticated and pernicious culture of organized crime. Gangsters were threatening to undermine and corrupt democracy.

Under the leadership and protection of the An Garda Síochána, the CAB also ensured that the criminals could no longer intimidate or attack the civil servants who quizzed them about their tax or social welfare payments. In 1989 Brian Purcell, the social welfare inspector who had terminated Martin Cahill's dole payments, was abducted and shot in the legs. In another incident when a revenue inspector went to interview Cahill at his home, the civil servant's car was torched as he sat inside with the crime lord. John Gilligan had also openly threatened revenue and social welfare officials who tried to investigate his affairs. The result had been that civil servants effectively refused to investigate the tax or social welfare affairs of known criminals. Despite the revelations that Gerry Hutch availed himself of the 1993 tax amnesty there is no evidence that Revenue ever carried out an investigation to rescind the amnesty. CAB's first boss was Detective Chief Superintendent Fachtna Murphy one of the gardaí's most experienced financial fraud investigators. His second-in-command was Detective Superintendent Felix McKenna who had spent most of his career on the front line with the Serious Crime Squad. The Bureau Legal Officer was Barry Galvin, the indefatigable State Solicitor for Cork who was instrumental in drafting the legislative powers of the new agency. Such was the level of threat against the courageous lawyer that Galvin became the first civilian ever allowed to carry a police firearm for his personal protection or to qualify to drive squad cars. Galvin's offices in Cork were even reinforced to withstand a bomb attack. Over the following years the crusading trio of Murphy, Galvin and McKenna would make their collective mark on gangland. The international law enforcement community had never seen the likes of the Criminal Assets Bureau. And neither had the Monk.

In his interview with Veronica Guerin, Gerry Hutch had been adamant that it was no one's business where he got his money. Unfortunately for him, the Criminal Assets Bureau had different ideas. While John Gilligan was given priority for obvious reasons, the Monk too was foremost in the minds of the hand-picked officers who attended the agency's first meetings in August 1996. Detective Superintendent Felix McKenna (now retired) who later replaced Fachtna Murphy as the CAB chief recalled:

> Hutch and his gang were always going to be top of the Bureau's list of targets and his name was one of the first mentioned at our initial meetings. He was the target of our first full-scale Bureau investigation. That is why we called it Operation Alpha. When we began looking at Hutch it was like dropping a stone into a pond – but none of us dreamt just how far the ripples on this particular pond would extend. As we examined the affairs of each gang member we uncovered other names and began probing them. Further searches and production orders led us to more assets and hidden accounts. For him it opened a hornet's nest.

Operation Alpha was launched in secret in August and centred on Gerry Hutch, Geoffrey Ennis and the others in the Monk's immediate gang. The four agencies accessed every piece of information they had on the serial offenders. Of particular interest were the files on Hutch's attempts to repatriate the money seized by the Belfast High Court in 1987 and his tax amnesty application. Although inadmissible in a criminal trial, the evidence was more than sufficient to support the assumption on the balance of probabilities that Hutch's money was from the proceeds of crime. That in itself would merit raising a big tax demand against him for starters. The team moved quickly as they were aware that Hutch would be cleaning house. Properties and bank accounts were identified in the Republic and financial institutions were served with production orders. Information from financial institutions outside the jurisdiction was obtained under international legislation. The offices of several solicitors, accountants and auctioneers were also raided and searched.

Hutch and his cohorts first learned of the investigation when the CAB team swooped one morning in February 1997 and searched ten addresses in the north inner city, including Hutch's home and his other properties. Instead of searching for the normal fare of evidence linking the suspects to crimes, the officers were looking for evidence of wealth. Initially the Monk offered the explanation that his wealth was generated after he wisely invested the £25,000 (€60,000) compensation award he received from the Department of Justice for breaking his ankle in Mountjoy Prison. He also pointed to the £8,000 (€19,000) whiplash payment he'd received from Securicor. But despite his protestations his claims just didn't stack up and were thrown out of court.

As the investigation progressed, CAB officers began unravelling a labyrinthine maze of front companies and bank accounts as they followed various money trails from the Republic to Northern Ireland, the UK, the Isle of Man, Jersey and Portugal. They identified several individuals and underworld financial advisers, including international crime figure John Carway, originally from County Clare.

As part of the complex financial web, the investigating team unearthed hidden accounts held in the name of Carway's female business partner which they believed were used to move the Monk's money. Between December 1994 and 1998 they discovered that over £1.1 million (€2.1 million) had passed through an account held in the National Westminster Bank in the Isle of Man. The money was later redistributed in 111 separate transactions to companies and banks in the United States, the Isle of Man, the UK, Ireland and Northern Ireland.

Other transactions were made to a hotel and apartment complex owned by Carway on Portugal's Algarve. The Bureau also traced the

Stg£130,000 (€289,000) payments Hutch made to Paddy Shanahan
to invest in his final development, the Drury Hall project, in 1993.
The investigation also discovered that Hutch deposited Stg£386,000
(€864,000) on 23 February 1994 to another account at the Halifax
International Bank in Jersey. That account was also in his wife's
name. The gardaí later confirmed that they suspected this money
had come directly from the Marino Mart heist. From a study of the
records the team could see that activity in the accounts dramatically
increased after the formation of the CAB was announced.

One incident during the investigation illustrated the painstaking
efforts made by officers to find and follow Hutch's money trail. They
received intelligence that he had been seen, about a year earlier, in
the offices of an international courier company in Dublin Airport.
Officers from the Bureau spent days searching the office until they
found a receipt for a package he had sent to an address in Jersey – a
post office box. When the officers went to check out the address they
discovered it was next door to a bank. Later it emerged that Hutch
had sent copies of his driving licence and passport in the package
so he could open an account with the bank.

As another strand of Operation Alpha the Bureau's Revenue
officers assessed Hutch for tax, based on the proceeds of the Marino
Mart robbery. On Friday, 13 June, a registered letter arrived at Gerry
Hutch's home in Clontarf. He later claimed that he learned of the
CAB's tax demand in the *Evening Herald* newspaper. When he got
home and discovered the registered letter had arrived for him four
days earlier, he complained: 'I thought tax demands were supposed
to be private.' For the tax year 1986/87 Revenue had assessed him
as owing £393,658 (€756,000). Until the tax demand was paid, the
debt would continue to rise as interest and further tax assessments
were added. Eventually the total bill topped over £2 million (€3.5

million). It was calculated on his notional earnings from the various armed robberies.

Hutch's initial reaction was to pack up his family and leave the country, like so many other criminals had done following the establishment of the Criminal Assets Bureau. Instead he decided to stay put and face the music. He said that if he ran people would speculate that he was a drug baron. The effect of the CAB attentions inevitably meant that he became a hot news story.

In the absence of a criminal conviction a known hood could previously sue the media if they suggested he was involved in crime. The Monk had done just that in the early 1990s and settled with the *Sunday Tribune* for a small sum of cash. But now there was no hiding place. The Bureau investigators could go into the civil courts and openly accuse organized crime bosses of illegal earnings. The proceedings could then be published for public consumption. In the process crime lords were stripped of their anonymity as well as their assets. The very fact that someone had become a target of the Criminal Assets Bureau meant that there was a tangible link to organized crime.

Gerry Hutch appealed against the demand at a hearing before the Revenue Appeals Commissioner on 12 June 1998. He was photographed leaving the building by the *Sunday World* and the image accompanied a report on his ongoing battle with the CAB under the heading: 'The Monk Comes Out to Pay'. While he was awaiting a decision on his financial future, Hutch continued to work on his public image, claiming that he had retired from crime. At the same time he was doing some genuine good for his old neighbourhood.

In the winter of 1998 Corinthians Boxing Club opened a new, fully equipped clubhouse and gym. The Monk had played a pivotal role raising the finances to complete the project. Locals say that he also put some of his own money into the club. One of the donors was the director Jim Sheridan who had met Hutch while filming the movie *The Boxer* in the area.

On Sunday, 8 November this writer attended the official opening of the new clubhouse as Gerry Hutch's guest. The invitation had been conveyed through a mutual garda contact. The launch was attended by a strange mixture of ordinary citizens, politicians, gardaí and criminals. I was the only media rep and this was to be off the record. After I took a few steps inside the door, the crowd seemed to part and a smiling Gerry Hutch was standing there with his hand extended in welcome. He was friendly and ordered me a pint. We stood talking under a large 'Drug Free Zone' notice hanging from the ceiling.

From our conversation it was clear that Hutch was genuinely trying to do something to help keep the local kids out of trouble: 'The club is a help to keep the kids away from heroin. It won't stop kids becoming addicts but we can save as many as we can with a place like this.' Hutch was passionate and sincere. He also said that he had come to terms with the media hype which was a relief to hear! Hutch stood in several pictures alongside local gardaí, politicians and even the Lord Mayor of Dublin. After that he shook hands with an Assistant Garda Commissioner. A truce had been declared in the interests of the local youths.

The biggest cheer of the night from the large gathering was for Gerry Hutch. He was singled out for praise by the master of ceremonies for being one of the prime movers in making the club a reality for the area: 'He is one of the most respected members of our community.'

In a subsequent interview with the *Sunday Tribune* Hutch spoke about his home turf with the passion of a community worker:

I love this area. It's my home. My heart is here. We've put this club back here. It's only one facility. There are many other facilities that are needed like pitches and play areas. Even the schools around here are losing out. Some kids around here need special education. But schools in Dorset Street and Sheriff Street have lost specialized teachers who taught children who needed special attention. What hope does an area like this have when that happens?

He also shared some criminological insights on the subject of prison: 'They want to build more prisons. But it costs £50,000 a year to keep a kid in prison. The only grant we got for this club was £250, which was pathetic. We can manage to stop a couple of kids taking gear in here. But we haven't been given any money and are in the red.'

Two months later the community of the north inner city extended a collective arm of comfort around the Hutch siblings after their beloved mother Julia passed away. Their father Masher had died sixteen years earlier. As Hutch mourned his mother's death there was more bad news. On 22 February 1999 the Revenue Appeal Commissioner officially rejected his appeal and confirmed that he owed £2,031,551 (€3.5 million). Hutch appealed against the demand in the Circuit Court, lost and later took his case to the High Court. In June, Mr Justice Fred Morris also upheld the CAB demand.

Negotiations took place behind the scenes between the Monk's representatives and the CAB to hammer out a settlement. Barry Galvin and former Detective Superintendent Felix McKenna normally attended such meetings on behalf of former Detective Chief Superintendent Fachtna Murphy who had final approval of any deal. In its first year of operation the Criminal Assets Bureau realized that they would ultimately have to negotiate with targets to obtain the highest realistic settlement figure. If they sought to completely strip their targets of everything the process could be tied up in the Irish courts for years. Even with this dispensation the negotiations between Hutch and the CAB dragged on for four years.

When Gerry Hutch continued to prevaricate the Bureau turned up the heat. They threatened to charge his wife with money laundering offences because the offshore accounts were in her name. Hutch was also threatened with the possibility of criminal proceedings based on tax and money laundering offences. The Monk dropped his guard during one particularly angry exchange with CAB detectives and warned that he 'might have to take action' if they pushed him too hard. At the time it was interpreted, not as a threat, but that he was contemplating another major robbery so that he could pay his tax bill.

Hutch was, however, a pragmatic man who solved problems one at a time. He wanted to protect his wife from exposure to the criminal justice system and the media. He also realized that he would have to make an offer that the Bureau would not refuse if he was to hang onto the rest of his hidden fortune. On 23 March 2000 Gerry Hutch officially became tax compliant when he agreed to pay the lesser amount of £1,200,000 (€2.1 million) in 'satisfaction of all taxes due by him'. As part of the deal he sold two of the houses he owned in Buckingham Street for £700,000 (€888,000) and agreed to hand over the balance in a bank draft.

To close the deal Gerry Hutch agreed to do something that he could never have dreamt of when he was growing up. He would walk into the Bank of Ireland on Talbot Street, central Dublin, with a haversack full of £500,000 (€894,000) in cash. Throughout his career he had specialized in doing the exact opposite. Hutch had set up a bizarre agreement with Felix McKenna that he would lodge the cash to the bank after opening an account in his own name. He would then withdraw the money in the form of a bank draft and hand it over to two waiting officers.

McKenna ordered a major security operation on the momentous day the Monk paid up. Detectives visited the bank branch to inform the nervous managers of what was going to happen. There was a fear that Hutch might organize an armed robbery to get the cash back after lodging it or have himself 'mugged' on the way. As part of the operation members of the Emergency Response Unit and armed CAB officers were deployed in the streets around the bank. A number of ERU snipers were positioned on the rooftops of nearby buildings and a security van was also on standby to transport the cash immediately to the bank's main cash holding centre. Hutch was shadowed as he walked through the streets of his old neighbourhood with a sack full of cash thrown over his shoulder. Nothing was left to chance in the garda plan. Hutch followed his instructions and duly handed over the bank draft. 'That's us square now,' he smirked at the CAB officers, before walking into the street as a tax compliant citizen.

While the loss of over a million pounds was undoubtedly painful for the naturally frugal Monk, he was still a very wealthy man. Years later in the interview with RTÉ's crime correspondent Paul Reynolds he said of the CAB settlement: 'I had a problem with the amount that they were looking for because I couldn't afford that amount. Well, we came to an arrangement and we settled.' When it was put to him that he still had 'money and lots of it', Hutch grinned and replied: 'Oh I still have a few quid, of course, that was the deal. They can't leave you in your nude; they have to meet people halfway.'

While the Monk was fighting his corner so too were many of his associates and family members. Paul Boyle, Geoffrey Ennis and William Scully between them were eventually forced to pay over £610,000 (€988,000) in individual settlements by the year 2002. An order was also obtained in relation to the estate of murdered gang member Gerry Lee. The Monk's drug trafficking brother Derek paid £120,000 (€194,000)and Eddie Hutch had a bank account seized containing over £156,891 (€252,000). John Good, the associate who had ordered the false registration plates for the Brinks job, agreed to pay £350,000 (€566,000) in January 2002. As a result of the CAB's investigation of Good they investigated one of his business associates and got another £150,000 (€242,000).

The owner of a taxi firm who was suspected of fronting the business for Gerry Hutch also came under the spotlight and was assessed as owing over £1 million (€1.2million) in unpaid taxes. Two property developers who were associates of Hutch were pulled into the net of Operation Alpha as well. The men were suspected drug traffickers with extensive connections to organized crime gangs in mainland Europe and the UK. They ran a number of property developments in conjunction with George Mitchell, the Penguin, and an English crime gang. They readily agreed to pay up £1 million (€1.2million) in taxes between them to get the CAB off their backs.

Matt Kelly was targeted with Hutch from the beginning of Operation Alpha. Felix McKenna revealed at the time: 'It was obvious from the beginning that Kelly had been closely linked with Hutch. We uncovered the various property deals between them and Shanahan. We discovered that he had become a very wealthy property developer, even though he was an undischarged bankrupt.'

Kelly had used a network of professionals and fictitious names to front his ownership of property valued at approximately £4 million

(€6.3 million). It was also revealed that he was the beneficial owner of three nursing homes in Lincoln and Gainsborough in the UK. Further investigations revealed that Hutch was also a secret investor in the homes.

CAB detectives uncovered secret bank accounts held by Kelly under the name Peter Kelly. They traced the lodgement of £419,000 from a total of £659,000 that they believed was paid to Kelly for Buckingham Village. This money was lodged in the name of Peter Kelly, with an address in Buckingham Village, and was held at the Ulster Bank in Blackrock in south Dublin. The detectives positively identified their target from the bank's CCTV security footage.

Between October 1992 and February 1993 a total of £385,250 (€793,000) was lodged to the same account before it was closed. It was also discovered that he had used a number of solicitors and a financial consultant to carry out various transactions. One of those transactions exemplified how the cash moved around. In March 1997 a solicitor obtained a bank loan to buy a property for £250,000 on Dublin's North Circular Road. The property, which was owned by one of Kelly's front companies, was actually valued at £650,000. The solicitor paid £220,000 of the purchase price to a financial consultant who had offices on the south side of the city. He in turn lodged the money into his bank account at Ulster Bank in Ballsbridge.

Five days later, the financial consultant returned to the bank and withdrew the £220,000 in the form of a draft made payable to one Peter Kelly. The following day the same Peter Kelly, alias Matt Kelly, opened a new account in the Ulster Bank in Blackrock by lodging the £220,000. He also lodged a further £10,000. Three weeks later Kelly closed the account when he ordered three separate bank drafts of £75,000, each in the name Peter Kelly. He then cashed them in at bank branches in Phibsboro. The money eventually trickled through to a number of businessmen associated with the former carpet salesman. The Criminal Assets Bureau managed to seize one of the drafts from Kelly's original lodgements. The money was paid over to the Official Assignee in Bankruptcy who had been appointed when Kelly's Carpetdrome closed in the early 1980s. In the meantime the CAB handed Kelly an assessment for £2,950,000 (€5.2 million) in unpaid taxes between 1985 and 1996.

Like his friend the Monk, Matt Kelly fought the CAB all the way and the case continued in the courts for three years. In sworn affidavits Kelly denied making money from criminal activity and claimed that he had been ready to pay off all his debts and come out of bankruptcy. But Barry Galvin accused the crime lord of simply stalling for time. Behind the scenes there were intense negotiations between Galvin and Kelly's representatives.

As Kelly prevaricated Galvin continued adding to the growing bill which eventually reached €3.6 million. In February 2000 the High Court granted the CAB a partial decree against Kelly for payment of €662,000. Over a year later, in July 2001, Kelly's lawyers said he had agreed to hand over the €3.6 million due. But his bill did not end there. Together with his tax bill and capital gains taxes, Matt Kelly paid over €7.1 million to the Revenue. In order to pay up he was forced to sell off part of his property portfolio but like Hutch he was left far from penniless. One of the properties he sold fetched €11 million. After he settled his tax affairs he was officially declared to be no longer bankrupt. Operation Alpha was making the criminals hurt and the CAB still hadn't come near completing their investigations.

During their trawl of Matt Kelly's myriad business dealings they discovered his links to Charlie Duffy the scrap dealer and motor parts trader based at Smithfield in Dublin's north inner city. Born in 1942, Duffy had previous convictions for serious assault and road traffic offences but was not involved in drugs or armed robbery. Instead he was a facilitator for gangs such as the Kellys and Hutches, and also handled stolen goods. He had known the Monk since he first appeared on the scene. In September 1997 the Bureau officers working on Matt Kelly's case found that Duffy had effectively laundered £250,000 (€317,434) for the former carpet king.

The Operation Alpha team traced two drafts worth £21,000 (€40,000) and £23,000 (€43,700), which originated from Matt Kelly, through a complex trail involving a solicitor and accountant. One of the drafts was lodged to Duffy's account and the other, made out in the name of Peter Kelly, was lodged to a second account Duffy owned. The investigators then discovered that Duffy had transferred over £800,000 (€1.2 million) to Barclays Bank in Jersey, where Gerry Hutch had also held accounts.

In legal documents sent by the CAB to the Jersey authorities Detective Superintendent Willy Ryan described Duffy as being '… associated with one of the most serious organized crime groups that operate in the Republic of Ireland' which he clarified was the 'Gerard Hutch/Matthew Kelly organized crime group'. In a sworn affidavit he also claimed Duffy 'has participated in criminal activity and he has also facilitated the concealment of the proceeds of his and their criminal activities. Duffy has committed serious criminal offences under the Revenue Acts, relating to failing to return income, and knowingly and wilfully making fraudulent returns.'

When officers subsequently travelled to Jersey and were given access to bank records, they discovered that one of Duffy's hidden accounts held over Stg£10 million. Back in Dublin, the CAB launched an official investigation of Charlie Duffy under the taxation laws and sought orders to freeze various accounts. After spending four years on Gerry Hutch's affairs the team was expecting a similar long drawn out battle. But the scrap dealer took them completely by surprise. Duffy offered no explanation for the provenance of the money but he agreed to close the Jersey account and handed over the contents by way of a banker's draft on 13 December 2000. When it was converted into euro the total payment came to a staggering €17,142,526 (€22,796,233). It was the largest single settlement in the CAB's twenty-four-year history. And the ripples from the CAB's investigation into the Monk and his gang did not end there.

The examination of Charlie Duffy had uncovered his corrupt links to former Assistant Dublin City and County Council Manager George Redmond, who had granted the planning permission for one of Gerry Hutch's first investment opportunities, Buckingham Village. As the investigation broadened out the CAB also uncovered direct links between Matt Kelly, Gerry Hutch and former IRA terrorist Thomas McFeely. The connection was made when the Bureau began examining Hutch and Kelly's secret involvement in an inner-city hotel and uncovered evidence of deals between Kelly, Hutch and McFeely.

Born in Dungiven, County Derry in 1948, McFeely was first convicted for terror-related offences in 1973 when he was jailed for eighteen months in the Special Criminal Court in Dublin. In February 1977 a Belfast court sentenced him to twenty-six years on two counts of attempted murder, robbery, possession of a stolen rifle and of bomb-making equipment. While in prison he took part in the hunger strikes staged by republican prisoners to obtain political status. Eight members of the IRA and INLA died during the hunger strikes in 1981.

Shortly after his release McFeely arrived in Dublin in 1990 where he began working as a sub-contractor. He became involved with various criminal figures including Matt Kelly and the young Gerry Hutch. McFeely was suspected of involvement in fraud and extortion including so called 'C2 VAT Fraud'. This was a highly lucrative IRA-controlled racket that used false tax certificates to obtain refunds from the Revenue Commissioners for non-existent building work. At one stage the racket was estimated to be costing the Irish taxpayer tens of millions each year.

At the same time McFeely built up a multi-million-euro property empire. When the CAB began looking into his affairs, they discovered the ex-Provo had never made a personal income tax return. In 2001 he had paid over €5 million for a mansion in Ailesbury Road, Ballsbridge, one of Ireland's most exclusive neighbourhoods. After lengthy negotiations McFeely agreed to pay €8.1 million in unpaid taxes and still walked away a wealthy man. Meanwhile Operation Alpha continued to make the Monk's associates pay.

Carlos Portalanza from Ecuador arrived in Ireland in 1984 at the age of twenty-five. He had four convictions for larceny and was the listed owner of a number of properties in the city centre including an electrical appliance shop. Intelligence received by the gardaí suggested that the businesses were in fact really owned by Gerry Hutch. Portalanza agreed to pay over €400,000 to the CAB. Another criminal to fall under the team's eye was Noel Duggan, Gerry Hutch's closest friend.

Duggan was the country's biggest cigarette smuggler, earning him the nickname 'Kingsize'. The convicted criminal operated a thriving cash and carry business with his business partner Christy Dunne on Queen Street, around the corner from Smithfield. The large complex also included a furniture business and a block of apartments. For many years he had featured prominently in the files of the Serious Crime Squad where he was described as a member of Gerry Hutch's criminal gang.

Born in 1958, and originally from Cabra in north-west Dublin, Duggan began his career as a butcher. But crime was a much more lucrative option and he received several convictions for receiving stolen goods, forgery and burglary. In the early days of his business Duggan dealt with major villains such as John Gilligan and George Mitchell when they specialized in robbing warehouses to order.

Duggan's smuggling business grew so large that the retailer's representative group RGDATA complained to the government that their members were losing huge amounts of revenue because Kingsize was undercutting them. Many jobs, they argued, were at risk because of the smuggling operation. In December 1996 a joint garda and customs investigation, codenamed Operation Nicotine, was launched to investigate the Monk's close friend. It was later brought under the aegis of the CAB's Operation Alpha. In October 2000 Duggan and his partner Dunne were both assessed as owing a total of €6 million in unpaid taxes.

After negotiations with the Bureau the two smugglers agreed to pay over €2 million to the exchequer. In December 2002 Kingsize handed over the keys of his Queen Street property in person to Felix McKenna and Barry Galvin. It was then placed on the market for auction.

The following night the colourful tobacco smuggler was in an upbeat mood when he told this writer:

They [CAB] have taken everything and now I haven't even got the price of a packet of smokes! It nearly fucking killed me handing over those keys; I'm on my second bottle of brandy already. I was in those

premises for over seven years and I have spent most of my life in that
area wheeling and dealing. Maybe if all those thieves over in the Dáil
paid up like me then we would have a decent health service.

In reality, like his best friend Gerry Hutch, Duggan was happy – he still had plenty of money and more irons in the fire.

The ripples of Operation Alpha kept spreading. Two brothers who owned a furniture business in Cork became the team's next target when they popped up on the CAB's radar. The brothers were close friends of the Monk and Duggan and both men had attended the wedding of one of the brothers. The Bureau suspected that the brothers were involved in smuggling and money laundering with the pair. Their association cost the Cork men dearly when the CAB hit them with a tax demand for €750,000. Another player on the periphery of the Hutch gang also agreed to pay €360,000.

By the tenth anniversary of Veronica Guerin's murder Operation Alpha, which began as an investigation of the Monk's finances, had brought in over €40 million in settlements. Several other businessmen and professionals with links to Operation Alpha targets were referred to the mainstream tax inspectors and assessed for taxes, netting another €2 million for the Irish exchequer.

Knowing Gerry Hutch had ultimately proven to be a costly business.

CHAPTER THIRTEEN

THE NEPHEWS

In the history of organized crime in Ireland the first decade of the new millennium stands out as an era of unprecedented mayhem, bloodshed and murder. From 2000 narcotics became the mainstay of organized crime as the hedonistic Celtic Tiger generation's insatiable appetite for artificial highs created an industrial-scale boom time for the majority of the criminal gangs. In 2003 the Irish Health Research Board estimated that the total retail value of the narcotics trade in Ireland was almost €650 million. Two years later the figure had almost doubled to over €1 billion. Gerry Hutch's reaction was to steer well clear of the unfolding madness and turn a blind eye to the involvement of many of his friends, associates and family members.

Gangland murders, shootings and bombings became a normative by-product of the drug trade as a virulent species of ruthless, volatile thugs slaughtered each other for the spoils. In 1993 there were three gangland-style murders in Ireland. A decade later in 2003 the figure had jumped to twenty killings, making it the most violent year on record in Ireland. Murder had become a way of life and hit men became as plentiful as drug dealers with most of them doing both. Killing was often how addicts and dealers paid off their debts. The first killing of that bloody year brought gangland violence to Gerry Hutch's door as the casualty was one of his closest friends.

Around 9.30 p.m. on Thursday, 23 January 2003, Niall Mulvihill went to a prearranged meeting with a criminal associate. The fifty-seven-year-old career criminal, who worked as a taxi driver in between times, parked his car near Spencer Dock Bridge beside the International Financial Services Centre (IFSC) in central Dublin and waited. He wasn't expecting any trouble but the Monk's partner in crime and underworld Mr Fixit got more than he bargained for.

A masked hit man suddenly appeared and fired five shots at the Silver Fox as he sat in the driver's seat. As the gunman made his escape, Mulvihill, who was badly injured, managed to drive off in the direction of the Mater Hospital. At the junction of the North Circular Road and Dorset Street he passed out, the car careering out of control and smashing into a line of parked cars. The veteran criminal was rushed to the hospital but died a few hours later.

In gangland terms it was one of the most significant executions in many years. Although a non-violent, charming character Mulvihill had been an important cog in the wheels of organized crime and was clearly not without his enemies. After all his list of associates in the underworld read like a who's who of organized crime and terrorism. He had been involved in every scam possible: fraud, money laundering, drug trafficking and fencing stolen art works. As a result of his close links to Gerry Hutch, the Silver Fox had also become a target for the CAB.

For most of 2002 Mulvihill was contesting an assessment by the CAB for €909,000 in unpaid taxes and interest which had been issued the previous May. The investigating team had located a complex web of international bank accounts used by Hutch's friend. The main line of enquiry by gardaí in the murder investigation was that the suspects had been Mulvihill's partners in the deal to sell the Beit paintings several years earlier. One of the last remaining paintings stolen by Martin Cahill in the famous 1986 heist, a work by Rubens, had been recovered in 2002 by police on the north side of Dublin.

Sources confirmed at the time that Mulvihill would have known where it was hidden and was possibly suspected of giving it up as part of a deal with the CAB. Whoever had arranged the fatal meeting with him on 23 January was the one who had set him up. Gerry Hutch was deeply angered and upset by the killing of his close friend. The partners-in-crime used to meet every day to gossip and discuss business at a small coffee shop in Sutton, north Dublin. It is likely that Hutch may have had no knowledge that Mulvihill was in trouble otherwise he would have undoubtedly intervened to save his friend from gangland's grim reaper. At the time Hutch blamed the media's coverage of the painting's recovery for causing Mulvihill's associates to suspect he had double-crossed them.

The Monk was also a friend of the hood who had ordered the killing. But the pragmatic godfather wasn't going to get sucked into a feud by seeking revenge. He only went down that route if someone crossed him or his family. Hutch had nothing to do with Mulvihill's predicament and didn't want to be involved after the fact. It was claimed that the criminal who had ordered the killing later explained why it had happened and reassured the Monk that there was no quarrel with him. He claimed Mulvihill had been responsible for his own downfall. Hutch seemed to accept that the execution was, in Mafia parlance, not personal but business. It was another example of how he compartmentalized problems. He mourned the passing of his friend and then got on with life. No one was ever charged with Niall Mulvihill's murder.

Just five days later, on the evening of 28 January, another killer struck. Former drug trafficker Raymond Salinger was having a pint in his local pub, Farrell's on New Street in the south inner city when shortly before 10 p.m. a lone gunman, armed with an automatic pistol, walked in and shot him four times in the chest. The motive for the murder was revenge. Fifteen years earlier Salinger, who had been a drug addict, was selling heroin on the streets for the Dapper Don, Christy Kinahan. When Kinahan was busted for dealing heroin in 1986 he blamed Salinger for setting him up. Kinahan subsequently got a six-year prison sentence and he never forgot who had caused it. During the investigation it emerged that the Monk's nephew, Christopher 'Bouncer' Hutch, and his associates carried out the assassination on Kinahan's orders.

The investigation of the Salinger murder also gave gardaí an insight into the extent and scale of Christy Kinahan's growing drug operation in Ireland. Kinahan and his partner-in-crime, convicted kidnapper John Cunningham, aka the Colonel, were already major targets of the gardaí and other European police forces. The organization was smuggling hundreds of millions of euro of ecstasy, cannabis, cocaine and heroin which it then supplied to other gangs. They discovered that they were also importing large amounts of weapons and had developed a sophisticated logistical infrastructure for storing and transporting product.

The enquiry in Dublin revealed how Daniel Kinahan, working for his father, controlled one of the biggest drug-dealing gangs in the country. By 2003 the emerging crime cartel was an amalgamation of individual groups of young, violent criminals from Crumlin and from the south and north inner cities. The group from Crumlin included brothers Liam and David Byrne, and their cousin Fat Freddie Thompson. At the time the Thompson/Byrne group was immersed in a ferocious gangland feud with their former partners. The warring faction was led by Brian Rattigan. The slaughter continued for most of the noughties claiming sixteen lives with many more left injured and traumatized for life. Paddy Doyle, from the north inner city and a close friend of Hutch's nephews, was one of the most prolific killers operating at the time. By his twenty-fifth birthday in 2005 Doyle was directly linked to six feud-related murders and that tally did not take into account other freelance hits he'd carried out.

Bouncer Hutch and his younger cousin Gary Hutch were still an integral part of the tightly knit team who controlled the distribution of ecstasy, cocaine, cannabis and heroin across the north inner city for Daniel Kinahan and his father. The group also included Bouncer's two best friends, Martin Cervi and Gary Finnegan. The officers who had targeted them in 1996 had proved to be prescient. By 2000 the young gangsters had graduated to carrying out several armed robberies and aggravated burglaries to raise money to invest in Kinahan's shipments. In 2001 Gary Hutch was jailed for six years for his involvement in a terrifying raid on the home of a businessman in north County Dublin. Hutch was eighteen when he acted as the getaway driver for four raiders involved in the shocking crime. The gang forced the businessman at gunpoint to unload his safe while his wife was held hostage. Gary Hutch's share of the jewellery and cash was used to fund his drug dealing.

Of the Monk's many nephews Bouncer and Gary Hutch were the closest to him. Bouncer hero-worshipped his uncle and was determined to emulate him. Cervi and Finnegan were also in awe of the crime boss and the connection bought the young criminals gravitas on the streets of gangland.

Cervi's talents as an armed robber and drug dealer had also been spotted by Christy Kinahan. The Dapper Don contacted the Monk to check him out. After receiving a glowing reference Kinahan took Cervi under his wing and treated him like a son. Bouncer Hutch, Finnegan and Cervi regularly visited Christy Kinahan in Amsterdam where he was based at the time and Cervi began spending more time there. In June 1999 the young trio were arrested when Dutch police discovered a handgun, overalls and balaclavas in a search of Cervi's apartment. Despite taking responsibility for the find, a technicality meant that he was never charged.

By early 2003 the gang had prospered and were one big happy family. The relationship, however, created some potentially awkward issues for the Monk in light of his rigidly held abhorrence of the narcotics trade.

From his earliest criminal exploits those who know him best used to say that Gerry Hutch preferred everything to be black and white in life. But the problem is that gangland is an amorphous, twilight world full of contradictions, hypocrisy and delusion. The lines blur into mist when an attempt is made to unravel the complex tapestry of Hutch's gangland relationships. To be fair the same can be said of every other veteran criminal. In Dublin's underworld Hutch could not get away from drug dealers. Practically every criminal he ever associated with, including his own close family members, were narcos. His tendency for rationalization and cognitive dissonance helped him to navigate around such ethical obstacles. A new shade of grey, however, would soon be discovered in the Monk's world.

Following the Salinger murder, gardaí compiled a detailed intelligence document on Kinahan and his emerging Dublin-based cartel. Included in the document was an interesting garda intelligence report from 2000 in which an informant told how

Daniel Kinahan regularly had meetings with Gerry Hutch in a pub in Thomas Street in the Liberties area of the south inner city. The report said: 'The informant states that Daniel Kinahan has had meetings with Gerard Hutch, the Monk, on Monday evenings in the Silken Thomas [pub], Thomas Street and that it is a regular occurrence for meetings to be held there.'

The report further stated that Eddie and Derek Hutch were regular visitors to a furniture store Daniel Kinahan owned in the same area. Gardaí investigating the Salinger murder identified the possible revenge motive and the suspects responsible for the shooting. It was decided to start arresting them from the beginning of April. One of the names on the list was Christopher Hutch. However, he was about to cheat the arrest warrant.

The aspiring international drug trafficker died from a cocaine-induced overdose on the night of Saturday, 29 March 2003. Family members later said that the Monk had tried to convince his nephew to get out of the drug trade, but he was not successful. On occasion, when gardaí asked him about his nephews' involvement in the drug trade, he would shrug and say that he wanted nothing to do with them. The Monk's children were the exception to the family rule. He had successfully steered them away from crime by rearing them in middle-class suburbia. His nephew had grown up in a dysfunctional family environment where domestic violence was a constant problem. His father Eddie was regularly the subject of barring orders for beating his wife Jane. On a number of occasions the Monk's older brother was locked up for breaching the court orders. Whenever the parents split up the kids would be moved between different homes. With the approval of his father, Bouncer had begun his criminal career in his early teens before eventually moving into armed robbery and drug dealing.

In the few years leading up to his death Christopher Hutch had developed a cocaine habit and was given to bouts of violence. Bouncer lacked his uncle's self-control. Some years earlier in a fit of rage he'd attempted to shoot the gay lover of his uncle, Derek Hutch, in a city centre pub. Luckily for the young robber – and his would-be victim – the pub had been the scene of several gangland shootings and its battle-hardened criminal clientele tended to be more alert than normal punters. As Christopher Hutch pulled out a .22 pistol and fired a shot in the air, he was wrestled to the ground and disarmed. The incident was the result of a row which broke out between Bouncer and his uncle's friend in a night club. The gardaí were not alerted and the row was resolved when the Monk intervened and made his nephew see sense.

On the day of the funeral Gerry Hutch and his family carried the coffin of the cherished son and nephew through the streets of the north inner city from his home to the local church. The entire community had come out to express their sympathy with the family. A friend told this writer at the time: 'Gerard considered Bouncer to be his protégé. He and the rest of the family are heartbroken by this tragedy.' But the bitter, deep-rooted antipathy between Eddie Hutch and his ex-wife Jane caused a major row about where Bouncer should be buried.

A fortnight after the funeral Eddie Hutch said: 'She wanted Bouncer buried in her family plot and I wanted him in ours. In the end we had to put him in his own plot.' The reason he decided to speak on the record was the result of a bizarre twist in the story of his son's tragic death. Jane Hutch who was heartbroken by her loss broke the family's code of omerta to give an interview in which she alleged her boy had been murdered. She claimed: 'He did not take more than two lines of cocaine at a time. I believe that he was held down and a large amount of drugs was forced into him. When I saw his body laid out it was covered in bruises on his arms and legs and there was vengeance in his face like someone had been forcing him.'

But gardaí and a post-mortem examination could find no evidence of foul play. Eddie Hutch agreed with their verdict, commenting:

Christopher and me were very close and I am heartbroken about his death but I have to accept what happened. His death was the tragic result of taking drugs and that's it. If my boy was murdered there would be serious inquiries going on. This is all very hard to take and we are all heartbroken. Christopher was like a brother to all my brothers including Gerard.

Four days after Bouncer's death, his close friend and ally Martin Cervi was arrested for questioning about the Salinger murder. Gardaí had found his thumbprint on a newspaper in the getaway car used by the killers. However, it wasn't enough evidence to sustain a charge and Cervi walked free.

A few days after Bouncer's funeral, Hutch's wife Patricia and their children threw a surprise fortieth birthday bash in the Monk's honour on Saturday, 6 April. The party was held in the Temple Theatre in the north inner city and the attendees included a who's who of what one cop dubbed the 'Irish Sopranos'. The cheeky invitation was on a print of a €500 note that featured the crime boss posing as Frank Sinatra, complete with a dark suit and matching trilby. The family had planned the surprise bash weeks in advance and a decision was taken to go ahead with the party despite the recent bereavement. By all accounts Hutch had a great time.

Gangland continued to thrive throughout 2003 and 2004 but Gerry Hutch had apparently gone legit. The Monk had taken up the first legitimate job of his life – driving a taxi. But he didn't get it without a fight. In 1999 while his High Court appeal against the CAB tax demands was pending, Hutch applied to the Carriage Office for a public service vehicle (PSV) licence. The application was refused on the grounds that the Monk was under investigation by the Bureau. When Hutch appealed the decision to the High Court the garda officer in charge of the Carriage Office said it had been turned down amid 'public disquiet' over Hutch being a 'notorious member of the criminal community'. Again the Monk's application was refused.

Following his settlement with the CAB, however, Hutch had returned to the District Court in June 2001 to appeal the decision of the Carriage Office. Inspector Philip Ryan, who had been involved in Operation Alpha, informed the court that the Monk was 'now fully tax compliant' and he had no other outstanding tax liabilities. In response to a question posed by Hutch's solicitor, Inspector Ryan said that he would not be nervous travelling as a passenger in the gangster's cab.

Based on the evidence presented the judge ruled that Hutch could apply for a PSV licence, much to the annoyance of the many gardaí who had investigated his serious crimes over the years. As he was leaving court Hutch was asked by a reporter about his involvement in organized crime. 'I haven't been involved in crime. I had a bit of a tax problem, like several other people – it's all over,' he replied with a smile before walking briskly away.

In the meantime his other ambitious nephew Gary had taken over where Bouncer left off and was rising through the ranks of the Kinahan organization. He was released from prison in June 2006 after serving sentences for armed robbery and theft of a motorbike. He continued to organize robberies and controlled a large drug distribution network, dividing his time between Dublin and Spain where the Kinahans had moved their operating base.

Six months after his release in November 2006 Hutch and a close associate were the prime suspects for the gangland murder of Raymond Collins from Matt Talbot Court in the north inner city. The forty-two-year-old was shot dead by the pillion passenger on a motorbike as he walked along Clonliffe Avenue on 14 November. Hutch and his associate had assaulted Collins in a pub a month earlier after they accused him of raping a young woman who was related to a family friend. They had been arrested and questioned but released without charge due to a lack of evidence. But while Gary Hutch may have aspired to fill the Monk's shoes, he, like Bouncer, did not possess either the brains or the composure of his uncle. A month later he was in trouble again for another shooting. It wasn't long before he needed his uncle's help.

In December 2006 Gary Hutch was charged with possession of a firearm with intent to endanger life after shooting his friend, Paul 'Dicey' Reilly. An associate from the neighbourhood, Reilly was left seriously injured after Hutch shot him in the chest and back. Reilly and his girlfriend identified Gary Hutch as the shooter and said the row was over a missing firearm. However, Reilly subsequently had a complete change of heart and withdrew his allegations.

When the case went to trial Reilly said that he was all mixed up and didn't know what he had been saying when he made his original statement to gardaí. Gary Hutch was acquitted of all charges and walked out of the court a free man. It was suspected that the Monk had intervened on his nephew's behalf and had a meeting with Reilly after which the shooting victim experienced a Damascene conversion.

The Monk later denied any interference in the case:

> No, I wasn't involved in any meeting with anybody. I mean, like, Dicey
> Reilly alleged that he was shot and the young lad was arrested and
> put in custody and he faced trial on it... I mean if people get shot and
> he's in hospital on a dying bed he's liable to say anythin'. It came to
> some arrangement or he must have realized that it wasn't him [Gary
> Hutch]. I don't know exactly the details of it but if he changed his
> statement, he changed his statement.

In September 2007 Gary and his younger brother Derek 'Del Boy' Hutch, were suspected of involvement in the gangland murder of drug dealer Derek Duffy in Finglas, north-west Dublin. Duffy was shot five times as he sat in his car at Casement Drive in the suburb and an attempt was made to burn the body and the car. The brothers were both subsequently questioned about the murder – Del Boy in 2008 and Gary in 2009. Neither of them was ever charged. While his nephews were gaining notoriety, their uncle was cashing in on his status as a celebrity gangster.

In 2005 Gerry Hutch had hit the headlines when he bought a stretched Hummer limo and posed for pictures beside the monstrous white machine, sporting a wide grin and a chauffeur's hat. He also set up a company called Cab – Carry Any Body – in a nod to the people who had dragged him out of the shadows. In many ways he was doing the very thing that he had so vehemently disapproved of in his old nemesis Martin Cahill – preening in the limelight. For a time Cab's services were in huge demand and pictures of him driving celebrities in the distinctive Hummer regularly adorned the society pages of glossy magazines. Reporters rarely got a quote from him, but they got plenty of smiling, silent, pictures.

The law-abiding people of Dublin loved the novelty of being driven in luxury to hen parties, stags, weddings and debs by the country's most enigmatic armed robber. Hutch the chauffeur became friendly with former world heavyweight boxer Mike Tyson and others in the boxing elite. He would drive them around Dublin in the Hummer and bring them to meet kids in his local Corinthians Boxing Club. And he was part of the entourage at all the big boxing events in Ireland and around Europe. After three decades of criminal enterprise the Monk was enjoying his retirement. The following year the once publicity shy mobster won another unexpected accolade when a women's glossy magazine voted him one of Ireland's 100 sexiest men.

In all the various articles on Gerry Hutch he was referred to as the 'former criminal'. But behind the scenes the Monk was far from retired.

———

CHAPTER FOURTEEN

STEPPING INTO THE LIMELIGHT

An extremely angry and agitated Gerry Hutch wanted some enquiries made. He was clearly rattled. This time he felt that he was being crossed in a big way and was determined to take action. It was February 2008 and the Monk had learned that he was to feature prominently in a TV series about the Criminal Assets Bureau. Specifically, the six-part *Dirty Money* series on TV3 (now Virgin Media One) was to devote an entire episode to his life, crimes and the hunt for his ill-gotten-gains. The series was produced and directed by the Emmy award winner Gerry Gregg of Praxis Pictures. Hutch's ire was firmly targeted on this writer, the presenter of the series, who he blamed for the unacceptable intrusion into his affairs in the best-selling book *The Untouchables* on which the series was based. Hutch decided to fight back – legitimately – through his lawyers.

The Monk first sent threatening legal letters demanding that the programme should not be broadcast and that in the event that it was, he was going to sue. After a decade or so of largely tolerating his exposure in the public spotlight it was out of character for him to come out fighting. Hutch seemed genuinely fearful about what the programme was going to reveal. Lawyers for the TV company

told his representatives that they were standing over the content of
the programme and confirmed that it would be broadcast on 17
March 2008.

For a while the producers expected Gerry Hutch to use the next
legal option available, applying for a High Court injunction to
block the broadcast. But such a move would ultimately fail and
probably exacerbate his situation. It would also be a very costly
waste of money. The Monk instead decided to go on the offensive
and reinvent himself using his new-found fame as a retired villain
and driver to the stars.

Hutch left his closest associates stunned when he decided to
do the unimaginable – launch a full-frontal media campaign to
mitigate the damage he felt he was going to suffer. And the Monk
decided the most effective medium was television. He reportedly
hired a public relations company which made tentative approaches
to RTÉ's *Late Late Show*. The offer was that Gerry Hutch would give
them an exclusive interview which would be a huge ratings booster.
However, there would be clear parameters imposed as he wanted
to convey the fact that he was a respectable businessman and not a
criminal. In the end the producers of the flagship chat show found
that it was an offer they could refuse.

Overtures were then made to RTÉ's crime correspondent Paul
Reynolds. It was eventually agreed that Hutch would do an extended
face-to-face interview for the news and current affairs programme,
Prime Time. It was a spectacular scoop for RTÉ. The only guarantee
Hutch received was that his genuine work with the Corinthians
Boxing Club would be highlighted alongside the fact that he was
now a legitimate businessman. The Monk was claiming that he had
retired from crime after serving his last prison sentence twenty-three
years earlier. Hutch also wanted the opportunity to reaffirm his

abhorrence of the drugs trade and to rebut what he felt was his unfair media portrayal, especially in the *Sunday World*. He was determined to get his side of the story in first.

Hutch seemed confident that the interview would be a pushover and he could swat away any awkward questions. That was a big mistake. Paul Reynolds is a vastly experienced and highly regarded crime journalist who has been on that beat for over twenty years. He had an encyclopaedic knowledge of the criminal underworld and his experiences interviewing slippery and often evasive ministers and garda chiefs had moulded him into a tough, formidable interrogator. Of all the journalists in Ireland, Reynolds was probably the last person the Monk should have targeted.

The interview was broadcast on Thursday, 13 March – four days before the *Dirty Money* episode aired. In order to contextualize the story Reynolds gave the viewer a pocket history of Gerry Hutch, citing the major armed robberies he had masterminded and his settlement with the CAB. The programme was rigorously fair and balanced. It was interspersed with shots of Hutch as a businessman and community worker. He was filmed driving his taxi and working with kids at the boxing club which it was pointed out he helped to fund from his own pocket. It quoted the locally held belief that Hutch was the victim of a campaign of vilification in the Irish media. In the voice-over Reynolds repeated Hutch's denials that he was a major league armed robber and his assertion that he had been going straight for over twenty years. But he also juxtaposed the two sides to the Monk's persona: a man of influence and power in the local community, and a man of respect and fear in the criminal community.

A statement from the *Sunday World* newspaper was also broadcast in which it said it stood by every allegation it had made against the mob boss. Reynolds also sought the views from the victims of the various crimes attributed to Hutch. A representative of the security industry described the often forgotten psychological trauma suffered by employees who found themselves being confronted by armed raiders. A number of senior gardaí also didn't mince their words in describing Hutch as a criminal godfather. By agreeing to be interviewed on national TV Hutch had handed the normally reticent cops a unique opportunity to put the public record straight and clear the fog of ambiguity that hung around the gangster.

Reynolds subjected the Monk to a robust, forensic inquisition the likes of which had not been seen on Irish television before. The normally clever gangster had voluntarily put himself on trial before the court of public opinion. Hutch ducked and weaved like a boxer but left himself open to a succession of body blows. In his answers he came across as evasive and more than a little shady. His only defence from the barrage of awkward questions were shrugged denials. It made for box office TV.

The following transcript is an amalgamation from the outtakes and the actual broadcast version of the interview between Paul Reynolds (PR) and Gerry Hutch (GH).

PR: OK, Gerard I suppose the first question is what are you doing here? Why do you want to do this?

GH: I wanna' tidy up a lot of things that have been writ in the paper. A lot of nonsense and lies, particularly the Sunday papers. That's basically it.

PR: Well like what?

GH: Well like you've the *Sunday World* in particular which is one of the main Sunday newspapers… if they're writing about incidents that's happening for the last ten, fifteen years, no matter who is shot in Dublin or who does a robbery or who is doing drugs, they throw my photograph in right beside them all the time. They make it out that Gerry Hutch is the boss of crime and if they put me in with a photograph of people who were shot and they're sayin' I'm the boss of crime, it makes me look like that I'm the leader of this pack and all that type of stuff which is totally untrue.

PR: But you are a convicted criminal.

GH: Oh yeah, a convicted criminal, I know that. But not a convicted armed robber, not a convicted hit man, ya' know? Not a convicted drug dealer, there's so many things like, ya' know?

PR: But you were a major criminal.

GH: Well I don't know what is a major criminal, like I mean, is a major criminal a guy who doesn't pay his tax, is that a major criminal?

PR: No, a person who is involved in two of the biggest robberies in the history of the State is a major criminal.

GH: Well that's not me.

PR: OK, well you're a multi-millionaire today, how did that happen?

GH: How did that happen? I got two years for £50 worth of damage to a motor car and I went into prison for two years. In prison I had an accident and I broke me ankle. I have three screws still in my ankle today and I was awarded £25,000. I went and I used that wisely.

PR: What did you do with it?

GH: I bought property. I bought a couple of properties in my neighbourhood which were very cheap at the time and done them up. I rented them out, remortgaged them, went onto another one and

another one. I had a claim off Securicor, a security van that ran into
the back of me, and I got £8,000 to £10,000 off them.

PR: Well coincidentally, it happened after the Marino Mart robbery?

GH: Yeah. I done a lot of business in property, it was a good time and
that's where I made me money. If people say armed robberies so be
it, I mean, I was questioned about these armed robberies yer' talkin'
about so we'll let them decide, the people.

PR: But the figures don't add up.

GH: Sometimes figures don't add up.

Hutch had offered the same explanation in his High Court battle
against the CAB which also found it incredible and ruled that the
money did in fact come from his armed robberies.

Reynolds then turned to the links between Hutch and the seizure
of some of the proceeds from the Marino Mart job when gardaí
arrested the bagmen, Lonan Hickey and Francis Sheridan.

PR: The gardaí recovered £129,000 from that robbery. They recovered
it from two men.

GH: Yeah.

PR: Francis Sheridan and Lonan Hickey. They said that was your
money.

GH: Yeah… [long pause] And?

PR: Is that true?

GH: [Shrugging his shoulders] No, the money they had wasn't my money.

PR: Well they said it was the money from the Marino Mart robbery.

GH: I don't know if it was the Marino Mart. It wasn't me.

PR: And they said they were holding it for you, they were laundering it for you.

GH: Yeah, well that's not true – they weren't.

PR: £75,000 of the money from the Marino Mart robbery ended up in your bank account in Belfast.

GH: No. I had a bank account in Belfast with money in it alright, but it wasn't from Marino Mart.

PR: It was found to be the Marino Mart money.

GH: In the end of the day they [Belfast High Court] weren't happy that I had proper title to it and they didn't give it back to me.

PR: They didn't give it back to you because it was the Marino Mart money.

GH: I don't know about that.

PR: It was Securicor's money. The Belfast High Court gave it back to Securicor and said that was the money that was stolen in the Marino Mart robbery. And you were trying to claim that was your money, so obviously you must…

GH: I did claim that that was my money, yeah. It was my money and I lost me case. It wasn't their money.

Reynolds moved on to focus on the most recent heist attributed to Gerry Hutch and his gang – the Brinks-Allied robbery at the depot in Clonshaugh, Coolock, north Dublin.

PR: What did you think of the famous Clonshaugh robbery?

GH: I think it was a good job, best of luck to whoever got the few quid.

PR: So you admire the people who carried it out?

GH: Probably so, yeah.

PR: What do you know about it?

GH: [Shifting in his seat] I know all about it. I have been arrested and questioned about it. I have been writ about that what happened in 1995, thirteen years ago.

PR: £2.8 million…

GH: Yeah.

PR: …the biggest robbery in the history of the State at the time.

GH: Yeah.

PR: They say you know all about it. Tell us about it.

GH: I've read all about it in the newspapers that's why I know about it. My photograph was thrown in. I was brought down to the station. Well they [Gardaí] interrogated me about the robbery and I think they were satisfied it wasn't me and they released me.

PR: I don't think they are satisfied it wasn't you.

GH: Well they released me at the end of the day.

PR: They had to because there was no evidence on you because it was such a well-planned job.

GH: Ah, when you have no evidence on something it's obvious that you didn't do it.

PR: No, it's not obvious that you didn't do it.

GH: If everyone knows you done it [looks away] like, everyone knows you done it, there has to be stuff to back it up.

PR: In fairness the gardaí believe you did it. There's enough intelligence to link you to that robbery. There's enough intelligence to link you to the Marino Mart robbery. The community believe you did it and every criminal in Dublin believes you did it.

GH: Yeah OK and why would they all believe that, not the guards, every criminal and every person in the city? I am beginning to believe I done it meself from reading it in the paper. When you read these things every week, week after week, there must be no smoke without fire. It looks that way, it sounds that way, if it barks it's a dog. I didn't do the robbery, you know.

PR: But why do you say that when you know you did and everybody else knows you did. The money that you made, the figures just don't add up, I mean we've just got into the Marino Mart one. I mean the compensation claim it doesn't really wash.

GH: It doesn't wash with you. It washes with me.

PR: Well the evidence is there in the money, in the figures that don't add up because one minute you're a guy who has no money who has grown up in poverty…

GH: Yeah.

PR: …you get a compensation claim…

GH: Yeah.

PR: ...and now you're a multi-millionaire, very suddenly you're a multi-millionaire and coincidentally around the same time two of the biggest armed robberies in the history of the State are carried out.

GH: Yeah.

PR: And you're linked to both of them.

GH: Yeah.

PR: Do you really expect people to believe that?

GH: I don't care what they believe to be honest but, eh, what can I say, if everyone believes I done it – hands up. I didn't do them that's all I can say.

PR: What about the CAB settlement. You paid them £1.2 million. Why?

GH: Because of me ignorance to the tax laws that's why I paid them that. I built up a portfolio of property and I had bank accounts and this is it, I didn't pay me tax. They didn't get paid on the proceeds of crime, they got paid on taxes.

PR: They taxed you on the proceeds of crime, that's what the Criminal Assets Bureau does.

GH: The Criminal Assets Bureau tax people. I mean, well, when you say the proceeds of crime it's tax, not paying your tax is a crime ...

PR: No that's a different crime.

GH: It's a crime. They probably taxed me on that type of a crime, but they didn't take money off me from security van robberies and say we want our tax outta' that. I had a problem with the amount they were looking for because I couldn't afford that amount. Well we came to an

arrangement and we settled.

PR: Well you still have money and lots of it.

GH: [Leaning forward, smiling] Oh I still have a few quid, of course,

that was the deal. They can't leave you in your nude; they have to

meet people halfway.

By way of balance, the journalist put Hutch's claims that his only offence had been not to pay his tax and it had nothing to do with the proceeds of crime to the then head of the Criminal Assets Bureau, Detective Chief Superintendent John O'Mahoney. Hutch called his taxi company, Carry Any Body (Cab) as a sly joke against his former tormentors. But the CAB boss turned the joke back on the Monk. Detective Chief Superintendent O'Mahoney didn't mince his words as he demolished Hutch's defence:

There are people out there who would have you believe that a

certificate of tax clearance meant that people were innocent of

criminality. A certificate of tax clearance is just that, it is not a

certificate of innocence. We tax the proceeds of crime. The Criminal

Assets Bureau by its very nature is about two things: it is about

criminality and it is about assets. It's about linking those assets

derived from criminality back to criminality before we can bring a

case before the courts.

Paul Reynolds then steered the crime boss back to more comfortable territory and something that he clearly didn't mind talking about – growing up in Dublin's north inner city and the impact of drugs.

GH: As a kid like I mean me first conviction was for stealing a bottle of red lemonade. I got a fine and then I was involved in other crime as a kid stealing and breakin' into shops. I was caught. I done lots of crimes, some of them I got away with.

Hutch turned to his concerns about being linked to the drug trade.

GH: What would concern me is the media linking me to the drug trade. The drug culture is the scourge of the country. All towns everywhere has it but I mean the justice minister and the department should make it illegal to have drugs in yer system and go into a party, people takin' drugs and arrest them, take a DNA, you've drugs in yer system it's against the law, now yer nicked.

Reynolds highlighted how some of the Monk's nephews – the late Christopher 'Bouncer' Hutch, Gary Hutch and Del Boy Hutch – had reputations as major criminals.

GH: I feel if they're involved in serious crime they're very foolish to be involved in serious crime but like I mean they're me nephews. There's probably fifty guys out there, or fifty family members, with the same name as Hutch and one of them gets into trouble, where he's a relative or a friend, it lands on my door with the media. I'm thrown in, my photograph is thrown in.

PR: But they are serious players; they are *serious* players.

GH: Well I have kids meself. I have a wife and I have five kids and my kids are not involved in crime.

Reynolds raised the shooting by Gary Hutch of Paul 'Dicey' Reilly which had taken place over a year earlier. He asked the Monk about Reilly's strange decision to retract his statement when the case

went to trial and if he had been involved in making sure his nephew Gary Hutch walked free.

PR: Wasn't there a meeting of the Hutches after that [Dicey Reilly shooting]?

GH: No. I wasn't involved in any meeting with anybody. I mean, like, Dicey Reilly was alleged that he was shot and the young lad [Gary Hutch] was arrested and put in custody and he faced trial on it.

PR: He made a statement identifying Gary as the shooter.

GH: Against him that he done it and then he [Reilly] retracted his statement and… [shrugs]

PR: And how did that happen?

GH: Well I don't know. I mean if people get shot and he's in hospital on a dying bed, he's liable to say anythin'.

PR: Well he's not really.

GH: It came to some arrangement or he [Reilly] must have realized that it wasn't him [Gary Hutch]. I don't know exactly the details of it but if he changed his statement, he changed his statement.

The journalist asked Hutch about his reputation as a man to be feared and respected in his inner-city neighbourhood.

PR: People don't mess with you.

GH: Yeah, yeah.

PR: Why? Is it because they know you're a man not be messed with?

GH: Well yeah, probably so, but it's not like, 'back off or I'll do this'.

PR: It doesn't have to be said.

GH: [Shrugs with apparent bewilderment] Yeah, well maybe so yeah, that's it, that's it. But I would have done that on numerous occasions I mean.

PR: A man of influence.

GH: Probably so, like I mean a guy came up to me one day, one of the local councillors, and he said, 'There's a guy there and he's owed ten grand for drugs and the drug dealer is givin' him a terrible time and he's tellin' him that he's goin' to get you to sort it.' I says: 'Well tell him that the kid gave me the money and that's the end of that.'

PR: It is the end of it.

GH: Rather than see some kid gettin' seriously injured because he owes a debt, which is disgraceful, but these things happen. And you just say it's nothing to do with me, which it isn't. If some woman comes over who you grew up with and says her son is… [in trouble], you have to kinda' give her a dig out, that kind of thing, you know.

Former Assistant Garda Commissioner Martin Donnellan was asked for his view on Hutch's reputation as a mediator for people experiencing problems with criminals. He commented: 'What I would say to people living in communities is to give anybody that sets themselves up in that position a very wide berth. What sanctions has that person and that can only lead to more criminality and more pain and trauma for people.'

One of the reasons for Hutch's fearful reputation was his connection to the murder of Mel Cox two decades earlier which Reynolds asked the Monk about.

PR: Did you know Mel Cox?

GH: No.

PR: You didn't know him?

GH: Didn't know him.

PR: He was from the north inner city

GH: From the north inner city and I didn't know Mel Cox. I heard of him being shot dead, but I didn't know him.

PR: A forty-three-year-old scrap dealer who was shot in the front garden of his house in Blanchardstown in the summer of 1987.

GH: Yeah

PR: He was from your community.

GH: Yeah, but I didn't know him.

PR: Do you think he's part of the reason why you have the reputation of a man to be feared?

GH: It probably is but I never met that man, and like I'd know his wife and their family, but I never met that man.

PR: Did you have a row with him in a pub?

GH: No.

PR: Because that's the word down there…

GH: Yeah, but that's all nonsense 'cos I've never had a row with the man.

PR: …and that that's the reason why he ended up dead.

GH: Well it's totally without foundation. It's not true.

Gerry Hutch's final remark in the Reynolds interview became the water cooler topic of the week. The reporter had asked him about crime and what he thought of it.

GH: My house was broken into twice. Talkin' about victims of crime, like, I've been a victim of crime.

PR: What did you lose?

GH: I called the ambulance for them.

Gardaí and Hutch's criminal associates alike thought that he had committed a serious error of judgement volunteering for a public interrogation. It was anathema to everything the Monk had stood for over his three decades as an ODC. He'd left himself with no choice but to come across as shifty, evasive and untruthful. After all he couldn't very well admit to crimes he hadn't been convicted of. Previously Gerry Hutch had only ever received such a grilling about his criminal activities in the more intimate surroundings of a garda interview room. But then it was just him and two cops in the room; and he could pick out a spot on the wall to gaze at while refusing to answer any questions he didn't like. This strategy wasn't possible in the glare of the spotlights on the *Prime Time* set.

But Hutch put a brave face on it and later told his associates that he was 'happy enough' with his performance – he'd got what he saw as his side of the story into the public domain first. He reckoned he had succeeded in controlling the narrative before *Dirty Money* tried to ruin his reputation. However, as someone who strategically planned his every move in life, this episode represented a spectacular miscalculation. All the Monk had achieved was to raise more questions than answers.

The following Monday night the *Dirty Money* programme was aired and pulled in a massive audience, which was no doubt bolstered by people wanting to find out what the godfather was trying to hide from the Irish public.

In the end, however, the secrets Hutch was so stressed about being uncovered were not actually revealed in the documentary. The Monk had been anxious to keep his latest criminal endeavours out of the public eye because he was being investigated by three UK police forces as a member of a major organized crime group based in the West Midlands. He was also the subject of a fresh investigation by the Criminal Assets Bureau.

By the time *Dirty Money* went to air, the UK security services had officially classified Gerry Hutch as a 'threat to national security'.

———

CHAPTER FIFTEEN

A THREAT TO NATIONAL SECURITY

In February 2008 a month before Hutch's television debut, the West Midlands police in the UK swooped on a Birmingham-based crime gang. Investigators believed the group was involved in fraud, extortion and money laundering 'on a massive scale'. The joint police and HM Customs investigation centred on the activities of the gang leader, Thomas Scragg from Solihull, a suburb of Birmingham. Between 2002 and 2008 he masterminded an elaborate racket to defraud the UK revenue of over Stg£34 million (€52.5 million). In the course of the investigation it was discovered that the fifty-two-year-old was a close friend and secret business partner of Gerry Hutch.

On 8 February 2008 police and customs arrested Scragg and twelve other co-conspirators including his minders, Carl and Anthony Johnson from Wolverhampton, who were both notoriously violent criminals. As part of the operation the UK authorities obtained High Court orders to seize luxury homes, bank accounts, jewellery, cash and high-performance cars, including a Lamborghini Murciélago, Bentley Continental, Porsche Cayenne and Ferrari Spider, from the gang. Realizing that the bubble had finally burst on his criminal empire Scragg made frantic efforts to put as much of his assets beyond the reach of the police as possible. Gerry Hutch agreed to take Scragg's Lamborghini to Ireland for safe keeping until the dust settled.

Within hours of the raids taking place the Proactive Crime Unit of the West Midlands police contacted the Criminal Assets Bureau in Dublin. They had discovered that the Lamborghini, which was subject to a restraint order in the UK High Court, had boarded the ferry at Holyhead and was bound for Dublin. CAB officers rushed to Dublin Port and stopped the luxury car as it came off the ferry. It was being driven by a business associate of the Monk from County Meath. One of Hutch's sons was in the passenger seat having gone along for the spin. They had travelled over to collect the car on the Monk's instructions. Hutch's associate told the CAB officers that he had taken the car for a week-long trial as he was considering buying it. He said he had been dealing with a guy called Sid Sheamer. The officers seized the car and gave the driver their number for the owner to call. An hour later Sheamer phoned the CAB officers claiming he was acting on behalf of the company who owned the car and demanded to know why it had been lifted. He was told to call the West Midlands police. It later transpired that Sheamer was a member of Scragg's gang. He was subsequently jailed for three and a half years on charges of perverting the course of justice, money laundering and conspiracy to defraud. The Lamborghini was returned to the UK authorities as part of the case against Scragg.

It was clear that former Chief Superintendent John O'Mahoney had plenty of reason not to mince his words when he was interviewed about Hutch on the *Prime Time* documentary. By then he was in possession of the intelligence reports from the UK police and had assigned a special team to begin a fresh investigation into the Monk's financial affairs. In the meantime the 'retired' gangster began popping up elsewhere in the UK. CAB officers received calls from the Economic Crime Unit of the City of London police and Scotland Yard seeking information about Gerry Hutch.

An internal CAB report noted: 'Following the action taken by CAB in February 2008 in relation to the Lamborghini motor car separate calls were received from police officers in the UK seeking information about Gerard Hutch as he had come to prominence in their respective districts because of his association with serious organized criminals.'

The Monk was now being investigated by the CAB, the West Midlands police, the London Metropolitan police, the UK Economic Crime Unit and HM Revenue and Customs. The UK authorities officially classified Hutch as a 'threat to the security of the State'.

The investigation revealed that Hutch had been a close friend of Thomas Scragg for several years. The discovery of the relationship raised justified suspicions as to whether Scragg had helped launder proceeds from some of the Monk's big robberies in Ireland. The investigation in the UK, which began in 2006, noted that Hutch had been spending a lot of time in Birmingham, Liverpool and London in the company of what they described as major organized crime figures. The Monk's large property portfolio in the UK included a pub in Liverpool where he had been observed on numerous occasions meeting with members of a well-known drug trafficking gang. The intelligence reports also revealed suspicions that Hutch was acting as a 'debt collector' and an enforcer for Scragg and other associates.

In 2006 an associate of Scragg from the Ruislip area of west London, was in dispute with two Dublin car dealers over a jointly-held debt. In March the businessmen met another car dealer from the north inner city to discuss the debt dispute with their UK partner. The dealer turned up with the Monk who stood impassively in the background and said nothing. He didn't have to. The Dublin businessmen knew about the Monk and his fearsome reputation. The car dealer warned the men that the debt had 'moved on' and that they now owed the money to someone else. As he left, he gave each of them a business card for Hutch's limo business. They got the message and the debt was paid soon afterwards.

Scragg and Hutch shared a life-long passion for boxing and they regularly attended big fights together. It was the Birmingham-based criminal who had introduced Mike Tyson to Hutch and the trio once took a helicopter trip together to Sligo. The Monk had often visited Scragg at his opulent residence outside Birmingham.

Using a large network of front companies, corrupt accountants and auditors, Scragg laundered money on an industrial scale for criminal associates which CAB suspected might also include Hutch. Scragg used one of his legitimate enterprises, 'Moya Payroll' which managed staff wages for construction companies, to steal Stg£34 million in employee PAYE tax over an eight-year period. In the ten months prior to February 2008 the sophisticated scam netted Stg£8 million. The proceeds of the fraud were then washed through a complex maze of companies and bank accounts. Over Stg£3.6 million was siphoned off in cash before the accounts were frozen. As one of Scragg's close associates, Hutch was suspected of helping to move the money. It was never traced.

Scragg nurtured the image of a brash, successful businessman who rubbed shoulders with celebrities from the world of showbiz and sport. Snooker legend Jimmy White was best man at Scragg's wedding a year earlier and a number of soap stars were guests. Gerry Hutch was also believed to have attended the nuptials.

But behind the purdah of respectability, Scragg had plenty of form as a serious criminal: he had convictions for fraud, extortion and assault. His connections were like a who's who of organized crime and his network of contacts also included the likes of Christy Kinahan who by this time had become one of the UK's single biggest drug suppliers. Scragg had good reason for wanting hard men around him.

On 16 May 2005 he had been abducted when he and an associate went to what he thought was a business meeting at the Prince William Henry pub in Coventry. Instead, he was set upon by a gang of up to twelve masked men, gagged and bound, and taken to a windowless room upstairs. Over the next six hours the men took turns to beat and torture him with weapons and threatened to burn off his skin with a hot iron. Metal cables and a machete were used to hack at their victim's face, slashing it down to the cheekbone. They also threatened to drill Scragg's kneecaps when he struggled to break free. In return for his release the gang demanded a ransom of Stg£150,000 in cash. The kidnappers also demanded the logbook to his cherished Lamborghini. Scragg's business partner, Paul Phillips, handed over Stg£72,000 to a corrupt West Midlands police officer, Colin Hester, who was double jobbing as a member of the kidnap gang. Hester arranged to collect the cash from Phillips in the car park of the police station where he worked. A year later Hester and four other gang members were jailed for the horrific attack.

Despite his grievous ordeal Scragg resumed his massive money laundering operation and recruited the notorious Johnson brothers' gang to act as his minders and enforcers. The UK police suspected that Hutch was also providing protection for the gangster. Following the arrest of Scragg and his co-conspirators, including his business partner Phillips, the group was released on bail. The gang leader did everything he could to thwart the State's case.

In December 2008 the Regional Assets Recovery Team (RART), the UK's equivalent of the CAB, sold the goodwill of Moya Payroll to a similar company in the process of liquidating Scragg's assets. A week after the deal was done Scragg became a director of the purchaser company – blatantly buying back his original business. For that stupid stunt he was hit with a third criminal charge of conspiring to cheat HM Revenue and Customs.

In February 2009 the West Midlands Police gave their colleagues in the CAB a progress report. The ongoing enquiries hadn't been able to identify a money trail between Hutch and Scragg's organization, however, the UK authorities were satisfied that the Monk was deeply involved in Scragg's organization. An intelligence report in 2009 stated: 'Gerard Hutch is now a partner or has taken a major stake in Thomas Scragg's company and is visiting the West Midlands regularly, meeting with Scragg and other criminals.'

While the investigations were continuing in the UK evidence emerged that Gerry Hutch had been cashing in on his fearsome reputation in more ways than one. He and his old friend Noel 'Kingsize' Duggan were secretly operating as loan sharks to desperate clients who couldn't borrow from anywhere else. Their victims were loaned sums of up to €500,000 and in return the pair charged ridiculously exorbitant interest rates of 50 per cent.

Hutch and Duggan would loan individuals cash on which an agreed sum of interest was paid every month until such time as the principal was paid off. On a €50,000 loan the borrower could expect to typically pay up to €2,000 per month for the entire lifetime of the loan. At the end of the agreed loan period the borrower then paid back the original €50,000 in one lump sum.

In 2006 a businessman in dire financial straits plunged himself deeper into trouble when he borrowed €520,000 from Duggan and Hutch. He told his story to this writer:

> I was stupid to get involved with him [Hutch] and Duggan. I was desperate and was introduced to them by a relation of Duggan. I had a property deal going which would pull me out of the hole but I had problems with the banks and couldn't go to them. Duggan's relation convinced me that the boys could help me. They all ripped me off. I borrowed this money from them when I was at a very low ebb in my life. I met with Gerard Hutch by arrangement one day and he arrived on a motorbike. He gave me two lumps of cash – €200,000 and €45,000. He just pulled the money out from under his biker's jacket. Duggan also brought the money to me in lumps. In all I got €520,000 but then they wanted 50 per cent interest.

The property deal took longer than anticipated and the businessman had trouble keeping up with the payments. The loan and the interest combined was going to cost him over €750,000. When he couldn't keep up with the payments the mobsters turned nasty. He received numerous abusive phone calls from Duggan, usually at night when the loan shark was drunk and at his most sinister.

The businessman recalled at the time:

> Duggan was ringing me at all hours of the night ranting down the phone and threatening to have me killed. He [Hutch] was always very nice but then he also turned nasty and threatening and I am scared that I will be seriously harmed. Hutch told me: 'You can bring us to court and the judge can say what he likes but in the end you WILL pay us what you owe.' He then told me that I could be beaten by men with baseball bats.

In November 2008, when he could no longer bear the stress of having one of the most feared criminals in the country on his case, the businessman went to the Gardaí. Hutch and Duggan faced the possibility of being charged with illegal money lending and making threats. The businessman's lawyers also threatened legal proceedings against Hutch and Duggan. The information was relayed to the CAB whose remit included continuing to act as the inspector of taxes for criminals they had targeted. In the same year Hutch gave notice to the Bureau that he was planning to leave the country and that his personal tax affairs would no longer be subject to the Irish tax system. Hutch was planning to move to Turkey where he owned property.

Despite the multiple strands of investigation Gerry Hutch avoided criminal charges or another big proceeds of crime payment – on both sides of the Irish Sea. The businessman withdrew his complaint when the pragmatic Monk was forced to back off because the case had received so much attention. This writer published a story about the loan-sharking operation which included an interview with the unnamed victim. The gardaí had also taken statements from the businessman, providing him with a layer of protection. Hutch and Duggan knew that they would be the automatic suspects if anything happened to their unfortunate client. They didn't need the aggravation from the law or the media. After some haggling, they agreed to take €624,000 for the debt, which still represented a sizeable return on the €520,000 loan.

But the businessman had been the lucky one. The gardaí were convinced that he was very much the exception to the rule. No one else had been brave enough to report Hutch and Duggan. An intelligence report on the case noted: 'Information suggests that Hutch is using his name/reputation to enforce repayment and that generally these debts are paid off without fuss.'

While Gerry Hutch was organizing his move to Turkey, his nephew Gary had become a senior lieutenant in the Kinahan cartel. The twenty-seven-year-old was also now a major drug trafficker in his own right. But to get there he'd had to demonstrate his loyalty to the leaders of the organization, Christy Kinahan and his son Daniel. In the Kinahan cartel, which was now one of the biggest crime gangs in Europe, Gary had learned that loyalty required the capacity to betray friends.

———————

On 4 February 2008 Gary Hutch was driving his X5 BMW jeep with his pals Paddy Doyle and Fat Freddie Thompson in Puerto Banus in the Costa del Sol, Spain, which had become the gang's operational hub. The Costa was the European playground and base of operations for the top international organized crime syndicates including the Kinahans. The British underworld dubbed it the 'Costa del Crime' – the little bit of Spain that fell off the back of a truck.

The three Kinahan gang members were returning to the apartment Doyle shared with Hutch in the Bel Air estate. The trio were all well-established lieutenants in the cartel. But behind the scenes Daniel Kinahan and his father suspected that Doyle and another cartel member, UK national Simon Cowmeadow, had stolen €500,000 of their drug money. In November 2007 Cowmeadow had been executed as he walked along a street in Amsterdam. He died from a single gunshot wound through the eye.

The suspected gunman was twenty-six-year-old Dubliner Eric 'Lucky' Wilson from Ballyfermot, west Dublin. Wilson was a contract killer who gardaí suspected was responsible for at least eight gangland murders in Ireland before he fled to Spain. He was classified as one of the most dangerous and psychotic of the new breed of gangland thug to emerge in the noughties. Paddy Doyle, who was also a prolific hit man with at least six hits under his belt, came a close second in the league of professional killers. He was about to become Wilson's latest victim.

Even though they were all supposedly close friends Freddie Thompson and Gary Hutch had secretly agreed to set up Doyle for Daniel Kinahan. It typified how treachery and betrayal had replaced loyalty in the psyche of the new kids on the block. Doyle had murdered five men on Thompson's orders during the Crumlin and Drimnagh feud – including two members of Fat Freddie's own gang who he suspected of disloyalty. The hit man was a lifelong friend of Gary Hutch and was the person who had introduced him to Daniel Kinahan several years earlier. In rationalizing their perfidy Hutch and Thompson knew that if the shoe was on the other foot, Doyle would have had no compunction killing either or, indeed, both of them.

Gary Hutch had tipped off Lucky Wilson, telling him where and when to ambush the jeep. The two friends also ensured that Doyle would be sitting in the front passenger seat. As they emerged from a side road heading towards the apartment a car pulled alongside. Lucky Wilson fired several shots through the passenger window with a machine pistol. Gary Hutch drove the jeep into a lamp post and the three drug dealers jumped out and made a run for it, fleeing in separate directions. Doyle, who hadn't been hit in the initial volley, was pursued by the gunman down an alleyway. Wilson fired another burst hitting Doyle several times in the body. As he fell to his knees, Wilson finished Doyle off with two more rounds in the back of the head. Post-mortem results later showed Doyle had been hit fifteen times. It was a textbook precision hit that Doyle would have been proud of executing himself. Perhaps it was a fitting end that one professional assassin was taken out by another.

The Kinahan mob initially put the word out that an Eastern European gang had been responsible. But gardaí and Spanish police later ruled out this theory and laid the blame where it belonged, with the Kinahans and their henchmen. The mob, however, kept up their fake news version and were prepared to stamp down hard to punish any loose talk, even amongst their own ranks. And that included Gary's wayward younger brother Derek 'Del Boy' Hutch.

About two weeks after Doyle's murder Del Boy Hutch was on a drinking binge in a Dublin city centre pub with members of the gang including Freddie Thompson. Unlike his famous uncle, twenty-three-year-old Del Boy was boisterous, volatile and fond of cocaine. He began mouthing off, making loud derogatory remarks about Paddy Doyle saying that he'd got what was coming to him. But the mob could not tolerate such loose talk in public and Thompson and his associates gave Hutch a punishment beating.

Hutch stumbled away and stopped a taxi. Within minutes Del Boy went berserk, and the taxi driver diverted to Fitzgibbon Street garda station. After arresting Hutch gardaí noticed that he had suffered a severe beating and called an ambulance. Del Boy was treated in hospital but refused to make an official complaint about his assault. In the complicated dynamics of the gang, there were no recriminations from Gary Hutch. His only response was a suggestion that his brother would keep his mouth shut in future. For his part, their Uncle Gerry steered well clear. He had his own fish to fry.

As part of Daniel Kinahan's inner circle Gary Hutch was becoming a powerful figure in the growing cartel. A garda intelligence assessment of the Kinahan organization noted: 'Gary Hutch based in Spain is one of the key Irish individuals within the Kinahan Organized Crime Group (OCG) responsible for regularly supplying drugs to Ireland.' The Monk's nephew had become a major supplier of the Kinahans' cocaine, heroin and cannabis to gangs across the country. Gerry Hutch maintained his anti-drugs stance, but he turned a blind eye to the activities of his nephew. And the Monk's ambivalence when it came to narcotics was not confined to his nephew's role.

A former associate of Gerry Hutch was one of the few people who was aware of his secret peripheral involvement in the narcotics trade. The Monk, who was still anti-drugs in public, was a silent investor in shipments but he kept it a closely guarded secret, even from family. Hutch was a regular visitor to Marbella on the Costa del Sol in Spain, where the associate was based and helped to organize appointments for him.

According to the source, Hutch would hold meetings with members of UK gangs in the upmarket Don Carlos hotel in Marbella – out of view of the Kinahan cartel. The Spanish associate gave an insight into the way the Monk did business:

> Gerard would come over in a group of about twelve other mad fuckers and check into a cheap hotel up the road in Fuengirola. But that was always just a cover because once they were pissed-up he would slip off on his own. He also went to Torremolinos every few months and sometimes brought his wife which was a good cover. He was always careful with money and stayed in the cheap hotels. An Irish guy who also worked with Daniel and Gary used to pick him up by arrangement. He was very discreet and

didn't want to know anyone's business. That was why Gerard used
him. He would drop Gerard off at meetings and wait for him.

Gerard was always intensely cautious and on his guard all the
time. He would never say much, and he would have a good look
around a place before going in and then again when he came
out. He seemed very uncomfortable in crowds and was always
suspicious and his eyes would be scanning the room. He avoided
doing business with people from home and whatever shipments
he was involved in went to the UK.

He was very close to the English gangs who were operating
out of the Costa and he had a lot of contacts in the UK. When he
was here he would meet with the Noonans from Manchester and a
guy called 'Turbo' and his brother called 'Fish'. One of them had a
cafe on a beach near Mijas. Another guy, Joe from Liverpool, was
very close to Gerard. He was caught bringing drugs into the UK
on jet skis over the Channel. Gerard was investing in drug deals
but much smaller amounts than what the Kinahans would be
doing. He didn't trust the Kinahans because he thought they were
too wild and loose.

The deals would be mostly weed or hash, but I think there
was also some coke. In fairness Gerard never touched heroin
and wouldn't deal with someone who was. Typically a shipment
would be a couple of hundred kilos at a time and split up
between different suppliers – 100 kilos here and another there –
to mitigate potential losses if stuff was seized. They were doing
it for years. He had contacts in the transport business that he
used independently of Kinahan. He never had any contact with
the stuff and there was no connection to him. Gerard was a
hands-off investor and he stayed on the periphery. He was very

careful, watertight, and would never get excited or let on he had something going on.

The former associate recalled how Daniel Kinahan and his most trusted sidekick, a former armed robber called Kevin Lynch, would 'slag off' Gerry Hutch when they were out on the town, drunk and stoned:

> One night in the Auld Dubliner pub the gang owned in San Pedro Daniel and Lynch were stoned and drunk and they started taking the piss out of Gerard. They were calling him Mr Bean and saying he was gay, schoolyard bully sort of stuff. They showed no respect to him at all and would say it in front of him. They always tried to act like they had the upper hand but that was probably because deep down they were afraid of him. Gerard would never show any emotion or rise to the bait.
>
> With him everything was controlled and reserved. He never had a rush of blood to the head. One night Daniel rang a guy who was with me and Gerard in a bar in Marbella. The guy put him on speaker and it was obvious Daniel was out of his head on coke. When he heard that Gerard was in the company, he [Daniel] started shouting down the phone telling him he was a faggot and stuff like that. Gerard just shook his head and laughed: 'They are fuckin' mad... they're off their bleedin' heads.' Gerard would sort of shake his head like the wise elder at the excesses of the younger crowd like Gary. They were all fairly nice lads but when they were on the booze and coke it was a different story.

While Gerry Hutch was dabbling in the drug trade, following his nephew's lead, Gary was planning to emulate his uncle with a historic robbery of his own. Spanish police intelligence placed the Monk's nephew at a position immediately below Daniel in the Kinahan organization's pecking order. Above Daniel were his father and his long-time partner, convicted kidnapper and drug trafficker, John Cunningham. Christy was in the process of relinquishing the reins of power to Daniel and his brother, Christy Junior, who was involved in the cartel's money laundering operation. Gary had ambitions to elevate himself from a gofer to a shareholder. But to achieve that goal he needed money – a lot of money – to invest in the business. Together with the rest of his gang from the north inner city and with some practical advice from the Monk, he set about planning a terrifying tiger kidnapping. However, as the gang prepared to carry out the robbery tragedy struck the Hutch family.

In early February 2009 the Monk's younger brother Derek walked into Store Street garda station and asked to speak to a detective he knew and trusted. Hutch had spent most of his life plagued by inner demons that manifested in substance abuse and violence. Over the previous few months Derek Hutch claimed to have become a born-again Christian. He had given up booze and drugs and renounced his criminal ways. He explained to the detective that God had told him to confess to the unreported murder of a former criminal associate nineteen years earlier. He described killing the man and then burying the body, giving the officer the location.

The confession was Derek Hutch's catharsis and the stunned detective immediately began an investigation. A week later, on 23 February, the youngest Hutch brother was found slumped unconscious in his bathtub after cutting his wrists. He died a day later in hospital. The confession was one of his last steps towards redemption. Gerry Hutch and his siblings were distraught at the death of their deeply troubled brother. But as the family prepared for his funeral the timing coincided with his nephew

Gary's robbery plot.

Gary Hutch had planned the operation meticulously. The gang had identified their target and carried out detailed surveillance over a number of months. Gary decided that, despite the fact that it was coinciding with his uncle's funeral the following morning, the job was going ahead regardless.

On the night of 26 February 2009 Shane Travers, a junior employee at the Bank of Ireland on College Green in central Dublin, was babysitting his girlfriend's five-year-old daughter at her home in County Kildare. When his girlfriend and her mother returned from a shopping trip, they were set upon by a six-member armed gang. During a scuffle Travers was beaten and the women were roughed up. Then the family were held hostage overnight.

The following morning the bank worker's girlfriend, her daughter and mother were bound and bundled into a van. The terrified Travers was handed a burner phone to receive instructions and a Polaroid photograph of his girlfriend tied up. The gang ordered him to go to the Bank of Ireland's cash processing centre at College Green and present the picture as proof to his colleagues that his family was being held hostage. If he didn't do what he was told, or called the gardaí, the gang would blow his girlfriend's head off. At the bank Travers told a superior what was happening and hurriedly filled four laundry sacks with cash. The gardaí were not informed. Travers was then ordered to drive his car to Clontarf Dart station and leave it with the money in the boot. Then he immediately went to the gardaí for help. Soon afterwards the three female hostages were released in Ashbourne, County Meath. The bank later confirmed that the gang had got away with €7.6 million, setting a new record for the biggest cash heist in the history of the State.

However, the gardaí scored an early success less than 14 hours

into the investigation when they arrested two men in possession of
€1.74 million of the stolen loot. One of them was twenty-five-year-
old Darren O'Brien, a close friend of Gary Hutch and a member of
his drug gang. O'Brien had given the money to an associate, Mark
Donoghue, who had agreed to hide it for him in Longford. O'Brien
was subsequently sentenced to seven years after pleading guilty to
handling the proceeds of the robbery. Donoghue got five years for
money laundering.

Gary Hutch was one of seven suspects arrested for questioning
in the follow-up operation. Under interrogation he claimed that
he had been at his uncle's funeral that morning. No one else was
charged in connection with the robbery and over €5.9 million was
never recovered. Immediately after his release from custody Gary
Hutch returned to the Costa del Crime where the Kinahans warmly
congratulated him on a spectacular success. The Monk's nephew was
now able to play in a bigger league.

Inevitably the Monk loomed large in the garda investigation of
the robbery. Detectives were happy that he had not been physically
involved but aspects of the planning bore the hallmarks of his
legendary work. There was also the distinct possibility that Gerry
Hutch would launder some of the proceeds through Thomas Scragg
and his associates in the UK. Scragg was still out on bail pending
his trial for fraud and money laundering and had remained active.
An internal report highlighted this suspicion: 'The possibility that
Gerard Hutch may use Thomas Scragg or his companies to launder
the proceeds of Irish criminality, particularly the proceeds of the
robbery on the Bank of Ireland, should be considered.'

In November 2010 Thomas Scragg was sentenced to thirteen years
for fraud, money laundering and conspiracy to cheat HM Revenue
and Customs (HMRC). In May 2011 he was found guilty on further

charges of conspiracy to cheat HMRC and received another four years, bringing his cumulative sentence to seventeen years. It was one of the longest sentences in British criminal history for fraud. His business partner Paul Phillips was jailed for nine years. By 2012 another eleven of Scragg's co-conspirators had been convicted and jailed on charges related to the tax scam.

And even though they could never prove it the UK authorities were satisfied that Gerry Hutch was a big player in Scragg's wider network. Their investigations had revealed the connection between Scragg and a man from County Meath who they believed was fronting property deals in Turkey on Hutch's behalf.

In a report sent by the West Midlands police to the CAB three days before the Bank of Ireland robbery it noted: 'Gerard Hutch is now a partner or has taken a major stake in Thomas Scragg's company and is visiting the West Midlands regularly meeting with Scragg and other criminals.'

Gary Hutch was also developing his set-up. Five months after the tiger robbery gardaí seized cocaine worth €3 million which had been supplied by the Monk's nephew. Two members of his distribution network were caught with the haul and later jailed.

Sources close to the Monk would later claim that Gary had invested his share of the robbery proceeds, €2.5 million, with Daniel Kinahan who then ripped him off. Gerry Hutch claimed the seed of the Kinahan/Hutch feud was sown in the aftermath of the tiger robbery.

CHAPTER SIXTEEN

———

DANGEROUS WORLD

The Monk's recent brush with the authorities had confirmed his decision that it was time to retire from most of his criminal activities and live off his wisely invested, hidden fortune. Not that a born criminal like Hutch would find it possible to avoid a deal or opportunity that was on the wrong side of lawful. But after his close calls with law enforcement during the Scragg investigation and the death of his younger brother, the Monk's survival instincts warned that his luck would not last forever. Ireland was also changing. In the wake of the financial crash in 2008 he'd taken a hit on the value of his property portfolio but still remained a multi-millionaire. When the recession ended he was sure he'd recoup his losses and continue to build on his fortune. Life was good for Gerry Hutch — or so he thought.

Hutch closed the 'Cab' company and sold off the Hummer as the recession tightened its hold on Ireland throughout 2009. It was more of a hobby and publicity prop than anything else at that stage. In any event people could no longer afford the novelty of being chauffeured around by a notorious criminal mastermind. Hutch began spending extended periods of the year in Kusadasi, Turkey, where he also had extensive property interests. It was a bolt-hole from the prying eyes of the gardaí and, more importantly, it was a safe distance from an increasingly chaotic underworld at home.

As the first decade of the new millennium came to an end Ireland's gangland continued to be characterized by treachery, betrayal and murder. It was driven by the twin evils of greed and paranoia which created an endless cycle of bloodshed. Sudden death of the violent variety remained an occupational hazard in the predictably 'nasty, brutish and short' life spans of wayward teenagers who transitioned from petty crime to drug trafficking. In the new underworld order young volatile men had plenty of firepower and the willingness to use it. Life had become as cheap as a bag of coke. Hutch's nephews and the rat pack of murderous thugs they ran with exemplified this new breed.

In the age of narcotics being the mainstay of organized crime the average gangland godfather tends to have a relatively short reign at the top which ends predictably, either in a prison cell or a grave – often in that order. Gerry Hutch had good reason to stay in the background. In gangland the laws of the jungle dictate the order of things. Power is maintained through fear and violence. In this predatory world potential challengers wait in the shadows for any sign of weakness or vulnerability on the part of the leader. Then power is taken at the point of a gun. In order to protect his business the boss must be prepared to murder anyone, even former friends, who he suspects are a threat. At the same time there is the omnipresent danger of being busted by the police.

Chaos had become the new norm in Ireland's underworld as gang wars raged in Dublin and Limerick throughout the decade. The old ethics of the ODC were no longer observed. This was no country for a perceptive old gangster. Gerry Hutch no longer recognized the underworld landscape where he grew up. Cautious and contemplative by nature, the Monk strived to maintain a safe distance so that he wouldn't be sucked into the vortex of madness.

Hutch had a similar reason for moving his family to the middle-class Dublin suburb of Clontarf several years earlier. He created a geographical buffer for his five children, away from the criminogenic environment that prevailed in his beloved old neighbourhood. With their offspring safely reared, Hutch and his wife Patricia had decided they could move on.

The Monk's approach to parenting and home life continued to be an exemplar of how he stood out from the rest of the criminal crowd. Unlike the majority of his friends and associates, Gerry Hutch's marriage to his childhood sweetheart had lasted the test of time and given their children a stable home life. The Monk had also done everything he could to ensure none of his children followed in their father's footsteps. He ensured that they got the chances in life that had been denied to their parents, particularly a good education. Like his legendary heists, his strategy was well planned and flawlessly executed.

The Monk's proudest achievement in life is the fact that his kids turned out to be well-educated, law-abiding adults who are respected professionals in their chosen careers. None of them have ever been involved in crime of any kind. Their only connection to crime is their dad and his family name. The Monk was aware of this and even took steps to insulate his children from the baggage carried with the Hutch name by ensuring that they used a different surname. He wanted to minimize the risk of them being embarrassed or labelled purely because of their father. Hutch's ability to compartmentalize issues in his life meant that he could draw a strict demarcation line between home life and his clandestine work. The Hutch children were no doubt aware of their father's reputation growing up: all they had to do was read the newspapers or watch TV. But the nearest they ever came to a physical manifestation of their father's work were on the rare occasions when gardaí called to the house with a search warrant or to arrest their father for questioning. Even then the Monk unusually had a sort of unwritten gentleman's agreement with the police. He showed courtesy to them and they reciprocated accordingly. The fuss was kept to a minimum in the interests of the children.

A family friend gave a picture of a criminal godfather who was also a good father:

Gerard and Patricia were very loving parents who wanted the best for the kids and ensured that they did not experience the same poverty and deprivation that they had growing up. The reason why he moved out of town was to give them a chance and keep them away from crime and drugs. It may be just a mile or so away from the inner city, but Clontarf was really a different universe. The kids went to private schools and they grew up with other middle-class kids, some of whose fathers were guards and even well-known celebrities. They were never exposed to criminal elements. There are not very many people in Gerard's line of business whose kids turned out so well. Gerard and Patricia got on very well with their neighbours who found it hard to believe that he was this big bad criminal that the media were harping on about. The children were always courteous and well-behaved. They were a model family really and that is a side that the public know nothing about. It shows how solid the man is and makes you wonder what he would have become if he had grown up in Clontarf instead of the poverty of Railway Street. Gerard provided the protective shell and Patricia looked after everything else – she was a good, attentive mother to her children. They turned out to be lovely people and they all have really good jobs which he is very proud of.

Once they were set up with lives of their own Gerard decided that it

was the right time to retire and he meant it too.

Gerry's children, however, were the exception to the rule of the younger generation in the rest of the Hutch clan. Several of his nephews, Gary being the most prominent of them, had followed their forebears into the family business and become immersed in the new crime culture. The Monk was concerned that they were already serious players in an increasingly dangerous world devoid of humanity. But there was nothing he could do about it. Instead he adopted his usual Zelig-like approach and stayed in the background. But then the most volatile and dangerous of the new kids on the block, a close associate of his nephews and the Kinahan mob, came looking for trouble. His fatal mistake lay in his arrogant belief that he could threaten and intimidate criminals like the Monk and his associates.

Gangland had never seen the likes of Eamon Dunne, aka the Don. The psychotic thug had earned his reputation as the most bloodthirsty gang boss yet seen in the Dublin underworld. Dunne exemplified the quintessential dangerous narco-terrorist. The thirty-two-year-old from Cabra on Dublin's northside had literally blasted his way to gangland prominence, on 12 December 2006, when he organized the execution of his boss, Martin 'Marlo' Hyland and took control of one of the biggest drug trafficking gangs in the country.

Hyland's murder was probably the most significant killing of a high-profile crime boss since that of Martin Cahill over a decade earlier. But Dunne's bloody coup had also shocked and outraged the nation when his assassins gunned down Anthony Campbell, a totally innocent twenty-year-old apprentice plumber. The young lad was fixing a radiator in the house where Marlo was staying when the killers struck. After shooting Hyland in the back of the head as he lay sleeping in a bed upstairs, Dunne's henchmen callously executed the apprentice because he might have been able to identify them.

A month earlier Dunne had orchestrated the equally shocking contract killing of Baiba Saulite, an innocent mother of two who was gunned down as she stood at the door of her home in Swords, County Dublin. Dunne and his crew had been recruited by Hyland to carry out the murder for the notorious McCarthy/Dundon gang, aka Murder Inc., in Limerick. Murder Inc. boss John Dundon had agreed to organize the killing on behalf of Baiba's estranged Lebanese husband, Hassan Hassan, with whom he was sharing a prison cell at the time. Paddy Doyle and other associates of Gary Hutch and Daniel Kinahan had also been involved in the horrific attack. It was another illustration of the complex web of relationships that exist in Ireland's gangland.

The murders of two totally innocent people and a notorious crime boss in the space of a few weeks sparked public outrage and revulsion. The fact that innocent people were being deliberately targeted was a profoundly worrying development and it was more evidence that organized crime was spiralling out of control. The two innocent victims were among twenty-two people gunned down in gangland-style executions in 2006, making it the bloodiest year yet in the history of organized crime in Ireland. At that stage, however, Dunne's nefarious activities were of no concern to the rest of the underworld. As long as it didn't impact them, or their all-important bottom line, they didn't care. Marlo's murder was necessary in the interests of the business. Gerry Hutch clearly had no objections and adopted his default position in such matters – while it did not directly affect him or his family, he stayed out of it.

The rise and violent fall of Hyland is a paradigm for the modern-day godfather – and one of the reasons why the Monk stayed out of the narcotics game in Ireland. Being a silent back room investor made much more sense. Marlo had embarked on his journey to the top of the heap when he got rid of his boss and mentor, PJ 'The Psycho' Judge, exactly ten years earlier in December 1996. He had built a powerful drug trafficking organization, maintaining control through violence and fear. Dunne was twenty-two when Hyland mounted his coup and had been in his gang ever since. He was one of Marlo's most trusted lieutenants and fearsome enforcers.

But Hyland had become a victim of his own success. He had been linked to several murders and was supplying weapons and killers to other gangs in Limerick and Dublin. At the same time he was one of the biggest drug traffickers in the country. In September 2009 the garda Organized Crime Unit (OCU) and the CAB had launched a major operation to bring Marlo down. A garda intelligence circular about the investigation, codenamed Operation Oak, summarized Hyland's position:

> Ongoing intelligence at this branch confirms that Martin Hyland continues to be heavily involved in serious crime. Hyland is recognized as the leading figure in a criminal gang based primarily in West Dublin. However, Hyland is linked to a substantial number of the crime gangs operating throughout the DMR [Dublin Metropolitan Region] and beyond. Hyland continually endeavours to establish links to the most violent criminals in this jurisdiction. His gang are involved in murder, armed robberies, procurement of firearms, drug distribution and major fraud. In recent times Hyland has become

closely linked to both Dessie O'Hare and Patrick 'Dutchy' Holland
[Veronica Guerin's assassin].

Over the following year Operation Oak pounded Hyland's organization. Gardaí seized several shipments of narcotics worth more than €20 million and several of his gang members were facing serious charges for drug trafficking, possession of firearms and attempted armed robbery. Unlike the Monk's tightknit gang, the police had infiltrated so deeply into the heart of the organization that they knew Hyland's every move. On two occasions when Hyland tried to replenish the cash flow crisis the drug seizures had caused, by organizing robberies from cash-in-transit vans, the cops were waiting to arrest the would-be raiders. Eamon Dunne had been caught in one of the attempted robberies and was out on bail awaiting trial. As far as he was concerned Hyland had become either a jinx or an informant. And there was only one remedy for either condition – death.

The loss of so much product meant that Hyland had been falling behind in his payments to his main supplier of cocaine, heroin and cannabis, the Kinahan cartel. His cocaine habit was exacerbating his paranoia: he accused associates of betrayal and ordered more killings. In the gangland jungle he was seriously weakened and was becoming a liability across the board, both to those above and below him in the pecking order.

When Dunne made his move no one stood in his way. The governance rules of the Dublin underworld meant that such a high-profile hit needed the tacit approval, or indifference, of the big players to avoid any unnecessary conflict of interests or loyalties. The Kinahans were happy that a loose end had been tidied away. The Monk had been acquainted with Marlo over the years but no doubt saw the flamboyant crime boss as the author of his own destiny. Another underworld personality who agreed with Marlo's cancellation was Hutch's old friend and former mentor, Eamon Kelly.

When Kelly was released from prison in 2003 after serving time for cocaine trafficking, he emerged into an alien environment. He had been one of the pathfinders for what had become a billion-euro industry – but now everybody was a cocaine dealer. Despite the extraordinary transformation that had taken place during his long absence, the fifty-six-year-old embraced the new reality and had quickly resumed his influential position. He was still a man of respect amongst the hardest veteran villains including Gerry Hutch and his associates, and former republican terrorists such as his close friend Dessie O'Hare, aka the Border Fox, the notorious INLA mass murderer.

Kelly was an influencer in the eyes of the younger generation and began mentoring hoodlums, including Marlo Hyland, just as he had done with a young Gerry Hutch thirty years earlier. Over time the former IRA member had become a central player in the drug market, brokering deals for large shipments of drugs and guns from his old criminal associate Christy Kinahan. Kelly had no problem callously agreeing that Hyland had come to the end of his run. Behind the scenes he had begun advising Dunne on how best to achieve a clean transition of power.

A former detective described how Kelly had established himself as the 'go to' guy for criminals and subversives alike:

He [Kelly] was a central player in the wider criminal network. He was the top man, the same as a mafia boss, and nothing happened without his knowledge or say so. He was very close to Kinahan and of course Hutch and all the big names. In his role as a mentoring boss he could effectively control the likes of Eamon Dunne. But that was only as long as he could control Dunne.

Over the following years Kelly fell into the role of Dunne's *consigliore*. On Kelly's advice thugs like O'Hare, who had been very loyal to Hyland, switched their loyalties to Dunne. Kelly and Dunne were regularly spotted together in pubs and parks around Raheny in north Dublin where Kelly lived. Whenever they had particularly sensitive matters to discuss the pair would meet in St Anne's Park, Raheny so they were out of range of garda listening devices. But it was only a matter of time before Kelly lost control of the Don.

The truth was that Dunne was an unhinged psychopath who could not be controlled by anyone. He wasn't an ODC in the mould of the Monk or his associates whom Kelly had dealt with in the past. The Don was a natural born killer.

Confident that he had the backing to do what he wanted, Dunne ruled his patch with an iron fist in an orgy of bloodletting. Between 2005 and 2010 he had either organized or carried out seventeen gangland murders. With the exception of Daniel Kinahan, no criminal in the history of organized crime has been personally linked to so much carnage. Kinahan has long since beaten that inauspicious record having been responsible for at least twice that number of killings, including sixteen of the deaths related to the Hutch/Kinahan feud.

After the execution of Hyland, Dunne was responsible for a further thirteen killings in a short three-year period. The death toll included one of his own hit men, Christy Gilroy, and his supposed best friend, Graham McNally, who he shot six times in the head and face because he thought his pal was plotting against him.

In January 2009 Christy Gilroy had murdered Dunne's rivals, Michael 'Roly' Cronin and James Maloney. Immediately after the shooting Gilroy panicked and fled the scene leaving behind vital evidence including the murder weapon, a jacket, a mobile phone and a treasure trove of DNA. When he discovered how badly Gilroy had screwed up Dunne realized that it potentially put him at risk. Christy was a weak junkie and likely to talk when he was arrested. Dunne turned to his pal Gary Hutch for help. Dunne sent Gilroy to the Costa del Sol where Hutch had booked him into a drug detox clinic which Dunne paid for. No one knew where he was, and it would buy Dunne some time while the police were making frantic efforts to find Gilroy. They had an open and shut case against the drug addict and they knew he would co-operate with an investigation. That could finally help them lay a murder rap on the new 'Public Enemy Number One'. But it was a race against time: if they didn't find him first Gilroy would never be seen again. And that's exactly what happened.

A few weeks later Gary Hutch collected Gilroy from the detox clinic and he vanished. Gardaí subsequently discovered that Hutch had teamed up for a second time with assassin Eric 'Lucky' Wilson to betray the trust of an associate. On Dunne's instructions, and with the approval of Daniel Kinahan, Wilson executed Gilroy and they buried him in an unmarked grave.

Around the same time the OCU launched an investigation into Dunne's operation, similar to the one they mounted against Marlo Hyland. It was called Operation Hammer. Over the first eight months of 2009 the gardaí seized over €1.5 million worth of drugs belonging to the Don's syndicate. Fifteen members of the gang were also arrested and charged with serious drug offences. As he was attacked by the police investigation Dunne grew even more unpredictable and paranoid.

The recession had seen a significant drop in drug trafficking revenues which led to gangs fighting among each other over unpaid debts. The seizures were also causing an impossible drain on Dunne's financial resources as he had to pay the Kinahans for the lost shipments. He decided to make up for the shortfall in income by putting the squeeze on other criminals for money. His gang also began targeting the now abolished Head Shops for protection money. He formed an alliance with the INLA and together they abducted individuals and tortured them to extort cash.

As Dunne became more emboldened, he made the catastrophic mistake of stepping across the line by trying to extort money from veteran villains who were close to Eamon Kelly. In late 2009 Dunne approached Noel 'Kingsize' Duggan and demanded €150,000 in protection money. Dunne bluntly told Kingsize that the INLA would deal with him if he failed to pay up. The move was greeted with astonishment, especially considering Duggan was a hard man in his own right but also the best friend of the Monk. Dunne also let it be known that he had no fear of Gerry Hutch or his cohorts, and if they wanted a row they would get one. He was becoming a threat to the Monk himself. When Eamon Kelly intervened Dunne also threatened him. He was making deadly enemies. In the depths of his psychosis the Don was blind to the fact that he was being backed into the same corner that Marlo had inhabited.

Hutch and Duggan had long-established associations with the various criminal factions in the IRA. Several of Gerry Hutch's associates through the years were from the INLA. Through their contacts a meeting was arranged with the leadership of the INLA crime gang in Belfast. Hutch watched from the sidelines as Duggan went to the meeting. When Kingsize arrived at the venue he was taken aback to see Dunne was already there with the republican thugs. He was even more surprised at the outcome of the meeting.

Kingsize was told that the Don had their full support – in other words pay up his demand or face the consequences. The ultimatum implied that Gerry Hutch was not exempt from the firing line either. Duggan was flabbergasted. When he returned to Dublin he met Hutch and Eamon Kelly to discuss their options. The paranoid, unpredictable Don was spiralling out of control. He was prepared to kill anyone who, in his cocaine-addled mind, was perceived as posing the slightest threat, whether real or imagined. Having successfully avoided trouble for most of his career Hutch was now facing the ridiculous situation that this madman was liable to shoot him or his friend in the street for no good reason. Kelly was coming to the same conclusion and washed his hands of his new protégé.

The Don had become the sole topic of conversation between the veteran hoodlums. Secret phone taps by the gardaí and their Spanish counterparts were picking up regular conversations about the 'baldy fellah' between gang members. There was only one way to deal with a psychotic madman – and Hutch, Duggan and Kelly had plenty of allies to help them sort out the problem. The Kinahan cartel was also seriously concerned about the chaos Dunne was causing in Dublin: bringing down heat from the cops and creating unnecessary rows between gangs. Like Duggan and the Monk, Daniel Kinahan and Gary Hutch were increasingly nervous that Dunne could just as easily 'pop' one of them on a whim. When Gerry Hutch contacted his nephew and the Kinahans he was pushing an open door.

A peace summit of sorts, ordered by Christy Kinahan, was held in Dublin in early December 2009. It was attended by the leaders of the various gangs, including Dunne and the INLA, to iron out issues and prevent any further hostilities. But by then it was nothing more than a symbolic gesture. Dunne's erratic personality meant that he could not be trusted. Behind the scenes the unofficial gangland council of Hutch, Kelly and the Kinahans had already sanctioned the Don's denouement. All that was left to do was to select someone to organize the hit. That job was given to Gary Hutch and his associates from the north inner city. This time the motivation would be both business and personal.

Dunne, however, was not an easy person to target. The most feared figure in gangland knew he was open to attack and was hyper-vigilant. He continuously changed cars and moved between different safe houses, never sleeping in the same place more than one night. On the morning of Friday, 23 April 2010 gardaí in Dublin received intelligence that two senior associates of Gary Hutch were in the process of planning a hit in north Dublin. From phone taps they knew that the two known thugs had been watching someone for a number of days. But they didn't know the identity of the victim or the time or location for the proposed assassination. They would soon find out.

That evening Dunne was attending a friend's fortieth birthday in the Fassaugh House pub in Cabra. Around 9.30 p.m. a car pulled up outside and three armed and masked men got out. One stayed outside while the other two ran into the pub. A number of Dunne's associates who were standing outside made a run for it when they saw the gunmen. Inside one of the hit men made straight for the table where the Don was sitting with his back to the door. The assassin fired two rounds directly into the side of Dunne's face. When he fell to the floor his executioner fired one more round into his head. The Don would not be making any more threats to men of respect.

Later that night a garda phone tap intercepted a conversation between Daniel Kinahan and Gary Hutch's friend, Gary Finnegan, who gardaí suspect was involved in the hit. Kinahan warned Finnegan to assume that his phone was being tapped by the gardaí and to say nothing. The public line was that the Kinahan cartel had nothing to do with the killing. Finnegan flew to Spain and stayed with his fellow gang members for a number of weeks after the killing. He was one of a number of the cartel members subsequently arrested and questioned in connection with the Dunne murder. However, the gang had planned the operation too well and no one was ever charged.

The elimination of Dunne tied up a lot of loose ends and restored calm. From Gerry Hutch's point of view, it demonstrated the folly of young hotheads trying to mess with seasoned gangsters. It also justified his reasons for retirement and getting away from the chaos. The killing was the unofficial enunciation of one super-sized, all powerful mob who controlled Dublin's gangland. It was clear that the various elements, including the Hutches, had been absorbed into one indistinguishable group.

Eamon Dunne had shown macabre foresight when he organized his own mafia-style funeral, complete with flamboyant casket, just like the one that would carry David Byrne six years later. He bought his grave plot so that he could be buried head to head with his friend and fellow killer, Paddy Doyle.

But no sooner had the mob cleared up one problem than another much bigger one loomed into view. As Dunne was being laid to rest a major international police operation targeting the Kinahan cartel was in the final stages of preparation. Ultimately it would have a catastrophic knock-on effect on the Monk's life.

CHAPTER SEVENTEEN

OPERATION SHOVEL

Gary Hutch and his compatriots in the ranks of the Kinahan cartel were all doing very well for themselves and rolling in more money than they knew what to do with. In fact the organization was experiencing such a level of commercial success that it was attracting the attentions of law enforcement agencies across Europe and the US Drug Enforcement Agency (DEA). Since the beginning of the decade both Kinahan and his partner John Cunningham were operating as major suppliers to the UK and Irish markets. When the Dutch jailed Cunningham, for running a huge arms and drug smuggling operation, it did nothing to stultify the cartel's progress. By the end of the noughties, Europol classified the Kinahan cartel as one of the top ten criminal organizations in Western Europe involved in murder, money laundering and trafficking in drugs and guns on a vast scale.

From its base in the Costa del Crime the organization had become the single biggest supplier of narcotics to the Irish market and one of the largest dealers in the UK. The gang had also been associated with a string of murders in Ireland, the UK, the Netherlands and Spain. The crime group was too big to ignore. In the summer of 2008 a major international police summit had been held in The Hague to formulate a plan of action against the mob. Officers from Ireland, the UK, the Netherlands, Belgium, and Spain were joined by representatives from Europol and Interpol. The high-powered group had agreed to target the cartel in a multi-jurisdictional, co-ordinated investigation. Over the next two years, in what would become known as Operation Shovel, investigators uncovered information that led them to estimate that Christy Kinahan's empire was worth a billion euro. The sheer scale of the Dapper Don's operation and wealth dwarfed anything the Monk had achieved – a situation that did not bother him in the slightest.

The investigation also involved close-up covert surveillance, both physical and electronic, as Spanish cops listened to the gang's phone conversations and watched its every move. From the intelligence gleaned, the Spanish, with the help of their garda colleagues, were able to identify the hierarchy of the organization and analyse its internal dynamics. It was clear that, like Gerry Hutch, Christy Kinahan Senior had decided to retire. Surveillance showed that he had entered a process of passing control over to Daniel and giving the job of money laundering to his younger son, Christy Junior. He was handing over a very healthy and well-connected business.

The multilingual, well-educated Dapper Don had established direct links with the mafias in Russia, Sicily and Israel, as well as with the main drug producers of hashish, heroin and cocaine in Morocco, Turkey and Colombia. In a ten-year period it was estimated that Kinahan had accumulated a personal fortune of €100 million. He was also the brains behind the cartel's complex money laundering activities.

The investigation uncovered evidence of a global property portfolio worth in excess of €800 million. Through a complex network of front companies, corrupt financiers, lawyers and brokers, the organization had invested in real estate and businesses in Ireland, Spain, Belgium, Portugal, Dubai, South Africa, China, Antigua, Namibia, Brazil, England and Cyprus. In Brazil the group owned six leisure complexes and a string of residential properties worth €500 million and it had another €150 million invested in Spain alone. The Operation Shovel team identified trips to South America, South Africa and the Far East by members of the group, including Daniel Kinahan, Gary Finnegan, Gary Hutch and Matthew Dunne. They had been dispatched to supervise investments.

The environmentally conscious mob also put money into waste disposal companies and renewable energies. It invested in food, cement and commodity markets. The laundering operation used a network of over thirty companies in different countries to channel the dirty money. The cartel owned its own transport companies and a string of warehouses dotted across mainland Europe, the UK and Ireland. The various premises were used to store the gang's drugs and guns which were usually smuggled hidden in the innards of domestic appliances, food stuffs, hardware goods and high-powered cars which were specially adapted to conceal shipments. In Ireland the cartel also owned a dry-cleaners and a ticket sales business.

In 2009 alone investigators discovered that the organized crime group had transferred over €16 million from twenty-two bank accounts. Money was sent to the UK, Spain and Holland to pay for drugs. The profits from the deals were then moved to countries all over the world. In one manoeuvre John Cunningham and Matthew Dunne visited Brazil to transfer another €15 million as part of a major property deal.

In October 2009 Daniel Kinahan went to Dubai in the company of two associates from England and Morocco to supervise the movement of cash to banks in the UAE state. Christy Kinahan

Senior travelled to China that November to set up a meat export business in conjunction with the Chinese mafia. It was suspected that the real purpose of the deal was to launder money through bogus companies in China while drugs were trafficked from there to the West. In the same month Daniel Kinahan and Gary Finnegan visited South Africa to do business with an international drug gang based in Cape Town. The hoods also visited Kenya. That same November the gang's English money launderer was known to have transferred Stg£10 million (approx. €11.1 million) to a bank in Zurich, Switzerland. The money was then transferred to an offshore account in Antigua. The gang's agents in cities such as Liverpool, Dublin, Amsterdam and Antwerp were also transferring huge amounts of cash through Western Union, using bogus names and documentation. It was a breathtaking operation.

Intelligence gleaned in the Operation Shovel enquiry also gave gardaí a major victory over the Kinahan mob – and a timely reminder of how potent the cartel had become. On 13 May 2010 the Organized Crime Unit (OCU) raided a warehouse that was being used by the Kinahans near Straffan in County Kildare. Detectives seized €700,000 worth of cocaine and an awesome arsenal of military-grade weapons. The cache included an AK-74 assault rifle, a M8 grenade launcher and two Russian-made RPG-22 rocket launchers, fitted with warheads and ready for use. Liam Byrne and three of his gang members were arrested and questioned in relation to the seizure.

Less than two weeks later, in the early hours of 25 May 2010, Spanish police spearheaded the international assault on what they described in press briefings as one of the biggest organized crime syndicates in Europe, with tentacles stretching across the globe. The operation was given the full media treatment with dramatic videos of the arrests of the Kinahans, John Cunningham and other members of the cartel being flashed across news services worldwide. The splendid homes of the gangsters and their fleet of top-of-the-range cars were also shown. The Dapper Don, a former fraudster, had been elevated to the same status as Mexican drug lord El Chapo.

A Spanish government minister later described the investigation into the 'Irish Mafia' as one of the biggest ever undertaken against organized crime in Spain. At the same time police in Ireland, the UK, Belgium and Brazil also carried out searches and made arrests. Gardaí carried out over forty searches and arrested a suspected bagman. At the time it was reported that 700 police were involved in the various swoops. Thirty-two people were arrested, including twelve Irish criminals. The suspects were arrested in connection with drug trafficking, gun-running and money laundering.

European Arrest Warrants (EAWs) were also issued for Gary Hutch, Fat Freddie Thompson and Matthew Dunne. In the warrants it was alleged that Dunne was involved in money laundering, while Hutch and Thompson were classified as Daniel's 'trusted right-hand men' who acted as drivers, minders and managers. Hutch and Thompson had been organizing a drug shipment in Amsterdam when the raids took place. A senior police source told this writer that the pair was 'going up the walls' and 'running around like headless chickens' trying to find out what was happening.

In the arrest warrants the Spanish police summed up the role of Gary Hutch and Thompson in the cartel:

> Thompson together with Gary Hutch are the men who are closest to Daniel Joseph Kinahan, as can be inferred from telephone tapping and surveillance operations. They are his most trusted right-hand men and carry out jobs directly in relation to the organization's

criminal activities. Freddie and Gary are just one step below Daniel,
are very close and share equal status. They sometimes give orders
to each other without being able to determine who is higher up in the
organization.

Thompson and Hutch remained at large and continued to move between the Costa del Sol and the rest of Europe while Operation Shovel was ongoing.

Christy Kinahan and his two sons, who were classified as the ringleaders, were detained in prison as the Spanish authorities continued the investigation. The detectives were determined to link them to murders, money laundering, arms dealing and drug trafficking. In Spain suspects can be held indefinitely while an investigation is pending. The rest of the gang, who were also under active investigation for similar offences, were released on bail within a matter of days. Given their status the Kinahans had to wait much longer and were not granted bail until seven months later, in November 2010. As a condition of bail all the suspects had their passports confiscated and were ordered not to leave Spain. The gangsters had no problem with either requirement. They had access to plenty of passports.

For the globe-trotting drug trafficker passports are an invaluable and much sought after commodity. Some of the top cartel members were using legitimate Irish passports, complete with their own pictures, but under a false name, date of birth and home address. During Operation Shovel Spanish cops seized several forged UK and Irish passports that they noted were of a high quality.

In the late noughties the gardaí received reliable intelligence that Gerry Hutch was supplying the precious documents to other criminals for up to €20,000 each. Apart from tightening up on

the security of the passport application process, nothing else ever
came of the information. In a separate enquiry into the Kinahan
organization, it was suspected that a corrupt garda detective based
in Dublin had been secretly assisting the gang members to obtain
passports under false identities. The cop was in a relationship with
a female relative of a cartel member. He was suspected of using an
official garda station stamp to endorse the passport applications
which then went through the system undetected.

The gardaí eventually caught up with Freddie Thompson in
Dublin on 26 October 2011 and invoked the European Arrest
Warrant. He waived his legal right to fight the Spanish extradition
order and consented to being returned to Malaga two days later.
After four days he was also released on bail – and went back to
working for the cartel as normal.

Gary Hutch remained at large and went into hiding in Amsterdam
from where he tried to keep the Dutch side of the Kinahan operation
afloat. He moved between Holland, Spain and the rest of Europe
using false travel documents.

Meanwhile on the Costa del Crime it was becoming apparent that
Operation Shovel had not been the glowing success the authorities
had hoped for. The mob was quietly confident that they would
beat the rap. So Gary Hutch decided there was no need for him to
continue living as a fugitive either. He gave himself up to Spanish
police on 8 November 2012. He was taken into custody but quickly
got bail on the grounds that he had voluntarily handed himself in.

The police investigation found no evidence to link Gerry Hutch
with the Kinahan organization, other than through his nephew
Gary. Inevitably the media coverage of the Spanish raids and Gary's
involvement in the mob included pictures of the Monk which, as he
saw it, made him look guilty by association. The short chaotic reign

of terror by Eamon Dunne and the fuss around Operation Shovel convinced the veteran gangster that he'd made the right decision to get out of the crime scene.

The weight, reach and sheer scale of Operation Shovel had caught the gang completely off guard and left them in disarray for several months. The arrests and searches seriously disrupted the cartel's business costing them a lot of money in lost revenue. They had also earned a level of public notoriety that was frowned upon in the international drug trafficking community.

The media were considered to be almost as big an enemy to the criminal world as the police. Publicity about the exploits and wealth of apparently untouchable criminal gangs aroused the public's outrage which in turn put pressure on the political establishment to be seen to take affirmative action. That meant giving the police the resources and impetus to bust the big players so that the State was seen to be protecting society against the gangs. Being under the media spotlight was bad for business.

The two-year surveillance operation at the heart of the investigation had also gleaned a huge amount of valuable intelligence about the organization's drug trafficking and money laundering activities, especially in identifying their networks. The gangsters had been completely unnerved by the depth and scale of the sophisticated police surveillance operation mounted against them. It was only after the arrests that they learned the cops had been watching and listening to them for over two years. The exposure of the gang's international money laundering operation was also a big problem. In Ireland the CAB used the intelligence to target several individuals associated with the gang.

Ultimately, however, Operation Shovel failed in its original aim which was to impoverish the Kinahan mob and put them behind bars. By 2014 the investigation had fizzled out. The targeted gang members still had most of their wealth and were off the hook. One by one the Kinahans and their henchmen were called before the investigating judge to be told that they were no longer suspects or under investigation. Luck had smiled on them when the judge decided the evidence wasn't strong enough to sustain a prosecution. If the investigation had been centred in Ireland or the UK, where the criminal justice system is based in common law, there might have been a better chance of bringing the mobsters before the courts.

The international law enforcement community made a valiant, painstaking effort to bring down the cartel. However, the exigencies of the law and lady luck had prevented them from succeeding. The multi-force police team had lost a major battle with the enemy, but war is a series of such engagements and this one was far from over. Within a few short years the same investigation files would become a valuable weapon in another battle with the gang.

In the meantime the cartel recovered from the shock and began recalibrating its operation. The police surveillance set-up had ended when the raids took place, but the gang's close shave with the law had taught its members a priceless lesson and internal security was tightened up dramatically. In order to recover and expand they would be a lot more vigilant in future. Within a year they were back bigger than ever and their prospects looked bright once more.

Gerry Hutch's former mentor wasn't so lucky. Less than a month after the arrest of Gary Hutch in Spain, gangland pioneer Eamon Kelly, one of the pioneers of gangland, fell victim to an assassin's bullet.

On the afternoon of 4 December 2012 Kelly was walking home from his local bookies in Dublin when a gunman shot him four times in the back. The once feared and respected criminal godfather, who had guided the Monk's early armed robberies, had become eligible for his State pension and bus pass when he celebrated his sixty-fifth birthday just two weeks earlier. It was an ironic end to a long criminal career of the man seen as the *Capo dei Capi* of organized crime. Kelly had become embroiled in a feud with the dissident republican crime gang, the Real IRA (RIRA), which was a hangover from his work with the Don's gang.

The RIRA had been trying to extort money from the Monk's old friend but he had refused to pay up. In 2010 Kelly had survived an attempt on his life when the shooter's gun jammed. The gang boss had chased the gunman on foot forcing him to flee. He refused to report the incident to the gardaí, saying he would deal with the situation in his own way. But the RIRA gang leader Alan Ryan was cut from the same cloth as Eamon Dunne – he didn't mind who he threatened or intimidated.

Garda sources later revealed that Ryan had also been putting the squeeze on members of the Hutch family and word was sent to Gerry Hutch and his brother Patsy – the father of Gary and Del Boy – demanding protection money from the younger generation's drug trafficking activities. Ryan demanded that they hand over guns and sent word back that in his eyes the Monk was 'yesterday's man'. He then went one further when Alan Hutch, Eddie's son, was beaten up and his taxi was set alight. Ryan was on a collision course with Gerry Hutch and his family.

The situation had escalated dramatically on 2 August 2009 when Gary Hutch's younger brother Derek 'Del Boy' Hutch was arrested by gardaí with a loaded weapon on his way to execute Ryan. Del Boy was carrying a loaded semi-automatic pistol equipped with a silencer which was ready to fire. He was also wearing the assassin's uniform: two sets of clothes to help dispose of forensic evidence after the hit. In March 2010 he was sentenced to ten years for possession of the firearm.

Alan Ryan had become an intolerable nuisance and Gerry Hutch, Kelly, the Kinahans and their assorted allies agreed it was time to level the playing field. Alan Ryan's temerity was punished gangland-style when he was gunned down in the street in September 2012 by two men working for a major league northside drug lord known as Mr Big. A long-time associate of the Kinahan cartel, Mr Big had survived a number of attempts on his life by Ryan and his gang. He was more than happy to get rid of the RIRA thug and earn some goodwill from his peers for getting him off everyone else's back into the bargain. Ryan's boot boys, however, blamed Eamon Kelly for his murder and exacted their revenge four months later.

Unluckily for them the gardaí had been shadowing Eamon Kelly when the hit man struck unexpectedly. Detectives caught him running away from the scene. Sean Connolly was subsequently jailed for life after he pleaded guilty to the murder.

The eulogy at Kelly's funeral was delivered by Dessie O'Hare who had become a close friend of Kelly's when they were incarcerated in Portlaoise Prison. In one of the most bizarre and delusional tributes ever heard in an Irish churchyard O'Hare described the slain crime boss as a martyr who had spent his life trying to achieve 'freedom and peace' for the people of Ireland. Quoting poet W. B. Yeats, and without a hint of irony, O'Hare said Kelly's death was part of the 'terrible beauty' of the struggle for freedom, adding that the 'British colonial wrong' had left a stinking legacy of 'servitude' in Ireland.

Gerry Hutch was sad about the loss of his old friend but the murder was not for him to avenge. Eamon Kelly knew he was sailing close to the wind for at least two years and did nothing to either de-escalate the situation or keep a low profile. Retiring to the sun was a change the Monk had made so that he could leave all this madness behind. Hutch was determined to enjoy life and moved with his wife from Turkey to the Canary Island of Lanzarote where he owned a villa in Puerto del Carmen.

But dark thunder clouds were beginning to form on the horizon. And when the storm finally reached him, it would bring devastation and destruction.

CHAPTER EIGHTEEN

———

TREACHERY AND BETRAYAL

The normally frugal Monk spared no expense when he decided to throw a lavish party to celebrate reaching a major milestone in his life – his fiftieth birthday. In April 2013 over 200 close family and friends flew out to join Gerry Hutch for the festivities in Puerto del Carmen in Lanzarote, where he and his wife Patricia now lived for most of the year.

A long-time friend from childhood later described it as a dual celebration marking the Monk's retirement from the 'life' – an option that had been denied to so many of his old friends and associates:

> The party was a big thing for Gerard because he wanted to celebrate the birthday and also the fact that he had actually survived long enough to retire and enjoy it. When you look at the way it [(gangland] has gone that is a big achievement. He wanted to share his good luck with his family and friends. It was the party of a lifetime and everyone was there.

Hutch footed the bill for flights for up to forty members of his family including his brothers and sisters with whom he was very close. Some of the biggest names in organized crime flew out to join the celebration with their old friend including former members of his armed robbery outfit. A party planner was hired and the venue, Mulligan's Irish Bar in the New Town, was block-booked for two nights on 11 and 12 of April. There was a free bar and food laid on for the guests each night. Three bands and a karaoke machine were also hired to entertain the revellers. The bill for the hooley was estimated to have set Gerry Hutch back around €30,000. But while the Monk may have thrown caution to the wind by splashing out on reaching fifty, he wasn't letting his guard down in other ways.

A team of bouncers was flown in from Ireland to provide security and prevent unwanted intrusions, especially from the media. When the Monk got on stage to entertain the guests with his favourite song – Frank Sinatra's 'My Way' – three bouncers patrolled the audience gently confiscating and deleting footage recorded on mobile phones. A clip of the underworld's most elusive godfather doing an impression of Frank Sinatra would have been a viral phenomenon.

Although the party had been kept under wraps the Irish media turned up to record the seminal event. An enterprising photographer working with Mick McCaffrey, a journalist with the *Sunday World* at the time, got a major scoop which ended up on the front page three days later. The Monk was pictured getting into a taxi at 3.30 a.m. looking the worst for wear. Hutch, who had only ever been a moderate, occasional drinker in the past, had been drinking much more heavily now that he was no longer masterminding major heists. One former associate said that alcohol didn't always agree with his personality: 'The Monk was one of those people that the booze didn't suit at all… you could see him going a bit dark and brooding when he was jarred.' By all accounts there was no evidence of that side of the godfather on his birthday weekend.

That same week Hutch shared the front page splash with his old friend Christy Kinahan Senior who wasn't in the same party mood. He looked less than happy when *Sunday World* crime reporter Eamon Dillon confronted him as he left a Spanish court. Kinahan was just after signing on as a condition of his bail during the Operation Shovel investigation.

Back in Lanzarote Hutch was bringing his entourage on pub crawls around Puerto del Carmen during the three-day party because he wanted the locals to benefit from the influx of guests. The party was a huge success and a cherished memory for Hutch and his family. But 1,100 miles to the north, on mainland Spain, trouble was brewing which would have dire consequences for the entire family. Within three years the impending conflagration would claim the lives of at least six of Hutch's party guests – either because they bore the same name or were his friends. His fiftieth birthday was to be the last happy occasion that the Hutch family would celebrate together.

One of the most predictable and defining traits of the gang culture is that members invariably fall out amongst each other and friendships end in bloodshed. The first tell-tale cracks were beginning to appear in the once cohesive Kinahan cartel. Gary Hutch, who had been Daniel's loyal right-hand man for many years, was beginning to suspect that he was being deliberately sidelined in the pecking order in favour of the Dublin-based Byrne brothers and their cousin Fat Freddie Thompson.

Gary Hutch, unlike his uncle, was volatile and hot-headed, character traits which weren't helped by his fondness for cocaine. He also had a reputation as a 'mouth' who wasn't shy about letting himself be heard, especially when he was drunk and stoned. Hutch began putting pressure on Daniel Kinahan for the return of the cash from the 2009 tiger robbery which he had invested with the cartel.

Hutch had committed a significant portion of the €2.5 million he got from the record heist and it was later confirmed to this writer by a source close to the Monk that Gary wanted his money back. But Daniel Kinahan played for time, urging his lieutenant to be patient and assuring him that the money would be returned with a healthy profit once the organization had returned to normality.

In turn Gary Hutch was coming under pressure from his own gang back in Dublin, including his relatives, who were convinced that Kinahan was trying to rip him off and had shown no respect for his hard work on the successful heist. They claimed that the Byrnes in Crumlin were getting a much bigger slice of the cake. The seeds of doubt had been sown and the situation wasn't helped by the ongoing impact of Operation Shovel on the cartel membership.

The revelations about the two-year surveillance operation had made the gang members look like idiots. Despite participating in an intensive counter-surveillance training course designed to spot undercover cops and shake off tails, the main leaders had been blissfully unaware that they were being followed all the time. It caused them to completely reorganize their internal security regime which included the purchase of the latest encrypted phone technology. The leaders of the group, Kinahan Senior, his sons and John Cunningham, were increasingly paranoid that they might also have spies within their midst. Faint whispers questioning Gary Hutch's loyalty began to circulate amongst the gang members.

The origins of the rumour could be traced to the seizure of a shipment of ketamine and cannabis by the UK police in February 2014. The haul, valued at over €10 million, came as a major setback for the recovering Kinahan cartel. The police had been acting on specific intelligence which could only have come from within their ranks. Gary Hutch was one of the people involved in organizing the shipment. The fact that he had been grumbling about the return of his money was enough for the equally paranoiac Daniel Kinahan to consider him a possible suspect.

The whispered rumours about Hutch's loyalty intensified in May following the funeral of Daniel and Christy Junior's mother Jean Boylan, who had tried in vain to stop her sons following in their father's footsteps. When the mourners reached Mount Jerome cemetery in south Dublin they were greeted with a bizarre sight. Graffiti had been smeared on the walls of the Russian-Orthodox church close to the crematorium proclaiming: 'Gary Hutch U Rat'. The spray-painted allegations in bright red also accused him of setting up a friend to be arrested: 'u set Fish up'. It was clearly intended to cause maximum embarrassment for the Monk's nephew in front of his bosses and associates. The incident was also extensively reported in the media. The vandal responsible had done his job well. The Hutch family believed that Daniel Kinahan was behind the mendacious stunt which was intended to make life uncomfortable for Gary in the gang.

The two people who least trusted Gary Hutch were Christy Kinahan Senior and John Cunningham. They thought he was arrogant, impulsive and a potential liability. They wanted a close eye kept on him. In the meantime Gary Hutch remained on friendly terms with Daniel who gave no clue as to his hidden suspicions. It was the same strategy deployed by Kinahan's celluloid hero in *The Godfather*: 'Keep your friends close and your enemies closer.'

At the same time Daniel Kinahan was pursuing his ambition to become a legitimate boxing manager and promoter. He had been using his dirty money to build a reputation as a serious player in the sport through his involvement with Matthew Macklin and his popular MGM gym in Puerto Banus on the Costa del Sol. Kinahan became the manager of the gym and was reportedly an investor. He signed a number of big names and managed his own stable of fighters from MGM. Former European boxing champion and Sky Sports pundit Jamie Moore, who had no connections with crime, had also come on board as a trainer for Macklin. Kinahan worked hard to ingratiate his way into acceptance by the elite of a sport that has a morally ambivalent relationship with organized crime.

During the summer of 2014 Gary Hutch simmered and grew ever more paranoid as he weighed up his options. He was conscious that a cloud of suspicion hung over him and was beginning to fear for his life. Daniel and his father might be creating an excuse to have him whacked so they could hang onto his dirty money. Hutch had first-hand experience of the treachery endemic in his chosen profession where close pals are prepared to kill each other on orders from the top. Hutch had done so himself when he set up Paddy Doyle and Christy Gilroy. He had also witnessed Daniel Kinahan's perfidy as he double-crossed business associates. One of those secrets concerned the betrayal of a Dutch drug trafficker.

Fifty-five-year-old Robert Mink Kok had been a long-time business associate and friend of the Dapper Don since the early 1990s when they met in a Dutch prison. Mink Kok, who had a string of convictions for gun-running and cocaine trafficking, was well connected. He was married to the sister of the Lebanese Koleilat Dalbi brothers who had close links with Hezbollah and were involved in international arms dealing and drug trafficking. Through Mink Kok they had also done business with Kinahan, supplying hashish from the Beka Valley, Lebanon, and heroin from Afghanistan. The brothers secretly supplied heavy military hardware, including helicopter gunships, to the one-time Liberian dictator Charles Taylor. They were both subsequently extradited to the USA by the Drug Enforcement Agency on drug trafficking charges.

Robert Mink Kok was arrested in Lebanon in August 2011, with two Palestinian accomplices, after undercover police seized 53 kilos of cocaine in what was described as one of the biggest drug busts in Lebanese history. The investigation team discovered that one of the men was in possession of an Irish passport in the name of a drug addict from Tallaght in west Dublin. They established that it had been supplied by the cartel. Mink Kok and his associates were subsequently jailed for eight years each.

An associate close to the Monk told this writer that Gary maintained that Kinahan had moved in on Mink Kok's operation behind his back following his arrest. To facilitate this Gary claimed that the cartel had organized the murder of the gangster's top lieutenant and made it look like the work of a rival gang.

> When Robert got sent to jail in the Lebanon, Kinahan killed his bag man in August 2013 in Marbella and robbed his South American connections [drug supplier]. He [victim] was in an Audi car and he had his wife and kid in the car with him. Daniel Kinahan sent an email to Robert by accident so Robert now knows that they killed his partner and double-crossed him and he will be seeking revenge for this.

Mink Kok was paroled three weeks after the Regency Hotel attack on 25 February 2016 but to date there has been no evidence of a revenge attack by him on Kinahan. The source also claimed that Gary Hutch had information that Kinahan had 'stolen' 30 kilos of cocaine from another Dutch gang and that the theft was blamed on a criminal group based in the south of Spain. Gary Hutch was well aware of the cartel's track record for treachery and had plenty of reason to be paranoid.

On 2 August 2014 Daniel Kinahan and his associates attended a birthday party in Puerto Banus. Amongst the revellers were Gary Hutch and his brother Patrick, who was also a member of the gang. Patrick was staying in Puerto Banus with Gary and was training with the MGM gym in the hope of becoming a professional boxer, but Daniel didn't think much of his chances. It was reported that a drunken row broke out between the Hutch brothers during the wild party. Patrick accused his brother of being 'weak' and after a scuffle the wannabe boxer was ejected from the party. Despite the simmering tensions in the background, outwardly Gary Hutch was still close to Daniel. He ended up leaving the party with his boss and going back to Kinahan's villa because it was closest to the venue.

Boxing pundit Jamie Moore, who was also staying in Kinahan's house for the weekend, arrived back from the party a few hours later. As he walked through the security gates a gunman wearing a 'ghoulish rubber mask' suddenly emerged from the shadows and fired a number of shots at him – hitting Moore in the hip and thigh. The gunman stood over his terrified victim as if to finish him off but suddenly stopped. To Moore it seemed like the shooter realized that he had the wrong man. He turned and ran to a waiting getaway car outside on the street. Moore called an ambulance on his mobile phone which probably saved his life as one of the bullets had narrowly missed an artery. It was only when the ambulance arrived that Gary Hutch and Kinahan were alerted to what had happened – or so it appeared.

The shooting incident sent shock waves through the organization as it became apparent that the intended target had been Daniel Kinahan and not Jamie Moore, the innocent victim. It caused panic and consternation from the top down. Daniel and his father were left seriously rattled by the unconscionable act of treachery. Someone within the organization was attempting to strike against the leadership of the cartel and that was unacceptable. Christy Senior and Daniel immediately launched an investigation.

The assassination bid also attracted more unwelcome media attention. The attempted murder of such a high-profile boxing pundit at the home of a suspected international crime boss made for big news across the sporting world. And that wasn't good for Daniel Kinahan's shot at being a legitimate power broker in the sport. The psychopath wanted the would-be assassin unmasked and brought to justice – of the gangland variety.

Initially an Eastern European gang was suspected but they were quickly ruled out. Then a corrupt cop from the local police gave Kinahan some very helpful information which narrowed the investigation down considerably.

After leaving the scene of the shooting the getaway car, a high-spec BMW, refused to stop at a routine police checkpoint and sped off as a chase ensued. The car was crashed a short time later. Before the police caught up with the two occupants, they fled on foot up a short hill where a second car was waiting to take them away. When police checked the getaway car they discovered that it was registered to Robert Mink Kok. He had left the bullet-proof luxury motor to his friend Gary Hutch for safe keeping while he was in prison. Armed with the information, in less than 24 hours, Kinahan had established the identities of the shooter and his two getaway drivers, both of whom were from Dublin's north inner city. Daniel Kinahan knew that the suspects were close associates of Gary Hutch. The fuse had been lit for the most violent gang war in Irish history.

There has been considerable speculation and confusion around what happened next in the explosive story which inevitably followed.

The underworld is a place of smoke and mirrors where nothing is ever quite what it seems. Criminals use lies, dissemblance, treachery and obfuscation to distort and manipulate the facts as it suits them. Gangsters are accomplished black propagandists. Some sources claim that Gary Hutch fled to Amsterdam following the attack and that negotiations between the main players took place over several months. The following version of events came from sources close to the Monk and others with a close knowledge of what happened. The known facts also corroborate important aspects of this account.

Kinahan claimed to have evidence that the shooter was Patrick Hutch and that the attack was plotted by Gary and his father Patsy, in a bid to take over the cartel. This was denied by the Hutches. But Patrick Hutch added fuel to the suspicions when he suddenly left Spain the next day and flew back to Dublin. The cartel theory went that the conspirators planned to steal a case containing €2 million in cash from Kinahan's house and make it look like a robbery carried out by another gang. The alternative theory is that Gary Hutch organized the hit simply because he feared Daniel Kinahan was going to have him whacked first. It was, they said, a case of kill or be killed. The least likely version is that Patrick did it on his own volition. To the Monk, whatever the exact cause it was an act of supreme folly which would only lead to disaster. He told associates that Gary was involved in the plot because he was in fear for his life. Either way his nephew was now in an even more perilous situation.

When the shooting took place Gary Hutch was supposedly conked out in Kinahan's villa after a night of partying. He and Kinahan were awoken by the arrival of the ambulance that Moore had called on his phone. When they found out what had happened, Gary denied any knowledge of the attack. Daniel wasn't taking any chances and had him placed under house arrest with a number of cartel henchmen in Marbella while he went about investigating and seeking retribution. In the hours after the shooting there was a flurry of activity as contact was made with the Hutch family, including Eddie and Patsy Hutch. A garda who was close to the investigation of the feud described the atmosphere in the gang:

> That Sunday there was suddenly a lot of activity amongst the gang members in the city centre and it was clear that something serious was up. When news of the Moore shooting broke, we realized what the commotion was about and then word filtered back that he wasn't the real target. The attack on Daniel really shocked the gang who were, you have to remember, all one big unit at the time. At this stage the lads who would soon be killing each other were still friends. Over the next several days you could see that they were on tenterhooks and there were a lot of people coming over and back from Spain. Our liaison officers were working with the Spanish police but it was very difficult to get accurate intelligence because the gang was being very tight.

The Hutches were given an ultimatum from Daniel – unless Patrick Hutch voluntarily returned to Spain for a punishment shooting his brother Gary would be seriously harmed or killed. At first the Hutches point blank denied involvement in any conspiracy and refused to give Patrick up. After a number of exchanges Kinahan Senior and his son said they would only negotiate with Gerry who, despite his retirement and removal to Lanzarote, they saw as the patriarch and leader of the family. They gave the Hutches a week to sort the situation out or Gary was going to be killed.

The truth was that the Kinahans were afraid of the Monk and were all too aware of his potential as a deadly foe. If Gary wasn't from the equivalent of Dublin gangland royalty, there would be no need for such tedious niceties. Within 24 hours of the shooting his bullet-riddled body would have been dumped on a Marbella street or ended up beside Christy Gilroy in an unmarked grave in the sunburned hills. His accomplices would have suffered the same fate in Dublin. And everyone would have moved on. Hutch's birthright, however, made things different.

The incident posed another dilemma for Christy Kinahan and his son. The Hutches and their network of associates, including proven killers, were an integral component of the organization in Ireland. Killing Gary Hutch would lead to a bitter internal split and an inevitable power struggle that would implode the cartel. Perhaps it was because of Hutch's standing in the gang that the Kinahans did not simply have Gary kneecapped instead of his younger sibling. They needed a clear route out of the crisis – but it had to be a course that reaffirmed their authority.

When word of the incident broke Gary Finnegan's cousin Barry and another member of the Hutch gang, James 'Mago' Gately, took the next available flight to Malaga to participate in the investigation. Gerry Hutch was in Lanzarote when he got a call from Patsy informing him of the Kinahans' ultimatum and their condition that they would only speak to the Monk in a face-to-face meeting. It was the last thing he needed. However, his rule of steering clear of trouble unless it came looking for him had always excluded family problems. The Monk later told a friend:

> I was doing my own thing and was perfectly happy. I didn't want to be involved in this. I was dragged into this because they [Kinahans] would only deal with me. They saw me as the leader of the family; I am not the leader of anything. But this is my family and I was asked to get involved. I couldn't leave my nephew hanging like that – I had to do something.

With the clock ticking, sources said Gerry Hutch took a flight to Malaga Airport where he had arranged to meet Daniel Kinahan. Hutch reckoned the safest place for a sit-down was in the secure environment of the airport. He had also spoken directly with the Dapper Don. Hutch first met an associate of Daniel's before the de facto leader of the cartel appeared and sat down to talk. Hutch did not try to defend the stupidity of his family members and made it clear that the shooting had nothing to do with him. But he also didn't want anything to happen to his nephew. Kinahan said that Gary would not be harmed but only on certain conditions.

Patrick Hutch, as a punishment, was to volunteer for the same kind of injuries that had been inflicted on Jamie Moore. He was to be shot once in each leg. After that Gary Hutch would be released and would no longer have any involvement with the cartel. Whatever money he was owed, would be returned but out of that €200,000 was to be paid in compensation to cover Jamie Moore's medical expenses. The Monk left to discuss the proposal with his family. In the meantime Gary Hutch remained under house arrest. One can only speculate as to the type of conversations that took place within the secret confines of the family when Gerry relayed the Kinahans' ransom demand. The Monk reckoned that the shooting had been reckless and wrong-headed and now it had come down to the difference between life and death. Patrick Hutch bravely agreed to take his punishment in the interests of his brother's safety. Of course the Kinahans believed that the fact that he agreed to such a primitive, brutal punishment was tantamount to an admission of guilt – no innocent man would volunteer to be maimed. But if no one died, then the two sides could retreat from the precipice.

The Monk contacted the Kinahans to say that his family agreed to the terms. As far as he was concerned his family had made a solemn, inviolate pact with Daniel Kinahan which they would not break. As long as Gary was spared, there would be no retaliatory action and no more violence. Instead, there would be peace between the two families.

Around 7 p.m. on the evening of Friday, 15 August Patrick Hutch and his cousin Derek Coakley Hutch went to an arranged meeting at a lock-up in Drumcondra. Coakley Hutch was one of Derek Senior's two sons. Daniel Kinahan had flown back to Dublin to personally administer the punishment and went with two henchmen to meet the Hutches. The crime boss produced a handgun and shot the would-be assassin in each leg. According to sources, Kinahan aimed to hit bone in each leg to cause maximum damage without inflicting a fatal wound. Seconds later the trio fled the scene. Twenty-two-year-old Patrick Hutch was bleeding and semi-conscious as his cousin bundled him into a car and drove at high speed to the nearby Mater Hospital. The car crashed into bollards outside it and Coakley Hutch jumped out shouting for help from passers-by.

Patrick Hutch underwent emergency surgery for shattered bones but suffered no lasting physical damage. The victims of shootings or stabbings are automatically reported by the hospital authorities. When gardaí visited Hutch he refused to make a complaint about the attack and didn't offer an explanation as to how he came by the gunshot wounds. He was subsequently arrested for questioning on the grounds that he had information relating to the unlawful discharge of a firearm. Patrick remained silent. The law of the land had no role to play in the mob's alternative system of justice.

Immediately after the shooting of his brother Gary Hutch was released in Spain and banished from the Kinahan cartel. According to the source, the Monk then warned his impetuous nephew to 'have manners, keep yer head down and no more fuckin' around'. The Hutches said the compensation was paid while the Kinahans have claimed that it was never received. Garda intelligence sources agree with the Hutch contention.

Following his fortunate escape Gary Hutch fled to Amsterdam where he had spent a lot of his time over the previous few years. He teamed up with his cousin Gareth Hutch, a son of John, Gerry Hutch's oldest brother. Gareth, who was of an age with Gary, had been hiding out in Holland after skipping bail in Ireland two years earlier after being charged in connection with the attempted armed robbery of a Securicor van carrying €1 million in May 2009. He'd organized the raid along with his cousin – Gary's younger brother, Derek 'Del Boy' Hutch – just three months after Gary was involved in the €7.6 million heist from the Bank of Ireland.

During the raid in Lucan, west Dublin, gang member Gareth Molloy had been s shot dead when he pointed his gun at armed gardaí who had confronted the gang. A second raider, Keith Murtagh, was also injured in the gunfire. In July 2012 Del Boy Hutch was sentenced to sixteen years for his role in the crime while in 2010 his close friend Murtagh had received ten years. Del Boy was also serving sentences for possession of a firearm and manslaughter. He was, in the words of the Monk, a 'bleedin' head case… a disaster area'. The other two men arrested in the failed robbery were acquitted.

In Holland Gareth Hutch had become involved in the cartel's operations. With his cousin by his side Gary felt more secure in Amsterdam. But the hiatus wasn't to last long. On 12 September 2014, a month after the shooting of Jamie Moore, Dutch police arrested Gareth Hutch on foot of a European Arrest Warrant. A fortnight later he was extradited to Dublin where he was remanded in custody pending his trial. He was subsequently acquitted of the charge by a jury. In the meantime Gary Hutch watched developments elsewhere with a growing sense of dread. The Kinahans had been tying up loose ends.

The week before the arrest of Gareth Hutch, Daniel Kinahan had ordered the murder of one of his most feared enforcers and debt collectors, Gerard 'Hatchet' Kavanagh. On 6 September Kavanagh was sitting outside an Irish pub in Elviria near Marbella where Kinahan had asked him to meet with someone who owed money to the cartel. Two gunmen suddenly appeared and shot Hatchet up to fifteen times, including several times in the head. It was the kind of brutal hit worthy of Colombian *sicarios*.

The motive for the murder was unclear but one theory pursued by investigators was that Kavanagh had been suspected of siphoning off cash from his debt collection duties. Another theory that could not be ruled out was that the assassination was connected in some way to the failed attempt on Kinahan's life. A Kavanagh was more expendable than a Hutch. The murder of 'Hatchet' provided an illustration of how the sociopathic Daniel compartmentalized his life: erecting Chinese walls between his lawful and unlawful pursuits. At the same time Kavanagh's son Jamie, a professional boxer, was signed up with MGM and was being promoted by Kinahan. Daniel somehow managed to convince the grieving boxer that he'd had nothing to do with his dad's tragic demise.

Like his con man father, Daniel was adept at setting up false trails to divert the focus from his own malfeasance. He spread a rumour that his enforcer had stepped on the toes of notorious Eastern European criminals. This was a delaying tactic, as the man who found inspiration in the fictional Michael Corleone still had unfinished business with the Kavanagh family. They were to suffer even more heartache when Kinahan had Hatchet's younger brother Paul executed in Dublin six months later. Paul Kavanagh was gunned down on 26 March 2015 as he got into a car outside his home in Drumcondra. He too had become a loose end after falling under suspicion of skimming the cartel's money. The prime suspects were two of Kinahan's deadliest hit men who would go on to play a major role in the savagery that followed the Regency Hotel attack. Kinahan and his henchmen were conspicuous by their absence at both funerals.

In the wake of the Moore shooting and his banishment Gary Hutch found himself being isolated and frozen out by some of his former associates and supposed friends, who had aligned with Daniel. It wasn't really surprising. No matter how it was rationalized, the plot to kill Kinahan had been an act of treachery. In his comments to associates and friends the Monk had said as much. Gradually, as more time passed, sides were beginning to emerge. Like a politician jockeying for position for a party leadership heave, Kinahan compiled a list of those whose loyalty he could depend on. Gary Hutch also had a strong support base of family and loyal associates from the north inner city, including his Uncle Gerry.

In the wary mind of a gangster the shooting plot lent credence to the suspicion that Gary Hutch might also be a rat and therefore have something to cover up. Gerry Hutch warned his nephew to keep his head down and steer clear of trouble. The murder of the Kavanagh brothers was a timely reminder of what Kinahan was capable of. But Gary Hutch was either too arrogant or foolish, or both, to heed the warnings. While he may have been still nervous, Gary viewed the presence of his uncle in the equation as a protective blanket and he continued drug trafficking as a sole trader waiting for things to settle down. But life was not that simple in a deceitful world.

By the summer of 2015 Gary Hutch felt confident enough about his situation to return to the Costa del Sol. He even started training again in Kinahan's gym. It seemed for a while that he was being gradually brought back into the fold. But, like his father, Daniel Kinahan was not the type to easily forgive or forget. He'd inherited Christy's feral instinct for double-crossing associates and reneging on deals whenever the need arose. At some stage he decided to have Gary murdered regardless of any covenant between the Kinahans and the Monk. The narcissistic boxing enthusiast was merely biding his time before landing the fatal knockout punch.

Gary was welcomed back by his fellow lieutenant Freddie Thompson and by James Quinn, another one of Kinahan's enforcers. Quinn, who was a nephew of veteran gangster Martin 'the Viper' Foley, was a cold-blooded killer suspected of being one of the gunmen in the murder of 'Hatchet' Kavanagh. The Spanish police surveillance operation had described the trio as key members of the gang who were also drinking buddies. The Hutch side believe Gary was deliberately lulled into a false sense of security which explains why he moved back to live in the area. He was unaware that in the background a double murder plot was being hatched – one that would spark a war.

On the morning of 24 September 2015 Gary Hutch left his apartment in the Angel de Miraflores complex in Estepona and walked to his car in an adjoining garage. As he did so a gunman emerged from the shadows, aiming a weapon at him. When it jammed Hutch ran for his life, racing around a nearby swimming pool towards a back gate where he could exit the complex. He was followed by the killer who continued firing shots in his direction.

When he found the gate locked, Hutch turned to find that the gunman had blocked him in. He was shot twice in the back and toppled over. As he lay on the ground reportedly pleading, 'No, no,' the assassin finished him off with two more shots to the head. It later transpired that Gary's 'friend' James Quinn had been part of the assassination team when police found his DNA in the killer's partially burned-out getaway car. At his subsequent trial in Malaga the prosecutors accused Quinn of being the gunman. He was convicted of murder and sentenced to twenty-two years by a Spanish court. Daniel's lieutenant, Fat Freddie Thompson, was also suspected of being involved.

Around the same time that Gary Hutch was meeting his gruesome end, another hit team was lying in wait for his father Patsy in Dublin. Kinahan had dispatched the same hit team he'd used to kill Paul Kavanagh six months earlier. The plan was the gunmen would get Patsy when he arrived to collect his grandson from St Vincent's National School in Glasnevin which was part of his regular routine. Kinahan wanted to take out the two important players in the family at the same time. He would deal with the Monk later. The proposed hit was a classic example of the mob's contempt for innocent civilians. It mattered little to Kinahan if Hutch was executed in front of women and children, including his grandchild. The hit team backed off when Hutch didn't show and another family member collected the child. Daniel's plan backfired because Patsy had just received the news of his son's death.

The spectacular double-cross came as a shattering blow to the close-knit Hutch family, especially his parents and siblings. The Monk was also devastated by his nephew's death and horrified by the Kinahans' cold-blooded treachery. Hutch had expected them to honour the agreement, as he had done. Another detective who knew Gerry Hutch for several years explained: 'Even though there is little doubt that he is a robber and a killer who has caused his fair share of heartache and fear, he is nevertheless a trustworthy criminal which may be hard for ordinary decent civilians to understand. When he made an agreement he stuck to it.'

The moment he received the news of his nephew's death and the implied betrayal Hutch must have realized that it was about to drastically alter the course of his life – and it meant the forced end to his retirement. A source close to the family believes Daniel Kinahan's real motive for the murder was to silence Gary Hutch: 'He knew all the information about Mink Kok and the other killings and rip-offs that the Kinahans had done. Daniel and the father couldn't take a chance on Gary spilling the beans to the people he had ripped-off and that is the reason why Daniel reneged on his deal with Gerard.'

The murder was a seismic development in gangland – it meant war between the two former allies. Criminals with the name Hutch were considered untouchable. The Monk and his family could not allow this grievous attack to go unavenged. If he did nothing, the Kinahans would hit the family again to ensure they no longer posed a threat. Gerry had an army of his own to call on with plenty of weapons and experienced personnel who were more than capable of using them.

The head of the clan cautioned Gary's hot-headed friends and associates against doing anything rash. Precipitative action led to failure and a long stint in a prison cell. Gerry Hutch was not a man given to impetuosity, even in the midst of the grief and intense anger he was experiencing. Like everything else he did in life, any retaliation would be carefully and meticulously planned out.

On 6 October 2015 Gary Hutch's funeral took place at Our Lady of Lourdes Church on Sean McDermott Street, in the heart of the old inner-city neighbourhood that has been home to his family for generations. Hundreds turned out to pay their last respects as family and friends carried the coffin the short distance from the Hutch family home on Champion's Avenue. The last time the clan had gathered together was for Gerry's fiftieth birthday which already seemed like a lifetime ago.

In the highly charged atmosphere the Monk opted to remain in the background and was nowhere to be seen. Making an emotional plea to the congregation, Gary's mother Kay laid down a marker that there was to be no revenge. The heartbroken mother said the pain she had endured at losing her son was unbearable and she would not wish it on others: 'We do not want retaliation. We don't wish our pain on any other family. I let God be our judge.'

Del Boy Hutch, Gary's thirty-year-old brother, was also absent. The prison authorities, in consultation with the police, decided that, even under close guard, his presence at the funeral posed a major security risk. Instead he sent a letter which was read out by a young relative. Del Boy said he would cherish the memories of growing up together '…me blaming you and you blaming me and ma killing the two of us'. Two weeks later the Kinahans sent a message to Del Boy but it wasn't contained in a letter.

The word had been sent through Mountjoy Prison that a bounty existed for anyone who would stab and seriously injure Del Boy. Kinahan was worried about the influence Hutch had on the outside and wanted to neutralize him. The first attack took place when two men armed with improvised knives jumped on him in the exercise yard. Hutch received a number of slash wounds before prison staff rescued him. A few months later there was a second attempt but this time he was saved by another inmate. After that Del Boy was moved to a segregated wing for his own protection.

In another incident Daniel Kinahan's violent sidekick Kevin Lynch, who was back in Dublin on a visit, smashed up Patsy Hutch's car outside his home. The attack was never reported.

On 7 November Gary Hutch's gang decided to strike back. Daniel Kinahan and several members of the cartel were in town for an MGM sponsored event which was due to be held in the National Stadium the following day. That night the mob was partying in the Red Cow Moran Hotel in west Dublin. As members of the gang stood outside smoking, a car drew up with two men inside. One of them pointed a firearm at gang member Liam Roe, but the weapon jammed. Roe ran inside to warn the rest of the group and they scattered in all directions.

The Kinahan crew suspected that the botched attack was the work of convicted drug dealers Darren Kearns and Daithi Douglas, both of whom were closely linked to Gary Hutch's drug gang. Douglas, a former IRA member, was also an old associate of the Monk.

Retribution for the botched hit came quickly from the Kinahan side. The following day Douglas was shot three times close to his home in Cabra, north-west Dublin. Although seriously injured, he survived the attack.

On 30 December the Kinahan mob struck again, this time with a greater degree of success. Darren Kearns was shot several times by a lone gunman as he left a Chinese restaurant with his wife. Gardaí later said they were satisfied Kearns had not been involved in the incident at the Red Cow Moran Hotel.

As the clock ticked down on the final 24 hours of 2015 Daniel Kinahan had more business to get out of the way. He wanted to start the New Year with one less reason to look over his shoulder. By the time the police were arriving at the scene of the latest gangland murder in Dublin, two more contract killers were in Lanzarote making final preparations to cross another gangland Rubicon. Their mission was to assassinate Gerry Hutch.

CHAPTER NINETEEN

WAR

The Monk spent Christmas 2015 with his family at home in Dublin as he pondered his next move. The year now drawing to a close had thrown his future plans into disarray. In the months since Gary's murder Daniel Kinahan had made overtures to Gerry Hutch requesting a parley and further face-to-face meetings but he had ignored all approaches. It would be a pointless exercise as they had broken a sacrosanct agreement. He believed that the requests for a sit-down were a ruse to set him up. A subsequent statement issued on his family's behalf said: 'We shook hands and agreed to walk away. Gary was then murdered for no reason. You cannot trust these people.' The Monk wasn't wrong.

Hutch's silence had rattled the Kinahans who knew he was a deadly enemy. The cartel had decided that the only way to neutralize the threat posed by the Hutch gang was to eliminate the Monk. By cutting the head off the dragon in a surprise attack the Kinahans predicted that the gang would be rendered a spent force in one fell swoop. With Gerry out of the picture the Hutches would no longer have any clout and could be quickly vanquished. For good measure, they also wanted to kill Patsy because Daniel blamed him for the Moore shooting. After that, the Kinahan cartel would be the undisputed and untouchable overlords of organized crime in Ireland.

On 28 December 2015 Hutch and his wife flew from Dublin to Lanzarote to spend the New Year at their villa in Puerto del Carmen. On the same day a man called Eamon Cumberton, from Dublin's north inner city, also arrived on a flight from Ireland with his partner and children. He was booked to stay for a week. Cumberton's sidekick had arrived with his girlfriend the previous day. A former cage fighter, Cumberton and his associate were members of the INLA and two of Daniel Kinahan's top *sicarios*.

Both men were ruthless experienced assassins. They had carried out numerous attacks for the cartel including the assassination of Paul Kavanagh nine months earlier. They had also been sent to murder Patsy Hutch on the same day that his son was whacked in Spain. The killers had no hesitation in accepting the lucrative bounty on the Monk's head – a development that would have been inconceivable a year earlier.

The murder plan was already in motion when they arrived. The weapons for the job had been transported to the island by associates of the cartel. Another gang member had been sent to act as a getaway driver and to dispose of the guns. They were there to kill the Monk and it was to be a typical gangland hit. They planned to shoot Hutch when he least expected it: while celebrating the New Year in his favourite pub, Mulligan's. It was a place where Gerry Hutch felt secure and they intended to catch him off-guard.

Over the next few days the assassins reconnoitered the pub, situated just off the main strip near the seafront. Once they had accomplished the mission and made their indelible mark on Irish gangland history, they planned to lie low for a few days before returning to Dublin with a tan and a big pay day.

Mulligan's was packed with merrymakers when Gerry Hutch and his wife arrived on New Year's Eve. The crowd was partying through the last remaining hours of what had been a stressful year for the godfather and his family. The Monk greeted staff and customers as he guided his spouse to a seat along a back wall. Being ever vigilant he wanted to be able to see everyone coming through the front entrance, at the top of stairs leading down from the street.

Hutch may have appeared calm but his survival instincts were on overdrive. Although he felt relatively safe the Monk was aware of the killing of Darren Kearns in Dublin the previous night. While gardaí had not yet worked out a definitive motive for the hit, Hutch's bush telegraph had already revealed that it was more than likely connected to the escalating feud and the shooting of his friend Daithi Douglas.

The Monk was scanning the crowd when he noticed two guys who had just entered and were walking to the bar. His body tensed when he recognized Cumberton who he knew by sight and reputation. He had grown up in Hutch's old neighbourhood and was a friend of his nephews. Hutch knew he was a cartel member and one of Daniel Kinahan's killers. Hutch also recognized the sidekick.

According to sources close to the godfather, Hutch's worst suspicions were confirmed when he glimpsed one of the men taking a furtive look in his direction. In that instant he knew they were there to kill him. Satisfied that they had eyes on the target, Kinahan's hit team promptly left the pub to get their guns. For Daniel Kinahan the Monk's death would mean starting the year with a clean slate.

As soon as the hit team disappeared Hutch grabbed his wife and quickly, but with no fuss, slipped out a back door and got away.

A few minutes later the killers returned wearing balaclavas and made straight for the spot where Hutch had been sitting a minute earlier. If Hutch and his wife hadn't already left, it would have been impossible for them to escape. Cumberton and his accomplice could be seen clutching the automatic weapons beneath their jackets. Some of the revellers thought it was a prank at first. The masked men appeared confused that their intended victim had suddenly vanished. They scanned the crowd before dashing back to the street.

Bar staff called the police, but the would-be assassins had vanished by the time they arrived. A short while later Hutch learned of his close call. His well-honed street instincts had saved his life and most likely his wife's too as she would have been in the clear line of fire.

The following day, when he was happy that the coast was clear, Hutch returned to view the pub's CCTV footage to see what had actually happened. He was also given access to the security footage from adjoining premises.

It wasn't difficult to identify the would-be assassins. The gunmen were wearing identical clothing to those worn by Cumberton and his accomplice. It was very sloppy planning. Had the hit men succeeded in getting their mark there would have been enough evidence with which to charge them.

The duo contacted Kinahan with the bad news that their target had evaded them. This was the worst news possible for the murderous godfather. If Hutch had been wavering about becoming fully involved in a feud the failed attack would help him make up his mind. The Monk would also tighten up his personal security and not leave himself open so easily in the future. Travel records show that the killers left Lanzarote empty-handed on 5 January. Hutch had no intention of sharing the fruits of his detective work with the

Spanish force. There was only one system of justice to prosecute his retribution – the gangland law of meeting fire with fire.

As the Monk viewed the CCTV images it must have come as an immense shock for him to actually see how close he came to death. The fact that his wife had also been put at serious risk was a step too far and a breach of his rules. Any lingering doubts he may have had about meeting the Kinahans or teaching them a lesson were erased in that moment. The genie was out of the bottle – he knew the cartel would keep coming until his eyes were permanently closed.

One of his associates later confirmed this: 'For Gerard there was no going back. He was in a corner and to protect himself and his family it was a case of kill or be killed. His old way of doing things wouldn't help him this time. He had a big crew of very able lads around who were more than willing to back him up.' Hutch lost no time in plotting his revenge.

Within days, word of the botched assassination attempt on Ireland's best-known crime boss filtered back to the media in Dublin where it was big news. At the same time gardaí were watching the unfolding events with an increasing sense of alarm. The Dublin underworld was a tinder box. But there was a paucity of intelligence coming from either of the two sides now clearly emerging from the split in the cartel. Everyone close to gangland – cops, criminals and crime reporters – agreed that there was major trouble on the horizon.

Gerry Hutch returned to Ireland on 14 January with a plan for a spectacular counterstrike against his enemies. To avoid attracting attention, he flew via Ireland West Airport in Knock, County Mayo. The cartel had spies everywhere and it was feasible that it could have spotters in Dublin to watch passengers arriving on flights from Lanzarote. The Monk was collected by a member of his family and driven back to Dublin where he kept a low profile.

A week later, on 21 January, Gerry Hutch travelled alone on a flight from Dublin to Brussels. He then hired a car and two days later caught a flight from Eindhoven in the Netherlands to the Polish city of Kraków. Flight records also show that Patsy Hutch, his son Patrick and two other members of the Hutch gang flew from Dublin to Kraków on 23 January. Gardaí believe that the gang then spent the next two days training in the use of firearms, including AK-47s, at one of Kraków's many shooting academies.

Since the noughties Irish drug gangs had been travelling abroad for weapons training at rifle clubs in Europe and the USA to brush up on their marksmanship. The training, combined with the ready availability of high-quality weapons, such as the Glock automatic which was normally used by Special Forces, had resulted in an exponential rise in accuracy – and deaths. Several members of the cartel, including Gary Hutch, had previously posted pictures of themselves brandishing military assault rifles on such trips.

On 25 January the gang members left Kraków and flew back to Dublin. Gerry Hutch returned by the same circuitous route he had taken earlier, flying back to Eindhoven, four days later returning the hire car and then flying from Brussels to Dublin. Gardaí believe the plans for the Regency Hotel attack were finalized during this period.

In typically audacious fashion Gerry Hutch and his gang had hatched one of the most dramatic assassination attempts ever attempted by a criminal gang. The target was to be the weigh-in for an upcoming WBO Lightweight title fight, organized by Daniel Kinahan and due to be held in the Drumcondra Regency Hotel on 5 February 2016. It was the only opportunity the Monk had identified where he could catch the boss and his minions together in one place, at the one time. He reasoned that the weigh-in would be the last place they would expect to be hit. The plan was to wipe out Daniel Kinahan and as many of his lieutenants as possible in one spectacular act of terrorism. The hotel was on Hutch home turf which was a major advantage for getting in and out quickly. If they pulled it off it would be the Irish equivalent of Al Capone's St Valentine's Day massacre.

The big fight between Jamie Kavanagh – whose father and uncle had been murdered on his manager Daniel's orders – and Antonio Jao Bento was scheduled to take place the following night at the National Stadium. The 'Clash of the Clans' was between Daniel's MGM gym and UK boxing promoter Frank Warren. It was another important stepping-stone for the gang leader's elevation through the ranks of the sport. But Kinahan was concerned that the widely publicized boxing tournament might present the Hutches with an irresistible opportunity to hit back and had already tried to make another approach to his enemies before the fight.

The divisions in the cartel following Gary Hutch's murder were broadly based on family blood and loyalty. The complex tapestry of relationships was unravelling, with Fat Freddie Thompson and the Byrne gang in Crumlin remaining staunch cartel acolytes. A significant number of Gary Hutch's fellow gang members from the north inner city had also decided to throw their lot in with Kinahan. Some of them had already proven their fealty by taking part in the murder of their former friend six months earlier. Other members of the same north inner-city gang, including a number of feared hit men, had sided with the Hutches.

One example of the emerging split between the once indistinguishable sides concerned a business partnership between James 'Mago' Gately and Barry Finnegan. The partnership was dissolved shortly after the Hutch murder. Gately stayed with the Hutches while the Finnegans remained firmly in the cartel. Like his cousin Gary, and indeed Gately, Barry Finnegan had a reputation as a violent and dangerous thug. He had also been jailed in the past for raping a fourteen-year-old girl. A Hutch associate told this writer:

> Gerard and his brothers had a good idea who was with them or against them based on who turned up at Gary's funeral. By staying away the other guys were expressing their allegiance to Daniel. Gerard, Eddie and Patsy were surprised at some of the people who sided with the Kinahans especially the likes of Gary Finnegan and Barry who had been very close to Gary and the lads. Gary Finnegan was Bouncer's [Christopher Hutch] best friend growing up and sure Eddie [Hutch] treated Finnegan like one of his own sons. Talk about treachery and betrayal? It says a lot about the people you're talking about.

Daniel had tested the old bonds of friendship when he dispatched the Finnegans to talk with Eddie Hutch two weeks before the boxing tournament was due to take place. Gerry's older brother had recently returned from a week in Lanzarote with some of his siblings. The two thugs called to Eddie around 8 p.m. on a Monday night and stood talking with him at the door. The meeting was recorded on CCTV cameras in the area. According to sources close to the Hutch family Gary first reminisced about his former best friend Bouncer who'd died from a drug overdose almost thirteen years earlier.

Then Finnegan moved on to the real purpose of the visit, what he called the 'hassle' over Gary's death and the attempt on the Monk's life. The gang didn't deny the killing but strenuously rejected any involvement in the incident in Lanzarote. The bottom line was that Christy Kinahan Senior and Daniel wanted Gerry to talk to them so they could iron out a lasting solution to avoid any more shooting. They said they didn't want any more incidents like the one at the Red Cow Moran Hotel. The Finnegans put Eddie on the phone to talk separately with Christy and Daniel. Hutch claimed that John

Cunningham had also called him to appeal for calm. Eddie later recounted the substance of the visit to a friend:

> Eddie said that Christy was playing the old pals game with the line, 'Look, we go back a long way, can we not sort this out?' sorta bullshit. Daniel said that he didn't want any bother at the boxing and was prepared to sit down and talk. Gary Finnegan said to Eddie: 'The only people who will make out of this are the guards… it's in all our interests to sort this out.' Adopting the position of a mere observer, he suggested that if a deal wasn't done there could be an escalation in violence and members of the Hutch family would be harmed. He said no one wanted that. Remember, this was coming from a lad Eddie treated like a son. Everyone who fell in with the Kinahans were infected by his poison, that's why we call him [Daniel] 'cancer'.

It is understood that the discussion lasted about 30 minutes. As the deadly Finnegan cousins left, Eddie said he would talk to Gerry and come back to them with a reply. But Eddie knew what the answer would be. He also had to be fully aware of the surprise attack being planned. At the same time as the approach was being made by the cartel minions, Gerry Hutch and other members of the gang were honing their shooting skills on the firing range in Poland.

A few days later Eddie called to Finnegan in Hardwicke Street with a message from his younger sibling. The Monk was standing by his position: the Kinahans had reneged on their agreement and tried to kill him – he wouldn't talk to people he couldn't trust. Daniel's diplomatic mission had failed.

At least fifteen people were involved in the preparations for the Regency Hotel attack which would be as elaborate an operation as any of Hutch's armed robberies. The main attack team, consisting of three men dressed in garda ERU-style SWAT uniforms, would be armed with AK-47s which were borrowed from their contacts in one of the dissident republican gangs styling itself the 'new' IRA.

The weapons were organized through IRA member Michael Barr from Strabane, County Tyrone. He worked as a barman in the Sunset House pub in Ballybough in the Hutch heartland. Barr's close friend and fellow terrorist from Tyrone, Kevin Murray, had agreed to be one of the five gunmen taking part in the attack. Murray and another gang member were to be the second team. His accomplice would dress as a woman and they'd pose as a couple. In his early years Gerry Hutch had often disguised himself in drag during armed hold-ups – old habits die hard.

Murray was photographed immediately after the attack and was dubbed 'Flat Cap' because of the headgear he was wearing. Patrick Hutch was subsequently accused of being the shooter in drag and was charged with the murder of David Byrne.

Gardaí also believe that the authentic-looking combat uniforms, 'garda' vests and Kevlar helmets worn by the hit team were obtained through a contact working in the props department of a movie production company. A van was stolen and parked offside to transport the squad for its lethal mission.

At the same time, Daniel Kinahan returned to Dublin to personally intervene with the Hutch family. The cartel filled the communications deficit by making fresh death threats and demanding more money from the Hutches. In the last week of January Daniel Kinahan called to Eddie Hutch's house at Poplar Row. The incident was recorded on CCTV. Eddie could be seen talking to Daniel Kinahan from an upstairs window. Kinahan was animated and appeared to be in a rage. The cartel boss was shouting abuse and making threats to the Monk's brother.

According to the Hutch family Kinahan demanded the payment of another €200,000 and said that if it wasn't paid family members would be shot and forced to leave their homes. He also said it could be sorted if Gerry agreed to a sit-down. As far as the Monk was concerned any such meeting would just be a ruse to lure him into the open and be a prelude to another attempt on his life. After a few minutes the CCTV showed Kinahan storming off, still fuming with rage. But by then the die had been well and truly cast. An unbilled alternative 'Clash of the Clans' was on the cards which would drastically alter the histories of two criminal families.

As Kinahan and his MGM staff made final preparations for the weigh-in and the big fight, the Monk and his mob were doing likewise. On Thursday, 4 February, the night before the event, Kevin Murray checked into the Regency Hotel under an assumed name. He was completely unknown to the cartel membership and could reconnoitre the hotel without raising suspicion. Flat Cap's room was booked using a credit card in the name of the wife of former Sinn Féin city councillor Jonathan Dowdall, a close friend of the Monk.

The thirty-six-year-old from the Navan Road in central Dublin had been a rising star in Sinn Féin and was elected to Dublin City Council in 2014. But just over a year later he stood down from his seat and resigned from the party amid claims that he had been the victim of bullying and a smear campaign. Dowdall had been a close constituency colleague and adviser to the party's then deputy leader Mary Lou McDonald. He was trusted enough by the Monk to be recruited as one of the six drivers selected to get the killers safely away after the hit went down.

Weather-wise Friday, 5 February was a perfect day for the attack. It was dark, miserable and cold as Dublin was battered by high winds and torrential rain. In the early afternoon Hutch's assault team rendezvoused in Buckingham Village, the development where he had first laundered some of his ill-gotten gains. The meeting place was not covered by CCTV cameras or prying eyes. In a bizarre twist, Kevin Murray initially got lost making his way in from the Regency as he tried to find the gang's meeting point. A member of the gang was sent down the street to meet him.

Apart from Flat Cap and his 'female' companion, gardaí believe that the three men in police uniforms and the driver were an even mix between Hutch's relations and Gary's former associates. It was very much a family affair.

The silver van left Buckingham Street around 2 p.m. with the six-man team on board – five gunmen and the driver. Around the same time a convoy of six cars drove into the grounds of St Vincent's GAA grounds a short distance from the hotel. Eddie Hutch was one of the getaway drivers. He was using a car he'd borrowed from another nephew, Jonathan Hutch – Gareth's brother. The GAA grounds was familiar territory for the Monk as it was the same location where he'd abandoned the security van following the Marino Mart robbery three decades earlier. Gerry Hutch was also there to ensure everything ran to plan.

The gang had planted a number of spotters to watch for the arrival of the cartel members in the Regency Suite where the weigh-in was taking place. The function room was packed with a crowd of over 200 people, including boxers, trainers, managers and members of the public. It included several children from boxing clubs around the country.

As the weigh-in commenced at 2.20 p.m. the silver van drove up and parked close to the hotel's service entrance. Eight minutes later Flat Cap and his partner got out and entered the hotel through a laundry room door.

Inside they asked a member of staff for directions to the Regency Suite. As the worker gave the 'couple' directions he noticed that the woman was 'actually a man with a Dublin accent'.

At 2.29 p.m. the murder van drove through a security gate leading to the front of the hotel. The gang used a fob to open the barrier. It was driven up to the main entrance and the three 'gardaí' jumped out, brandishing assault rifles. They ran into the hotel lobby firing shots in the air to create panic and confusion.

Seconds earlier the 'couple' had entered the function room, just as boxer Gerry Sweeney was having his weigh-in completed. One eyewitness later recalled noticing a man and a woman linking arms who 'seemed out of place'. The woman he said was 'bockety on her legs and unsteady on her feet'. As they passed, he could see that the person in the wig was a man dressed as a woman. As someone shouted, 'Gun, gun!' he saw the pair pointing handguns over the crowd and a number of shots rang out. People began diving for cover and scrambled to get out of the room as panic spread.

At the same time the deafening blast of the AK-47 rifles could be heard coming from the hotel lobby. The plan was to create a trap for Daniel Kinahan and his associates so that they ran directly into the fake ERU team as they fled the shooters in the function room. The same eyewitness recalled a man shouting, 'It's okay, the ERU is here,' and feeling relieved that the gardaí had arrived so quickly. Within seconds the 'ERU' had shot dead cartel member David Byrne and injured two of his associates, Sean McGovern and Aaron Bolger.

But Daniel, Liam Byrne and the other top-tier gangsters escaped what would have been a massacre. They were bundled to safety by their minders through a rear entrance and were gone as the death squad frantically searched adjoining rooms and corridors. The hit man wearing the wig was heard shouting: 'He's not fuckin' here...I can't fuckin' find him.'

The horrific attack was over in less than five minutes. The hit team returned to the silver van and left the complex through the security gate. The gang drove towards the Charlemont Estate in north Dublin where the van was abandoned and set alight.

At 2.40 p.m. the six men were seen on CCTV footage running down a lane towards the GAA grounds where they were taken away in the convoy of getaway cars, most of which were driven by taxi drivers.

As they exited the sports grounds the cars peeled off in different directions. In the follow-up investigation gardaí were able to identify and track each of the cars by examining CCTV footage from across the north inner city. By piecing together the footage detectives established that the Monk had returned to his home at the Paddocks in Clontarf shortly after the attack. A taxi driver dropped him off on a side street and he returned to his house via a back lane. He had often used the lane to get in and out of his house in the past while being watched by the police. When gardaí later called to check his alibi, Gerry Hutch said he had been in all afternoon. The hard drive for the CCTV cameras at Hutch's home had been wiped.

By the time the cops came asking awkward questions Hutch had realized that the most crucial 'job' in his career was a stunning failure. The attack revealed a fatal flaw in Hutch's normally meticulous planning. He had assumed that Kinahan and his associates would automatically run from the function room to the lobby. But he had overlooked the number of other exits from the building. Hutch's omission had inadvertently saved the lives of his hated enemies. Another problem he hadn't allowed for was the likely presence of the media who would want to get pictures of the notorious cartel membership.

Gardaí had no prior hints from their sources that there was going to be an incident at the weigh-in and it was not considered to be a security risk. No one thought to deploy a surveillance team, an armed unit or uniformed officers to police the potential target. The immensely embarrassing security lapse was exacerbated by the fact that journalists had captured dramatic images of the hit team, before and after the attack, which were flashed across the world. The reason for the oversight was due in no small degree to several years of swingeing budgetary cutbacks. The force's capacity to mount proactive investigations had been drastically diminished due to a lack of resources and the prioritizing of expenditure control over operational imperatives. A ban on recruitment and an incentivized early retirement package, motivated solely to save money, had depleted the strength and expertise of practically every unit in the country.

Over the following years, however, An Garda Síochána more than compensated for the initial shortcomings. They met the most intensive gang war ever seen in Ireland with an equally intensive counter-offensive which ultimately busted the once powerful international cartel. Their reaction more than justified Gary Finnegan's warning to Eddie Hutch that the only winners in a war would be the police. They were probably the only true words the dangerous thug ever uttered.

But before the gardaí gained the upper hand Daniel Kinahan and his army of psychopaths were responsible for an unprecedented cycle of violence which would claim another fifteen lives.

CHAPTER TWENTY

———

WINNERS AND LOSERS

In the weeks immediately following the Regency shooting the gardaí compiled a list of over seventy people in the extended Hutch family and gang who were seen as potential targets for revenge attacks. A massive security operation involving specialist armed units swamped the neighbourhoods where the protagonists lived in Crumlin and the south and north inner city. Checkpoints manned by armed and uniformed gardaí became commonplace.

However, it later emerged that despite the blind, murderous hate between the two gangs, there was an unspoken agreement that neither side would attack mothers, wives, daughters or children in the slaughter. It was to be the only concession to civility in the war that followed.

When Daniel Kinahan and Liam Byrne had recovered from the profound shock of the Regency attack, they held a meeting with their top lieutenants. The order was given to unleash chaos on the streets of Dublin in their quest for revenge. Huge sums of money were made available to hire a small army of hit men to kill anyone who was either related or close to the Hutch gang. Threats were being thrown around like confetti.

The Byrnes scrambled to find scapegoats and even tried to

intimidate a number of crime journalists who had to be given armed police protection. Like the Monk had often done in the past, the Byrnes and their thugs chose to blame the media for escalating the situation. The cartel also waged an insidious campaign against the people of the north inner city in a bid to turn them against Gerry Hutch and his clan. It was narco-terrorism on a scale not seen since the McCarthy/Dundons, Murder Inc., laid siege to Limerick City for over a decade. Through its network of spies and double agents, the cartel members quickly identified most of the people who had been involved in the Regency attack. Kinahan and Byrne drew up a hit list of people and passed it to the assassins as they went out to work. An inner-city cop who witnessed the unfolding mayhem recalled:

> The Kinahan and Byrne side deliberately set about terrorizing the people of the north inner-city. Junkies and dealers who owed money were being forced to set up their neighbours and friends or else get shot themselves. People were terrified of them in the inner city because literally anyone who knew the Hutches could be a target. You had people reporting the movements of friends and neighbours to the gang so they could be shot in the street. There are people who ended up in prison because they were coerced by the gang to get involved in murders and there are others who took their own lives over the pressure they were placed under which are not included in the overall death toll. After a while the Hutch family were treated like pariahs as people steered clear of them in case they were caught in the crossfire, which is understandable. It had a big effect on the younger children in the family because worried parents wouldn't allow their kids to play with them in case they were shot. The family began finding it difficult to even get tradesmen to do work on their houses such was the level of fear. It was all designed to isolate Gerry Hutch

and his family and turn them into prisoners in their own homes. The Hutch family were strictly home birds: the inner city was their home for generations and they never lived anywhere else. Apart from Gerry they had nowhere to run to when the murder spree kicked off. This was nothing more than terrorism of the worst kind. That is why the gardaí put in such a huge effort to loosen their [cartel's] grip on the community's throat.

On 8 February, the Monday after the attack, an attempt was made to muddy the waters when the Continuity IRA (CIRA) in Northern Ireland issued a statement claiming responsibility for David Byrne's murder. 'This will not be an isolated incident. Continuity IRA units have been authorized to carry out further operations. More drug dealers and criminals will be targeted,' warned a caller, claiming to be a spokesperson for the gang, in a statement to the BBC in Belfast.

But the claims were quickly rubbished as nothing more than an amateurish ruse orchestrated by the Monk and his republican accomplices in an attempt to divert blame and also scare the Kinahans and Byrnes into submission. It failed miserably as the gang members wasted no time claiming their first victim. A few hours after the call the backlash began when Eddie Hutch, one of the first names on the hit list, was gunned down in his home.

Daniel Kinahan ordered the assassination of 'Neddie' Hutch because he knew it would drive a stake through the heart of the family, especially the Monk who was very close to his older sibling. Eddie had always been Gerry's trusted confidante. A source close to the cartel later said that Eddie's murder was very personal to Daniel. That was why the cartel leader, who normally sat back and ordered murders, insisted on taking part in this one.

Around the time that the CIRA were claiming credit for the Regency attack, Daniel Kinahan was making final preparations with three associates in an apartment at Harte's Corner on the North Circular Road in Dublin city centre. Gardaí believe one of them was Gary Finnegan and the other two were also well known to gardaí as killers for hire. The four men left the apartment around 7 p.m. and just 45 minutes later a lone gunman shot Eddie Hutch five times in the living room of his home.

Gardaí have since established that Daniel Kinahan drove one of the getaway cars used by the hit team. According to a cartel source, who subsequently spoke to the Hutch family, the four men returned to the apartment at Harte's Corner in a panic a short time after the killing. The stolen BMW they had used in the attack wouldn't burn when they tried to set it alight. They had good reason to be concerned. Vital DNA evidence was later retrieved from the car. As a result Kinahan, Finnegan and their accomplices are wanted in connection with the murder. A source later confirmed to this writer:

> There is reliable information that Daniel Kinahan was hands-on involved in the murder of Eddie Hutch and drove a car used in the attack. He wanted to be involved because this to him was very personal – Eddie had been the go-between, so he was the first person he wanted to exact revenge on. Kinahan and the Finnegans are wanted for questioning about this crime.

Daniel Kinahan left Ireland for Spain shortly after the killing. He returned to Dublin again with his brother Christy Junior on 14 February, St Valentine's Day, for the funeral of David Byrne. They left again immediately afterwards and have not returned to Ireland since.

Finnegan also fled the country two days after the murder. At the time of writing he is believed to be living with the Kinahans in Dubai. The gang decamped to the UAE state in 2017 as a result of the intensive pressure from the gardaí and other police forces across Europe. Despite the intense heat, the desert bolt-hole was ideal as it has no extradition agreements with Ireland or other countries in the EU.

Meanwhile the Hutch family were left distraught by the death of their brother who was described as a genial gentleman and very popular in his community. A family member said: 'He was a lovely man, an innocent man who was the centre of the family and very close to his brothers and sisters and their children. He was a workaholic who always helped his neighbours out. Eddie wasn't involved in organized crime.'

The Monk was reportedly heartbroken. The night after the murder he sat alone in the dark in the front room of his home in Clontarf, watching the street outside as he contemplated his next move. He told a trusted associate that he still didn't regret mounting the disastrous attack:

> Gerard was determined that he had been justified doing what he did because he had no choice. The Kinahans and the Byrnes were going to wipe out him and members of his family even if they never retaliated. That's how this mad game works. You just have to keep killing because once you start when do you know when to stop? Gerard was trying to protect his family. He never wanted any of this, but they forced the situation. His biggest regret is that he didn't get him [Kinahan].

The same day that Daniel Kinahan returned for the funeral of his henchman, the *Sunday Times* published a statement issued by the Hutch family that articulated the Monk's position. It stated:

Gary had a falling-out with the Kinahan organization. This matter was resolved and €200,000 in cash was paid over to the Kinahans. We shook hands and agreed to walk away. Gary was then murdered for no reason. You cannot trust these people. The Kinahan organization has attempted to kill Gerard on several occasions in recent months. We are being terrorized by the cartel. Kinahan's representatives said members of our family would be killed or forced to leave their homes and Ireland if their demands for money were not met. We believe the Kinahan drugs cartel murdered Eddie at his home in Dublin last Monday, having approached him days before with demands for money. Our extended family are under threat from these people. Our family are not involved in any drugs war. We are well known in the north inner city and have no involvement in drugs. Our family are involved in various charitable, religious and sports groups which help young people. We are not involved in drug dealing.

In the meantime gardaí were making progress in the investigation. Undercover specialist officers had secretly planted eavesdropping devices in a number of vehicles used by members of the Hutch gang. One of them was on a jeep owned by Jonathan Dowdall who featured as a suspect when it was discovered how Flat Cap had booked into the hotel.

A few weeks after the Regency attack Dowdall drove Gerry Hutch to a meeting with Kevin Murray and other IRA members in Northern Ireland. It was suspected that Hutch was making arrangements with Flat Cap to acquire explosive devices, possibly for use as car bombs, and to arrange the safe return of the borrowed weapons. However, bombs were never used in the conflagration that followed. On the journey the Monk let his guard down and the two men were recorded discussing aspects of the Regency job.

Security sources confirmed at the time that the recordings contained enough incriminating material to charge Hutch in connection with the crime. The surveillance operation also led to the seizure of the AK-47s which were on loan to Hutch. On 9 March the anti-terrorist Special Detective Unit (SDU) seized the weapons as they were being transported back to the North. Ballistic tests later confirmed they had been used in the murder attack.

Based on the information gleaned from the secret recordings the anti-terrorist SDU obtained a warrant to search Dowdall's home for arms and ammunition. The house on the Navan Road was raided on 10 March, the day after the weapons were seized. An extensive search of the property found no evidence to link Dowdall with the audacious crime. But in a bizarre twist they did uncover damning proof of another serious offence.

A memory stick retrieved from a fish tank in the house contained footage recorded on a mobile phone showing Dowdall and his sixty-one-year-old father, Patrick, torturing a man who they wrongly suspected of trying to scam them. Dowdall held a towel over his victim's face before pouring water over his head in a torture technique known as 'water boarding'. The former Dublin city councillor threatened to cut his victim's fingers off and talked about chopping him up and feeding him to dogs. He bragged that he was a member of the IRA and close friends with Gerry Adams and Mary Lou McDonald.

The terrified victim was warned that he and members of his family would be killed within 48 hours if he went to the gardaí. Over the following weeks the police identified the torture victim. When he was approached, he agreed to testify. As a consequence of his involvement with the Monk, Dowdall and his father got their just deserts when they were subsequently jailed for false imprisonment and making threats to kill.

But by then Gerry Hutch was in the wind.

————————

The Monk had expected to come under pressure from the cops, as did the rest of the gang. His home had been one of a dozen searched on 23 February by officers from Ballymun garda station who were investigating the Regency attack. But he left the country for the last time before the seizure of the murder weapons and the raid at Jonathan Dowdall's property. The raids had convinced Hutch that the gardaí were closing in.

The shocking pictures captured by the media at the scene had fuelled a political furore. Coming as it did in the midst of a general election, the attack had seriously threatened the re-election chances of the outgoing government who were criticized over their handling of law and order. Gerry Hutch knew that meant no stone would be left unturned in the cops' efforts to bring him to justice. The iconic images of his handiwork had also propelled the Monk into the international media spotlight as pictures of the audacious assault had gone viral.

At the same time Hutch had heard that the Kinahans and the Byrnes had offered a €1 million bounty to anyone who could deliver him to them alive. Liam Byrne wanted to give Hutch a slow and agonizing death. While his boss found inspiration in the fictional *Godfather*, Byrne looked to Quentin Tarantino for his motivation. The Monk had a network of loyal spies and double agents filtering information back to him. An associate close to the Monk told this writer at the time:

They have sent the word out to everyone, including outfits in the
UK, Spain and Holland that they will pay a million if Gerard Hutch is
taken alive and then handed over to them. They want him held at a
safe location until they get there and then Byrne and Kinahan plan to
enjoy torturing him – they want to give him a slow and painful death
in revenge for what happened to David Byrne. That won't be allowed
to happen.

Although Hutch never showed emotion and kept his innermost thoughts locked away, the loss of his beloved brother Eddie and the deadly threat now looming over his family, left him desolate and alone. For the first time in his life Gerry Hutch was no longer in control of his own destiny.

It is difficult to imagine what must have been going through his mind when he realized that his only option was to flee Ireland and go into hiding. The once respected criminal mastermind has been reduced to the status of a stalked outlaw – making a run for it before either the gardaí or the mob get to him first. Hutch has not been seen in public since then and gardaí have received scant information on his possible movements. He has reportedly been moving between Turkey, Spain and the UK. His departure came as the Kinahans intensified their murder campaign.

On 23 March Noel 'Kingsize' Duggan was shot five times in the chest as he sat behind the steering wheel of his car, after pulling up outside his home in Ratoath, County Meath. He had been targeted because the Monk was his best friend. Kingsize also had good contacts in the IRA which made him a strong possibility for procuring the murder weapons. The prime suspects for the hit included Eamon Cumberton and his accomplice, the duo who had tried to assassinate the Monk in Lanzarote.

A few weeks later the cartel struck again. On 14 April a Kinahan hit man was sent to shoot Keith Murtagh. The Hutch gang member was standing outside Noctor's pub on Sheriff Street in the north inner city when he spotted the shooter coming at him on a push bike, holding a gun in his hand. As Murtagh ran for cover the fumbling assassin, Glen Clarke from Cabra, fired a number of indiscriminate shots in his direction.

One of the stray bullets hit twenty-four-year-old Martin O'Rourke, an entirely innocent man who was in the wrong place at the wrong time. The harmless drug abuser died instantly from a single gunshot wound to the head. Murtagh escaped uninjured and went on to survive at least two further attempts on his life over the following months. A year later in November 2017 the gardaí saved him from any further shootings when he was charged with an armed robbery and remanded in custody. In prison Murtagh was placed in segregation for his own protection as there was no shortage of prisoners happy to accept a contract to kill him. He was subsequently sentenced to twelve years.

The cartel struck again on 25 April 2016. This time IRA man Michael Barr was shot five times in the head as he worked behind the counter at the Sunset House pub. A month later, the cartel attacked the heart of the Hutch family. The Monk's nephew, Gareth Hutch, was gunned down getting into his car outside his apartment complex in the inner city.

Gardaí caught up with Eamon Cumberton who was arrested and subsequently sentenced to life imprisonment for the Barr murder. His accomplice is also wanted by the police for the same crime. Jonathan Keogh, Cumberton's fellow INLA member, was one of three people later sentenced to life for the murder of Gareth Hutch. Keogh was a neighbour of his victim. A year later, almost to the day, the Hutch side exacted revenge by murdering Jonathan Keogh's brother, Michael, who also lived in the area. It was the second and last murder attributed to the Hutches but which they deny. Over the following four years the other sixteen killings in the ongoing feud were credited to the Kinahan and Byrne organized crime gangs.

Meanwhile the level of fear and apprehension was palpable on the streets of the north inner city as over seventy members of the extended Hutch family and close friends were officially informed by gardaí that they were under threat. The chaotic situation prompted Diarmuid Martin, the Archbishop of Dublin, to denounce the killers and their bosses as 'animals' who were 'despicable and evil'.

On 1 July the bloodthirsty cartel members caught up with Daithi Douglas who was still recovering from the injuries he'd sustained seven months earlier. This time the killers were determined to get the job done properly. Douglas was shot several times in the head and chest as he stood outside his partner's shop on Bridgefoot Street in the south inner city. The follow-up investigation led to the conviction for murder of Fat Freddie Thompson who personally supervised the hit. During Thompson's reign of terror, which spanned two decades, he had been linked to at least a dozen murders. His incarceration was a major victory for the gardaí.

The killing spree then shifted to Majorca in Spain where the lethally inept Kinahan cartel hit man Glen Clarke claimed the life of a second innocent man in four months. Dublin city council worker Trevor O'Neill was enjoying a holiday with his partner and three young children in Majorca. Jonathan Hutch, whose brother Gareth had been shot in May, was also staying in the same holiday complex. He was having a well-earned break from living in the constant shadow of the Kinahan gunmen back home. But the cartel had learned of his plans through its spies in the north inner city and dispatched Clarke and an accomplice to kill Hutch when he least expected it.

On 17 August Trevor O'Neill and his family were going out for a meal with their children when they bumped into the Hutches. Their wives knew each other from school. The two men walked in front of their wives and children making small talk as Clarke ran up from behind. He fired a shot hitting Trevor O'Neill in the back. It was another catastrophic case of mistaken identity. The victim, who died later in hospital, was of similar build to the intended target. After the shooting Jonathan Hutch left the island with his family.

The murder of a decent, law-abiding family man in front of his wife and three young children while on holiday caused an outpouring of public outrage and revulsion. It also gave the Spanish police a new impetus with which to target the Kinahans – murdering blameless tourists in the crossfire of the feud was an intolerable situation. But none of that mattered to Daniel Kinahan or Liam Byrne who were insouciant about the fear and trauma they were inflicting on innocent people.

Glen Clarke had also been a suspect in the killing of Noel 'Kingsize' Duggan and a separate murder three years earlier. The hit man's DNA had been found on the butt of the discarded firearm used to kill Martin O'Rourke. But before the gardaí caught up with Clarke, other victims were spared when his ineptitude brought his career as a contract killer to an abrupt end.

On 2 December 2016 the bungling hit man was found unconscious with a head injury in a stolen car which was parked with its engine running in a housing estate in Leixlip, County Kildare. Gardaí believe that he was on his way to carry out another contract killing at the time as he was wearing gloves, overalls and had a canister of petrol with him so he could destroy the car after the hit.

Investigators think that he had accidentally shot himself in the eye while looking down the barrel of his revolver.

A few weeks later the Kinahans dealt another blow to Gerry Hutch. On 22 December, the Monk's lifelong friend and confidante, sixty-three-year-old Noel 'Duck Egg' Kirwan, was shot dead by a lone gunman equipped with a silenced firearm. Like Kingsize Duggan, Noel Kirwan was shot just because he was Gerry Hutch's friend. The two men had been pictured together at Eddie's funeral ten months earlier. Duck Egg Kirwan became the eighth victim to be claimed by the cartel in as many months. In the interim gardaí had prevented at least another ten attempted hits.

Since the murder of Gary Hutch fifteen months earlier, the death toll in December 2016 now stood at eleven lives. For anyone keeping a macabre score sheet it would have read: Kinahans 10 – Hutches 1. Describing it as the Kinahan/Hutch feud was no longer an accurate portrayal of what was really happening. 'Feud' suggested that both sides were in some way evenly matched. The reality was that the so-called war had become a very one-sided affair. It was better described as the attempted annihilation of one family-based group by a much more pernicious mob with a lot more money, guns and killers. Even experienced and hard-bitten gardaí would openly express their utter amazement and shock at what had unfolded between the two gangland tribes. As a result of the slaughter the Monk's family had won considerable public sympathy while Daniel Kinahan and his cartel became the most hated criminal organization in the history of the Irish State.

The murder spree continued over the next two years. Daniel Kinahan's lust for bloodshed had jeopardized his father's lifetime work of building a powerful drug syndicate. Once the killings started it appeared that Christy Senior had no control of events or over his twisted son.

In December 2017, exactly a year after the murder of Noel 'Duck Egg' Kirwan, the cartel also executed his son, Kane McCormack, because they feared he was preparing to take revenge. Derek Coakley Hutch, another of the Monk's nephews, was the next casualty to add to the death toll. In January 2018 he was ambushed outside Wheatfield Prison in west Dublin. By this stage, the Monk, still in hiding, had lost a brother, three nephews and two close friends. At Hutch's funeral a grieving friend had a poignant reminder for the congregation and the rest of the world: 'This is a family not a cartel.'

But there was no respite from the carnage. On the day of Derek's wake his friend Jason Molyneux was shot six times in the chest after paying his respects. He had gone to a meeting with someone he trusted who had obviously been turned by Kinahan's murder machine.

The garda response to the unprecedented violence was implacable, unrelenting and comprehensive. The impressive strike back was spearheaded by the newly established Garda Drugs and Organized Crime Bureau (GDOCB) and involved every resource available to the force. The approach was multi-pronged. Apart from individual murder investigations, the GDOCB actively targeted the Kinahan's drug and arms supplies, aided by police forces across mainland Europe. The CAB aggressively pursued the money trail and heavily-armed units were permanently deployed in the north inner city to protect the Hutch family from further attacks. At the same time the gardaí penetrated into the heart of the cartel. Undercover specialists planted tracking and listening devices in vehicles and properties used by the gang. The net effect was that at the time of writing the Kinahan cartel is on the brink of implosion. The combined operations saw the seizure of over €170 million worth of drugs in four years and over €12 million in cash. Several properties, high-spec cars, gold, jewels and other luxury items worth millions were also seized from the Kinahan mob.

The gardaí also succeeded in neutralizing the cartel's bloodthirst by foiling over seventy assassination attempts. In the four years since the Regency Hotel attack the GDOCB's work led to the conviction of twenty-six cartel members including Kinahan and Byrne's contract killers and their back-up crews. Using high-tech surveillance, the GDOCB teams were able to listen live as sub cells of the mafia-style organization planned murders – and then swoop in as the hit men were about to go into action.

One such elaborate operation saved the life of Gary Hutch's best friend James 'Mago' Gately, who was one of the top names on the cartel's hit list. In April 2017 the GDOCB arrested colourful Estonian contract killer, 60-year-old Imre Arakas, who had been hired by Daniel Kinahan to whack Gately who was hiding out in Newry, north of the border. Variously described as an actor, freedom fighter and wrestler, Arakas was better known as a leading member of the Estonian mafia. He was a ruthless criminal with the nickname 'the Butcher' who had been involved in a ferocious gang war with the Russian mafia in the 1990s which claimed the lives of over 100 people. Gately was an important target for Daniel Kinahan and he agreed to pay Arakas €100,000. Fortunately for the targeted gang member the gardaí had been tipped off by their international colleagues that one of Europe's top hit men was on his way. When the killer was arrested detectives found text messages on the encrypted phone supplied to Arakas by Kinahan in which he told his employers that he would finish Gately with 'one shot to the head' using a silenced weapon. In 2018 the hit man was jailed for six years after pleading guilty to conspiracy to murder Gately. A month after the arrest of Arakas another hit man almost got lucky when he shot and seriously injured Gately while sitting in a car at a petrol station in north Dublin. Although shot five times, including in the neck, Gately made a full recovery.

A similar garda operation also saved the life of Patsy Hutch in March 2018. Gary Hutch's father had escaped at least three attempts on his life since the Regency attack and gardaí had placed full-time armed protection at his home. He had been arrested and questioned about the attack in May 2016 but was released due to lack of evidence. That same month his son Patrick had been charged with the murder of David Byrne. The case against the Monk's nephew was based on his identification from the photographs taken by the *Sunday World* newspaper. In September 2016 Kevin 'Flat Cap' Murray was arrested in Northern Ireland on foot of a warrant seeking his extradition to the Republic. But Lynch escaped his date with justice when he contracted motor neurone disease and died a year later.

As the cartel continued its efforts to get Patsy Hutch the real ERU members swooped on a killer team as it was about to ambush him. A total of nine men were subsequently convicted for conspiracy to murder, possession of firearms and aiding a criminal gang.

The Hutches had another pyrrhic victory of sorts when Patrick Hutch's trial for the Byrne murder collapsed in February 2019. The State entered a *nolle prosequi* following the tragic death of a senior investigator in the case, Detective Superintendent Colm Fox, who took his own life during the Hutch trial a year earlier. There was no explanation for the death of the much respected and dedicated police officer other than that the intense pressures of the investigation caused him to suffer a catastrophic psychological meltdown. In many ways he became another victim of the gangland carnage. Immediately after the DPP's announcement Patrick Hutch left the Dublin Courts of Criminal Justice complex by the rear entrance. He joined his father Patsy who was waiting on a motorbike. Father and son sped off into an uncertain future. At the time of writing they are still looking over their shoulders.

For his part Gerry Hutch is still a man on the run with an ever more uncertain future before him. The unprecedented violence has left his family and friends emotionally scarred, bereft and traumatized. The same can be said for the people of Hutch's beloved inner-city neighbourhood who became the victims of the collateral damage. He has also forfeit the liberty to ever again walk freely through the streets where he grew up or to coach the kids in the local boxing club.

Over time, however, the chances of the Kinahan cartel catching up with the Monk are diminishing. Hutch may find some solace in the fact that Daniel Kinahan and his cartel are facing an even more uncertain future than he is. The foiling of so many murder attempts has meant that no one is prepared to do any more killing for the mob. The last feud-related murder took place in 2018.

At the time of writing the cartel is on the brink of collapse as it continues to be pummelled by the Irish police and their European colleagues. Such has been the intensity of the garda operation against them the cartel's top killers and managers are behind bars in Ireland and the UK, leaving only a handful on the outside to control operations.

Daniel Kinahan's ambitions to become one of the world's top boxing promoters have been beaten onto the ropes by the revelations about his reputation as a ruthless, murderous drug trafficker. In June 2020, to universal acclaim in the sport, Kinahan brokered an historic two-fight deal between his client, heavyweight world champion Tyson Fury, and Anthony Joshua. Kinahan was also hired by KHK Sports, a boxing promotions company owned by a Bahraini prince. The mob boss's strident efforts to erase his bloody past and become legitimate seemed to be working. They had involved a multi-pronged offensive which included a barrage of fake news on social media and glowing endorsements from such luminaries as top US boxing guru Bob Arum and a host of champion pugilists. At the same time he hired a top UK legal firm to fire off threatening legal missives in a bid to silence the Irish media. Kinahan was believed to have funded a nonsensical *Regency Hotel Attack* movie on YouTube which promulgated the preposterous theory that the attempt on Kinahan's life was the result of a grand conspiracy involving the Monk's gang, the gardaí, the media and Fine Gael to scupper Sinn Féin's chances in the 2016 general election a few weeks later. They even produced an online 'book' which named this writer as being one of the conspirators.

However, the chorus of support for the murderous mob boss gave way to silence as evidence stacked up on the stage of public opinion. The Irish High Court and the Special Criminal Court acknowledged that Daniel Kinahan and his cartel comprised a major organized crime gang involved in murders, drugs trafficking and gun-running. Such has been the reverberations from his narco-terrorism that the Irish Government has intervened and sent diplomats to brief the UAE authorities about his blood-soaked past. The fallout resulted in Kinahan being publicly sacked by Tyson Fury and KHK Sports. Adding insult to mortification, an announcement was made on his behalf that Daniel Kinahan was taking a step back from boxing promotion on the grounds that his involvement was an unnecessary distraction.

Daniel Kinahan's bolt-hole from justice is anything but secure, and even less so for the entourage of thugs around him. The cartel leader cannot risk leaving the United Arab Emirates where he holds citizenship for fear of being arrested and extradited back to Ireland. He is effectively a prisoner there. At the time of writing the Garda Drugs and Organized Crime Bureau (GDOCB) are finalizing a file for the Director of Public Prosecutions (DPP) which will recommend that Kinahan face charges of leading an organized crime group. He is also likely to face charges for the murder of Eddie Hutch. Daniel Kinahan's days as a crime boss are numbered.

The media campaign to expose Kinahan to the rest of the world was helped in no small way by the Monk. From the safety of his hideout Hutch has been using Twitter to wage a propaganda campaign against Kinahan who he refers to as 'cancer'. Using the supremely ironic title of 'Whistleblower', Hutch declares on his account that he will not stop until Kinahan is brought to justice for the murder of his brother.

Almost a year after the Regency attack and Hutch's disappearance, this writer spoke to one of his closest associates. He said that after all that had happened to the Monk and his family, Gerry Hutch was resigned to the reality that he would not pass away peacefully in his sleep. But he wasn't going down without a fight:

> There are guys out everywhere trying to locate Gerard and lure him into a trap so that is why he is being so vigilant and watching every move… he can trust very few people and he has no intention of giving up without a fight. He has lost so many friends and family now that he has no fear of death and he will go out by bringing some of them down with him.

As time goes by the likelihood of the Monk's assassination at the hands of the Kinahans or the Byrne gangs is subsiding. And many will hope that they never get to him. After all he is, by any comparison, the nearest thing to an ethical criminal.

At the time of writing the gardaí investigating the Regency Hotel attack have submitted a file to the DPP regarding Hutch's involvement in the incident. Only time will tell if he faces criminal charges and the possibility of the long stint behind bars that he has so adroitly avoided for almost three decades. Or maybe he will be free to walk the streets of the north inner city again.

The €1 million bounty for capturing Gerry Hutch still stands but it is highly unlikely that it will ever be claimed or that the cartel could now afford to pay it. The mobsters are more concerned with staying out of prison. For now, the elusive, enigmatic godfather is still in the place where he prefers to be – in the shadows and out of sight.

Acknowledgments

This book is the culmination of thirty years spent chronicling the life and crimes of Gerard Hutch, the enigmatic gang boss called the Monk. Much of the material is based on first-hand accounts from the main players in this dramatic story over the decades: cops, criminals and associates of the eponymous anti-hero. I would like to sincerely thank them all for their generosity along the way – they would prefer to remain anonymous for obvious reasons. I would like to thank the sources, some of them close to the man himself, who agreed to be interviewed as part of the research for the book; particularly in untangling the complex web of events which led to the notorious Regency Hotel attack and one of the bloodiest gang wars in the history of organized crime in Ireland. Thank you all for your trust.

My thanks to photojournalist Derek Speirs for the use of his powerful images (1, 2, 10 and 15), which capture the different moods and faces of the elusive Monk down through the years. Derek was the first photographer that the publicity-hating criminal ever actually posed for! My gratitude and thanks also to the indefatigable Charlie Collins of the Collins Photographic Agency for the use of the pictures at 6, 17 and 36 and to my colleagues at the *Irish Independent* for pictures 8, 11 and the iconic image, 39, captured by a courageous INM photographer at the scene of the Regency Hotel attack. The rest of the photographs were sourced by the author. My gratitude to my colleagues at the *Irish Independent*: editor Cormac Bourke; head of news, Kevin Doyle and news editor Gareth Morgan for giving me the space to write the book, kindly allowing use of the pictures and serializing the book.

As always, my deepest thanks to my extremely talented, and patient, editor Aoife Barrett, of Barrett Editing, who works her magic on the manuscript every time to make it both legible and understandable. Over the years Aoife has become an expert on the subject of organized crime. And to Ireland's top libel lawyer and my dear friend Kieran Kelly – the Consiglieri – of Flynn O'Driscoll Lawyers, who has always been a rock of strength in the most difficult of times.

Thanks also to the doyen of Irish publishing Jonathan Williams of the Jonathan Williams Literary Agency, for his kindness, hard work, wisdom and impeccable advice. I would also like to sincerely thank my publisher, Will Atkinson the MD of Atlantic Books and Atlantic's group associate publisher, Clare Drysdale, who are about to take the Irish publishing world by storm.

And lastly, as always, my love and gratitude to Anne, Jake, Irena, Archie and of course 'Bunny' for making life worth living.

Index